D0121790

ENTERPRISE 2.0

ENTERPRISE 2.0

How Technology, eCommerce, and Web 2.0 Are Transforming Business Virtually

Volume 1: The Strategic Enterprise

Tracy L. Tuten, Editor

 PRAEGER

AN IMPRINT OF ABC-CLIO, LLC
Santa Barbara, California • Denver, Colorado • Oxford, England

Library of Congress Cataloging-in-Publication Data

Enterprise 2.0 : how technology, ecommerce, and web 2.0 are transforming business virtually / edited by Tracy L. Tuten.
    p. cm.
    Includes bibliographical references and index.
    ISBN 978–0–313–37239–1 (set : alk. paper) — ISBN 978–0–313–37241–4 (v. 1 : alk. paper) — ISBN 978–0–313–37243–8 (v. 2 : alk. paper) — ISBN 978–0–313–37240–7 (set : ebook) — ISBN 978–0–313–37242–1 (v. 1 : ebook) — ISBN 978–0–313–37244–5 (v. 2 : ebook)
1. Electronic commerce. 2. Web 2.0. 3. Information technology. I. Tuten, Tracy L., 1967– II. Title: Enterprise two point oh.
HF5548.32.E567   2010
658'.054678—dc22   2010006057

ISBN: 978–0–313–37239–1 (set)
ISBN: 978–0–313–37241–4 (vol. 1)
ISBN: 978–0–313–37243–8 (vol. 2)
EISBN: 978–0–313–37240–7 (set)
EISBN: 978–0–313–37242–1 (vol. 1)
EISBN: 978–0–313–37244–5 (vol. 2)

14 13 12 11 10   1 2 3 4 5

This book is also available on the World Wide Web as an eBook.
Visit www.abc-clio.com for details.

Praeger
An Imprint of ABC-CLIO, LLC

ABC-CLIO, LLC
130 Cremona Drive, P.O. Box 1911
Santa Barbara, California 93116-1911

This book is printed on acid-free paper (∞)

Manufactured in the United States of America

For Luke

CONTENTS

ACKNOWLEDGMENTS

Every accomplishment, every project, and every success are ultimately the result of a team of people working together, directly and indirectly, and in no situation is that truer than in the completion of *Enterprise 2.0*. *Enterprise 2.0* is ultimately the work of the authors who contributed to its development—I extend my most sincere gratitude to them for contributing their expertise, knowledge, and time to the development of this book. On their behalf, I also recognize the support and commitment they had from family, friends, and colleagues who listened, waited patiently while they wrote, cheered them on, and offered the intangible resources all authors require. Though these "silent contributors" are not recognized by name, I feel certain they will nod knowingly as they read this, recognizing the role they played. I thank Jeff Olson (and the rest of the Praeger family) for believing in this project and for his encouragement and advice as it developed. I also thank Brian Romer for seeing this project through to its completion. I expressly thank my new colleagues and the administration at East Carolina University's College of Business and Department of Marketing and Supply Chain Management for their support of this project. Finally, I am thankful for my "silent contributors," David, Dad, and Susan, who inspire me to be better in all that I do, whether it's making the evening's meal or editing a volume on technology in business.

1

THE STRATEGIC ENTERPRISE

Tracy L. Tuten

The term "Web 2.0" was coined in 2004 in a meeting organized by O'Reilly Media to describe the innovative online applications developing.[1] By 2006, a term used to describe the organizational uses of Web 2.0, "Enterprise 2.0," followed.[2] Though Web 2.0 technologies were not exclusively consumer-centric, sites such as Wikipedia, Napster, Flickr, and YouTube catered to the self-expression, life sharing, and entertainment and resource needs of the tech-savvy consumers. Strategically, the key question posed (and still posed) was (is) "how will said site monetize its offering?" not "how can organizations utilize the benefit of this service capability to build a competitive advantage?" Whether by strategic intervention or, more likely, serendipity as tech-savvy employees used social-media tools at work, the Enterprise was born.

Ron Miller, of CIO, explains the concept of Enterprise 2.0, writing,

> Enterprise 2.0 lets you implement a multiparty conversation to share information and manage knowledge inside and outside the organization using blogs and wikis, social networking and tagging, rating systems and the like. The link among these tools is the ability of the individuals involved to participate and to control the process while they work together, share information, and create networks of people with similar interests.[3]

The tools used in the Enterprise are the tools used to fuel the content and network of the Social Web. The differentiator is not the tool or the technology, but rather the goal. The Enterprise is about meeting organizational objectives—strategic, managerial, and marketing objectives—to develop and sustain competitive advantage.

Indeed, this two-volume set views the essence of Enterprise 2.0 as the use of integrating collaborative technologies for competitive advantage. Consequently, Volume 1 focuses on strategic and corporate topics while Volume 2 focuses on behavioral topics, including managerial and marketing aspects of the Enterprise.

DEFINING WITH CHARACTERISTICS

Without doubt, whatever Enterprise 2.0 is, it evolves from the applications of Web 2.0. Further, both concepts are often explained using a list of characteristics, comparing what was to what is. Let's review these characteristics briefly.

Tim O'Reilly, in an article entitled "What Is Web 2.0: Design Patterns and Business Models for the Next Generation of Software," available (and highly recommended reading) on the O'Reilly Network,[4] explains that as he and his colleagues attempted to clarify the meaning of Web 2.0, providing examples of the differential between Web 1.0 and Web 2.0 was paramount. Some of the examples involve product evolutions and capabilities, while others are about behavior. For instance, in the product evolutions category, we have the following comparisons. In Web 1.0, DoubleClick was the answer to advertising metrics, but in Web 2.0, Google AdSense is the gold standard. In Web 1.0, Britannica Online was the go-to resource, but in Web 2.0, Wikipedia rules. Ofoto (now Kodak Gallery) was illustrative of Web 1.0 abilities, while Flickr is all Web 2.0. In the behavioral category, we have the following examples. Personal Web sites were so Web 1.0, while blogs are Web 2.0. Measuring page views was Web 1.0, but measuring cost per click is Web 2.0. Enhancing site stickiness was Web 1.0, while syndicating site content is Web 2.0. Publishing was Web 1.0, but participation is Web 2.0. Ultimately, O'Reilly devised a list of seven core competences of Web 2.0 companies:

- Services with cost-effective scalability (e.g., Google)
- Control over rich data sources
- Interdependence and trust with users as codeveloper
- Leveraging collective intelligence
- Reaching the long tail
- Software beyond the single device platform
- Lightweight user interfaces, development models, and business models

These concepts form the basis for our understanding of Enterprise 2.0 and its value to creating sustainable competitive advantage. For instance, as you continue through the chapters presented herein, you'll read of cloud computing as an alternative to traditional software systems for organizations.

Cloud computing refers to computing utilities including subscription-based and pay-per-use services provided over the Internet. You'll also learn about how we leverage collective intelligence with wikis and folksonomies, among other approaches. (Wikis, sites that enable open editing and the inclusion of hyperlinks and extensions, can be used to solve problems and, importantly, maintain a trail of the discourse and ultimate solution. A folksonomy is a method of categorizing and filing information using keywords determined most appropriate by a crowd rather than an individual expert. The term can literally mean management by the people [onomy: meaning management, and folks: meaning people].)

An article by Whitney Michael, for the Enterprise 2.0 conference, entitled "Enterprise 2.0: What, Why and How" takes a similar approach (although with a focus on characteristics rather than product capabilities) to exemplify the differences between Enterprise 1.0 and 2.0.[5] He uses these descriptors for Enterprise 1.0: hierarchy, bureaucracy, top down, centralized, silos, taxonomies, complexity, and scheduled. In contrast, the descriptors for Enterprise 2.0 include flat, agile, flexible, user-driven, bottom up, transparent, emergent, folksonomies, simple, and on demand.

Perhaps these characteristics sound familiar to you, as they did to me. Having studied organizational theory during my doctoral program, the list of characteristics put forth by Michael brought back memories of Tom Burns and G. M. Stalker's characteristics of mechanistic and organic structures in organizations.[6] Mechanistic organizations were described as closed systems—stable, hierarchical, contractual, centralized, and top down, with knowledge residing at the top of the hierarchy and tasks assigned by functional role; organic organizations as open systems—ever-changing, networked, comprising a committed community of interest, and community valued, with specialized knowledge contributed to others and knowledge based all over the network. If you aren't familiar with the Burns and Stalker book, *The Management of Innovation*, consider this: it was first published in 1961. It's as though they anticipated the rise of Enterprise 2.0 fifty years ago.

In truth, these classic management theorists likely recognized the need for organizations to master collaboration to achieve competitive advantage. Enterprise 2.0 does not represent a new kind of organization. Rather, it is a fresh iteration of the organic organization. The organic organization is reborn with capabilities to share specialized knowledge, network, change, and benefit from community cooperation made possible by technology, e-commerce, and all that is Web 2.0 and beyond. And, this is Enterprise 2.0.

THE SHIFT TO ENTERPRISE 2.0

We've seen that the shift to Enterprise 2.0 (E2.0) was simply a natural evolution to enhance organic organizations with Web 2.0 technologies. In today's age, technology makes the organic open-system organization not only possible but also efficient and effective. Importantly, the capabilities and low barriers to adoption for social tools mean that even traditionally mechanistic organizations are more likely to embrace knowledge media in the workplace. For instance, Sarah Perez notes that 51 percent of global companies with 2,000+ employees are investing in Enterprise 2.0 solutions.[7] Though large organizations struggle with collaboration and coordination, typically organizations of this size tend to the bureaucratic, mechanistic approach to structure and processes, illustrating the pull to E2.0 solutions. Still, context is king. As Whitney Michael points out, Enterprise 2.0 is a result of access to Web-based tools that enable and encourage user participation, the socialization of business applications (people-centric over data-centric), and a new business culture that encourages people-centric—social—applications in the business world.[8]

Just consider the following terms, all of which are now buzzwords of the 2.0 generation: connectivity, collaboration, conversation, community, engagement, democracy, and collective. The vernacular of the rise of 2.0 is upon us and clearly portrays the cultural transformation leading from individual entertainment and activities via the Web to consumerism to E2.0 business applications.

PEOPLE-CENTRIC E2.0 WEB APPLICATIONS

Essentially any Web 2.0 application is capable of supporting an organic organization. As social-media tools experience phenomenal growth and publicity, it becomes tempting to take a myopic view, thinking social applications are irrelevant, or worse—distracting—to business. Why is that the case when so many of us are avid users of social-media tools (albeit perhaps limited to our personal lives)? Before continuing, take a moment and think about what the word "social" means to you. If you were to describe a friend as social, or consider attending a social affair, how would you use the word? The answer to the question of why organizations may resist the power of socializing business procedures lies in our biases toward the word "social." Merriam-Webster's Dictionary[9] offers several definitions of the word "social," some of which are noted below:

- Involving allies or confederates
- Marked by or passed in pleasant companionship with one's friends or associates
- Of or relating to human society, the interaction of the individual and the group, or the welfare of human beings as members of society
- Tending to form cooperative and interdependent relationships with others of one's kind

Likely, your definition of social was closer to the second definition offered— marked by or passed in pleasant companionship with one's friends or associates. Consider, though, the final definition—tending to form cooperative and interdependent relationships with others of one's kind—and the use of the words cooperative and interdependent. These words are also associated with the organic organization. A tweet by @MatthiasKoller puts this discussion in perspective. He advised that in business settings, you exchange the word social for knowledge. Instead of social networking, it's knowledge networking; no more social media, it's knowledge media. The social Web—no, a knowledge Web. After all, the goal is the management of knowledge to gain competitive advantage.

ENTERPRISE 2.0 TOOLS AND TECHNOLOGIES

Enterprise 2.0 tools enable participants to work together without the limitations of geographic and temporal distances. These tools, in a nutshell, do what the Web first promised to do for the organization. Using a functional classification, we can categorize E2.0 tools as content or content interaction and delivery. Most of the Enterprise 2.0 applications discussed in this volume fall into the content interaction category, but three in particular represent pure content: wikis, blogs, and casts. Wikis are collaborative documents that can be edited by multiple users while maintaining a trail of changes. Blogs, short for Weblogs, began as online personal journals with chronological entries. Blogs have evolved over time, with increased functionality, popularity, circulation, and influence. Once reflecting the made-public private thoughts of individuals seeking a platform, blogs may now reflect content more indicative of trade journals, newspaper articles, and op-ed pieces. Casts primarily refer to podcasts (also known as netcasts for those who wish to avoid infringing upon Apple's copyright of the word pod), videocasts, and mediacasts (also called cybercasts). Casts themselves represent content; however, casting is a content delivery tool (discussed further in a following paragraph).

The other Enterprise tools are content dependent, but essentially represent the delivery and interaction of content more so than the content itself. While wikis, blogs, and casts present the original thought of their authors, content delivery and interaction tools are the basis for knowledge management in the Enterprise. These include social software, social networks, microblogs, games, virtual worlds, social news, social bookmarks, tags, casts and RSS (really simple syndication) feeds, and widgets and mashups. Content delivery and interaction tools vary in functionality and potential for interactivity and collaboration, but ultimately this set of E2.0 applications enables organizational members to search, access, share, organize, assess, and interact with content. We'll briefly define each one.

Social software refers to software applications that enable users to interact with and share data. The term "social software" may be used to refer to collaborative systems such as Microsoft's SharePoint, but it also refers to communication applications such as instant messaging, online chat, and text applications.

Social networks are online services that enable individuals to create and publish profiles, share opinions, express their identities, and interact with others with whom they have chosen to share a connection. Further, networks are visible to others within the system. LinkedIn is perhaps the best example of a social network with organizational value given its focus on business opportunities, professional affiliations, and credentials. Still, social networks generally enable the sharing of professional and personal data, as well as links to content housed external to the system.

Microblogs may prima facie seem better suited to the content categorization, but they are identified here as a delivery mechanism due to the character restriction upheld by microblogging services. Some microbloggers use these services as an abbreviated personal journal, but in business practices, they are used as a sort of headline news service to link others to valuable content. Twitter is the juggernaut of microblogs, and if you aren't already tweeting, a quick visit will illustrate the business uses of microblogs.

Casts and *RSS feeds*, also content delivery tools, enable content to be delivered via syndication, thereby reducing the need for an ongoing "pull" command from the intended recipient of the content. Users subscribe to casts and feeds such that updated content is fed as available. There are many forms of casts (e.g., anycasts, BerryCasts, TreoCasts, and Phone.CASTs), the specific names of which primarily reflect the devices used in the sending and receiving of content.

Widgets and *mashups* are a special case of content delivery and interaction in that they enable end users to access and manipulate available information. A widget refers to small applications that provide a focused information "at a glance" from a defined data source. Mashups integrate two or more data sources and applications into a single tool. Andy Mulholland of Capgemini defines the term "widget" on the CTO blog, writing that "a 'widget' is correctly defined as a (small) portable piece of code that can be added by a user to an existing Web page running on HTML and will run to produce an extended and personalized extra capability without any technology skill being required to make it work."[10] While widgets have been around since the early days of the personal computer, Mulholland attributes the power of widgets today as a function of the ability for the widget to deliver a service in a manner controlled by the organization offering it, but in a format that is customizable by the user. Enterprise widgets exemplify the "service beyond a single device" principle of Web 2.0. For example, UPS (United Parcel Service of America) developed an enterprise widget that would track packages, display delivery status, and provide a link to more detailed shipping information.

Chris Warner, posting on The Enterprise 2.0 Web Blog, explains that mashups are made up of three fundamental parts: (1) mashables, (2) mashups, and (3) shareables.[11] Warner's explanation helps to clarify why a mashup is a content delivery and interaction tool. A developer takes mashables, data sources and service applications, to create a mashup, which is then shared using a mashlet or similar "shareable." Warner defines a mashup as a "user-driven, user-focused thing that encapsulates the kind of data processing and manipulation actions a user would normally do to turn any data into real information." Mashlets enable mashups to be shared on Web sites and mobile devices. The Programmable Web Web site (www.programmableweb.com) offers a list of mashups, including those specifically for the Enterprise. For instance, a mashup on *BusinessWeek* magazine online provides links to company names on LinkedIn to determine to whom readers are connected. Faceforce is a mashup that integrates Facebook profile data with Salesforce data to provide detailed personal data about business prospects and colleagues. The Wii Enterprise Remote mashup enables project managers to plan on the Nintendo Wii.

Two forms of content delivery and interaction stand out due to their immersive nature: *games* and *virtual worlds*. Games include the use of online video games as well as alternate reality games (ARGs). They deliver content but in an interactive and immersive fashion. For this reason, consider gaming as an immersive content delivery tool in the Enterprise 2.0 arsenal. ARGs are interactive narratives that comprise fiction and nonfiction, mystery and detection, and scripted and unscripted scenes played out by characters and real people. Primarily used for branding purposes (e.g., The Lost Ring, McDonald's ARG tied to the Olympics), the games unfold over multiple forms of media and utilize many types of game elements, each tailored for the media platform used. Though typically used for branding, such games are also engaging tools for training and development. For instance, the Web site www.pietheory.com introduces an ARG designed to teach coding of JavaFX.

Virtual worlds, also known as "metaverses," refer to three-dimensional communities that mimic the real world without its physical limitations. In a virtual world, people are represented by their avatars. Like games, virtual worlds can be categorized as immersive content delivery tools. Virtual worlds include both social worlds (e.g., Second Life) and game worlds (e.g., World of Warcraft). Social worlds are game-like but lack the goal orientation of virtual games. Social virtual worlds offer opportunities for learning, entertainment, shopping, working and doing business, and socializing, but no objectives are inherent to the community. That said, organizations can utilize the three-dimensional lifelike environments of virtual worlds in many ways. For example, the U.S. Army uses a virtual-world environment to train soldiers for combat experiences.[12] International Business Machines Corporation (IBM) has created software to facilitate conducting meetings in virtual worlds. The software is called Sametime 3D, and it enables colleagues to chat, instant message, share presentations, and discuss ideas, while using turn-key meeting spaces (including boardrooms, amphitheaters, and classrooms) in several virtual worlds.[13] Second Life is used to present crisis situations to health-care professionals in training, allow architects to conceptualize and design spaces before creating physical prototypes, and enable companies such as Amazon to host virtual job fairs.

The final two forms of Enterprise 2.0 tools in use, *social news* and *social bookmarks*, are also content delivery and interaction tools. However, because content delivered via social news and bookmarks are annotated and enhanced by the collective intelligence, they are termed collective content management tools here. Both rely heavily on tagging with folksonomies and the ability to search in order to identify, access, sort, and manage content. Tagging refers to the categorization of content; folksonomies are tags chosen by individuals in a way that makes sense to them as opposed to using predefined keywords. Tagging results in a tag cloud, which provides additional data on the popularity of each tag used, making tracking content more efficient. Collective content systems may also include ratings that enable users to assign a value score to the content delivered, thereby making the content delivery more effective.

Social news Web sites are social communities that allow users to share content, including news stories, blog posts, articles, multimedia files, and more. The collective intelligence of users determines which content files are featured, tags enhance the searchability of the content noted in the social news community, and the ratings inform users of content value judgments. This functionality creates a collective content management system that organizations can use to find the best content available. For instance, an employee may use a social news site to identify the best vendors for Enterprise 2.0 solutions or to find answers to a question on troubleshooting a new piece of software.

Social bookmarking communities are similar to social news communities in that users can share material from around the Internet with each other and the size and influence of a user's network affects the ultimate influence of the resource in question. Users store and organize bookmarks (using tags) to online source materials with the social bookmarking site (instead of storing bookmarks with one's Web browser). The community aspect comes into play with the network of users. Within each community, users can share bookmarks with colleagues, resulting in a shared wisdom effect. Delicious is the leader among social bookmarking sites. While similar to social news in that both tools enhance the retrieval of relevant information with minimal duplication of research efforts, bookmarks represent more of a shared content delivery model while social news sites lean to the collective content model.

To summarize, the Web 2.0 tools available for application in the Enterprise include wikis, blogs, podcasts and videocasts, microblogs, feeds, widgets and mashups, games and virtual worlds, and social news and bookmarks. To better understand what these tools offer the Enterprise, we can categorize them as content and content delivery/interaction mechanisms. Further, the content and content delivery mechanisms may be controllable, immersive, or collective in nature. See Table 1.1.

BENEFITS OF ENTERPRISE 2.0 SOLUTIONS

The overarching reason to embrace the technological solutions associated with Enterprise 2.0 is to facilitate the organization's ability to gain competitive advantage. Ultimately, that's what it's all about. We've already discussed specific examples of organizations using enterprise solutions to enhance competitive advantage. Many of these showcased the specific benefits available to the E2.0 organization.

Tools are easy to implement and generally inexpensive. They do not require complex maintenance. What's more, implementing Enterprise 2.0 solutions in an organization enables the organization to behave as an organic organization with all the value associated with the open-systems structure. Specifically, communication and collaboration among colleagues are improved. Internal communication is more efficient, and a decision trail of information is maintained by the technology. Staff members are more engaged as a result of an improved capacity to collaborate and participate in critical decisions. Additionally, team building is prevalent, and a sense of trust grows from the transparency of the organization. Decision-making is enhanced by information that is vetted, readily accessible, and relevant. When information is lacking, connecting with content experts is feasible. All in all, E2.0 organizations achieve better communication, collaboration, and knowledge management, which results in a more efficient path to competitive advantage.

BARRIERS TO ADOPTION

Given these benefits, why would any organization refrain from shifting to Enterprise 2.0 solutions? When considering the barriers to adoption,

Table 1.1 Typology of Enterprise 2.0 Tools

	Controlled	Immersive	Collective
Content	Blogs Podcasts and videocasts		Wikis
Content Delivery/ Interaction	Microblogs RSS feeds, Casting widgets Mashups	Virtual worlds Games	Social networks Social news Social bookmarks

five characteristics are commonly used to explain whether an innovation is adopted: (1) relative advantage, (2) simplicity, (3) compatibility, (4) observability, and (5) trialability. Relative advantage refers to the perception that the innovation under consideration offers the prospective organization an advantage over its current approach. Simplicity highlights the hesitation for organizations to adopt innovations that seem too complex to implement easily and inexpensively. Compatibility emphasizes the importance for new tools to interact with tools already in use by the organization as well as the tendency for organizations to continue to operate according to the status quo. Observability enhances adoption by association and modeling. In other words, organizations are more likely to adopt innovations that are also adopted (and visible) by their peer organizations. Finally, trialability means that organizations will be more likely to adopt an innovation if it is easy and inexpensive to try before a full implementation is undertaken.

The Enterprise 2.0 Adoption Survey,[14] conducted in May 2009, identified the primary concerns limiting the adoption of Enterprise 2.0 technologies. Resistance to change was the challenge most commonly named by participants (52.3 percent), followed by difficulty in measuring return on investment (42.1 percent). Other concerns included the ability to integrate Enterprise 2.0 technologies with existing organizational systems (40.6 percent), security concerns (31.5 percent), budget restrictions (25.4 percent), product knowledge (22.8 percent), and tools are not fully enterprise ready yet (22.3 percent). Note the relationship between these responses and the characteristics explaining adoption of innovation. Resistance to change and the ability to integrate Enterprise 2.0 technologies with existing systems both relate to the compatibility characteristic. The readiness of the tools and security concerns may reflect a relative advantage issue. Fortunately for Enterprise 2.0, the characteristics of simplicity, observability, and trialability are readily in place. The vast majority of Enterprise 2.0 technologies are inexpensive, accessible, and easily implemented. Because Enterprise 2.0 began with Web 2.0 consumer-centric tools, many of the decision makers involved in transferring technology to organizational uses have much experience using the tools. Finally, industry conferences such as the Enterprise 2.0 conferences, Web 2.0 sessions, and TechWeb ensure that exemplar organizations and solutions are featured.

GROUND RULES FOR E2.0

Despite what's been presented here thus far, critics contend that Enterprise 2.0 technologies are more appropriate to satisfying consumer whims than to meeting organizational goals. Arguments against suggest that applications already available are underutilized, the social nature of Web 2.0, whether applied internally to organizations or not, enhance the risk of lost productivity, and the tools may result in an even greater sense of information overload. These arguments are not without merit. Ethan Yarbrough explains in his blog, Emerging Web Memo, the five key concepts important for pursuing Enterprise 2.0.[15] These concepts, when embraced before, during, and after the implementation of Enterprise 2.0 technologies in the organization, will help to ensure the desired outcomes.

- Enterprise 2.0 is about context, not just content. Libraries house vast quantities of data, none of which would aid in problem-solving and decision-making if the data were not searchable and accessible. It is the context that enables the content to provide value.
- Enterprise 2.0 should replace processes, not add processes. These solutions should enable employees to spend more time on accomplishing the core functions associated with their jobs and less on procedures and paper trails.
- Simple wins. As we noted, simplicity aids in adoption. Even if the organization recognizes the value of Enterprise 2.0 tools, they will not add value unless the organizational stakeholders embrace and use the tools. Yarbrough wisely notes that some of the best tools are also simple ones (e.g., Q-tip and toothbrush).
- Enterprise connections lead to retention (employee and knowledge) that leads to success. Employees operating in collaborative and interactive work environments are more likely to feel that their jobs are enriching and, consequently, feel satisfied and fulfilled with their work. Higher retention helps to maintain institutional knowledge on its own, but in addition, the ability for social tools to maintain documentation on the evolution of communication and decisions in the organization means that even as employees move on to other organizations, knowledge is retained.
- Changing an organization through Enterprise 2.0 is incremental. (Or as Yarbrough writes, "It's a glacier, not fireworks.") Organizations, particularly large ones, do not accept and integrate changes in operational procedures quickly and easily. Fortunately, adopting Enterprise technologies can be managed in small steps over time, rather than in a single overhaul of the system. Still, it is best to set expectations realistically during implementation and after, as employees begin to adopt and use the technologies provided.

Thus, we find ourselves in the position of acknowledging that our economy is one based on knowledge and the knowledge is social. It is shared. It is collaborative. It is ever evolving. What we know and how we use it are the components leading to competitive advantage.

ENTERPRISE 2.0—THE STRATEGIC ENTERPRISE

In this, the first of two volumes exploring Enterprise 2.0, our focus is the strategic enterprise. We begin with a contribution by Dr. Andrew McAfee of the Center for Digital Business in the MIT Sloan School of Management, which explains McAfee's SLATES mnemonic as a framework for effectively implementing Enterprise 2.0 technologies in the organization. In Chapter 3, we hear from Robert Rose, Vice President of Marketing and Strategy at CrownPeak Technology, which is the market leader for on-demand content management. Rose highlights the major trends leading to the need for and use of Enterprise technologies. Next, a case study on Handshake 2.0 illustrates the potential successes available for those who embrace social technology in business. In Chapter 5, legal expert Ken Maready explains the legal environment facing Enterprise 2.0 organizations, providing a primer on the legal challenges for organizations using social technology as well as best practices and protective steps. Chapter 6 focuses on content management systems for the Enterprise. From there we shift to cultural and tactical implications of Enterprise 2.0. Lauren McKay of *CRM* magazine tells stories of organizations practicing transparency and those which are not. The ability to strategically use social media as a service quality tool, and particularly as an approach to service recovery, is presented in a chapter by Dr. Deborah Cowles. Public relations is ever important to the strategic enterprise; Bob Witeck, CEO of Witeck-Combs Communications, presents the five characteristics facing the public relations function in the Enterprise. Dr. Lisa Spiller, the nation's leading direct marketing educator, elucidates on digital applications of direct marketing. Marketing with Web 2.0 technology means reaching the "long tail" of the Internet; in Chapter 11, Rose interprets the potential for the mass-servicing of micro markets. In Chapters 12 and 13, we hear more on the concept of cloud computing. First is a primer on cloud computing from James Elliott Brown of Emulsion Marketing, followed by the significant shifts in the practice of accounting for the Enterprise given the power of cloud computing. Dr. Anja S. Goritz presents the ability for Enterprise 2.0 organizations to embrace social technologies as a method of reducing the expenses and inefficiencies of marketing research. Finally, Judy Payne of the Henley Knowledge Management Forum presents the influential role of social software as the collaborative spine of the Enterprise. These 15 chapters make up our coverage of the strategic Enterprise. In Volume 2, our focus is the behavioral enterprise, with an in-depth look at the managerial and marketing applications and issues faced by the Enterprise.

NOTES

1. Tim O'Reilly, "What Is Web 2.0: Design Patterns and Business Models for the Next Generation of Software," O'Reilly Network, September 30, 2005, http://www.oreillynet.com/pub/a/oreilly/tim/news/2005/09/30/what-is-web-20.html.

2. Andrew McAfee, "Enterprise 2.0: The Dawn of Emergent Collaboration," *MIT Sloan Management Review* 47, no. 3 (2006): 21–28.

3. Ron Miller, "Enterprise 2.0 101: An Executive Guide to Enterprise 2.0," CIO, November 21, 2008, http://www.cio.com.au/article/268364/enterprise_2_0 _101_an_executive_guide_enterprise_2_0.

4. See Note 1.

5. Whitney Michael, "Enterprise 2.0: What, Why and How," Enterprise 2.0 Conference, May 2009, http://www.e2conf.com/whitepaper.

6. Tom Burns and G. M. Stalker, *The Management of Innovation* (London: Tavistock, 1961).

7. Sarah Perez, "Enterprise 2.0 to Become a $4.6 Billion Industry by 2013," ReadWriteWeb, April 20, 2008, http://www.readwriteweb.com/archives/enterprise _20_to_become_a_46_billion_industry.php.

8. See Note 5.

9. Merriam-Webster OnLine, http://www.merriam-webster.com/dictionary/ social.

10. Andy Mulholland, "Enterprise Widgets Join Enterprise MashUps," CTO Blog, June 16, 2008, http://www.capgemini.com/ctoblog/2008/06/enterprise _widgets_join_enterp.php.

11. Chris Warner, "The 3 Parts of Mashing," The Enterprise Web 2.0 Blog, November 3, 2008, http://blogs.jackbe.com/2008/11/3-parts-of-mashing.html.

12. Michael Peck, "Soldiers Learn Hazards of War in Virtual Reality," *National Defense*, February 1, 2005, http://www.encyclopedia.com/doc/1G1-128600658 .html.

13. IBM, "Made in IBM Labs: IBM Creates Software for Holding Face-to-Face Meetings in Virtual Worlds," March 4, 2009, Press Release, http://finance .yahoo.com/news/Made-in-IBM-Labs-IBM-Creates-iw-14541498.html.

14. See Note 5.

15. Ethan Yarbrough, "The 5 Big Ideas of Enterprise 2.0," Emerging Web Memo, May–June 2009, http://www.emergingwebmemo.com/search/label/The%205% 20Big%20Ideas%20of%20Enterprise%202.0.

2

ENTERPRISE 2.0: THE DAWN
OF EMERGENT COLLABORATION*

Andrew McAfee

By the fall of 2005, the European investment bank Dresdner Kleinwort Wasserstein (DrKW) had just completed a rollout of three new communication technologies to most of its employees. The tools—which included blogs, wikis and messaging software for groups and individuals[1]— caught on first among IT staffers, who soon realized that the initial wiki environment lacked a feature called *presence display*. That is, it didn't offer a way to tell if another employee was at his or her computer.

At 10:44 London time on October 11, 2005, an IT employee posted to his blog: *... it's about squeezing as much as we can out of what we have in place now ... The [presence display] idea for example can be achieved with ease [in the wiki] by simply adding the link below to an image tag ... It's a bit rough round the edges and the icon could be much better but does do what you want.*

At 11:48, a colleague posted a comment on the same blog: *Cool, I have then taken your [link] and (pretty nastily) hacked presence display into [the wiki]. I'll let Myrto [Lazopoulou, head of user-centered design at DrKW] know ... and ask her to look into perhaps getting her team [to see] whether we can do this better ...*

Within 64 minutes and without any project definition or planning, a presence display solution had been spontaneously taken from concept to implementation, then submitted to the person formally responsible.

*Reprinted with permission from Enterprise 2.0: The Dawn of Emergent Collaboration by Andrew McAfee, *MIT Sloan Management Review*, volume 47, no. 3, 2006, pp. 21–28, by permission of publisher. Copyright © 2006 by Massachusetts Institute of Technology. All rights reserved.

Why are these new technologies particularly noteworthy? After all, companies already have plenty of communication media—e-mail, instant messaging, intranets, telephones, software for document sharing and knowledge management, and so on. As the vignette above suggests, the new technologies are significant because they can potentially knit together an enterprise and facilitate knowledge work in ways that were simply not possible previously.

To see how, we need to first understand the shortcomings of the technologies currently used by knowledge workers, then examine how the newly available technologies address these drawbacks. We'll then return to the DrKW case to see how to accelerate their use within an enterprise, and highlight the challenges of doing so. Most of the information technologies that knowledge workers currently use for communication fall into two categories. The first comprises *channels* —such as e-mail and person-to-person instant messaging—where digital information can be created and distributed by anyone, but the degree of commonality of this information is low (even if everyone's e-mail sits on the same server, it's only viewable by the few people who are part of the thread). The second category includes *platforms* like intranets, corporate Web sites, and information portals. These are, in a way, the opposite of channels in that their content is generated, or at least approved, by a small group, but then is widely visible—production is centralized, and commonality is high.

Knowledge management (KM) systems have tried to have it both ways. They have sought to elicit tacit knowledge, best practices, and relevant experience from people throughout a company and put this information in a widely available database. It seems appropriate now, however, to refer to KM systems in the past tense; they didn't even show up in a recently published (2005) survey of the media used by knowledge workers.

This survey, conducted by knowledge researcher Thomas Davenport,[2] shows that channels are used more than platforms, but this is to be expected. Knowledge workers are paid to produce, not to browse the intranet, so it makes sense for them to heavily use the tools that let them generate information. So what's wrong with the status quo? One problem is that many users aren't happy with the channels and platforms available to them. Davenport found that while all knowledge workers surveyed used e-mail, 26 percent felt it was overused in their organizations, 21 percent felt overwhelmed by it, and 15 percent felt that it actually diminished their productivity. In a survey by Forrester Research, only 44 percent of respondents agreed that it was easy to find what they were looking for on their intranet.[3]

A second, more fundamental problem is that current technologies for knowledge workers aren't doing a good job of capturing their knowledge. As Davenport puts it, "The dream ... that knowledge itself—typically unstructured, textual knowledge—could be easily captured, shared, and applied to knowledge work . . . [has not] been fully realized. . . . Progress is being made . . . [but] it's taken much longer than anyone expected." In the practice of doing their jobs, knowledge workers use channels all the time and frequently visit both internal and external platforms (intranet and Internet).[4] The channels, however, can't be accessed or searched by anyone else, and visits to platforms leave no traces. Furthermore, only a small percentage of most people's output winds up on a common platform. Thus, the channels and platforms in use aren't much good at providing answers to such questions as: What's the right way to approach this analysis? Does a template exist for it? Who's working on a similar problem right now? When our Brazilian operation reorganized last year, who were the key people? What are the hot topics in our R&D department these days? Indeed, it's probably safe to say that within most companies most knowledge work practices and output are invisible to most people. The good news is that new platforms have appeared that focus not on capturing knowledge itself, but rather on the *practices* and *output* of knowledge workers.

ENTERPRISE 2.0 TECHNOLOGIES: BLANK SLATES

These new digital platforms for generating, sharing, and refining information are already popular on the Internet, where they're collectively labeled "Web 2.0" technologies. I use the term "Enterprise 2.0" to focus only on those platforms that companies can buy or build in order to make visible the practices and outputs of their knowledge workers. The excerpts from the DrKW blogs, for example, record an interaction *and* its output, as well as the identities of three people involved. These blog entries are part of a platform that's readable by anyone in the company, and they're persistent. They make an episode of knowledge work widely and permanently visible. Technology paradigms are often made up of several components. For example, the components of Windows, Icons, Menus, and Pointers (mice) combine to yield the WIMP user interface of most personal computers today.[5] Similarly, I use the acronym SLATES to indicate the six components of Enterprise 2.0 technologies:

Search

For any information platform to be valuable, its users must be able to find what they are looking for. Intranet page layouts and navigation aids can help, but users are increasingly bypassing these in favor of keyword searches.[6] It might seem that orderly intranets maintained by a professional staff would be easier to search than the huge, dynamic, uncoordinated Internet, but this is not the case. In the Forrester survey, less than half of respondents reported that it was easy for them to find what they were looking for on their intranets. A 2005 study by the Pew Internet & American Life

Project, on the other hand, found that 87 percent of Internet searchers report having successful search experiences most of the time.[7] The second element in the SLATES infrastructure helps explain this surprising difference.

Links

Google made a huge leap forward in Internet search quality by taking advantage of the information contained in links between Web pages. Links are an excellent guide to what's important and provide structure to online content. In this structure, the "best" pages are the ones that are most frequently linked to. Search technology like Google's works best when there's a dense link structure that changes over time and reflects the opinions of many people. This is the case on the Internet, but not on most of today's intranets, where links are made only by a relatively small internal Web development group. In order for this to change within companies, many people have to be given the ability to build links. The most straightforward way to accomplish this is to let the intranet be built by a large group rather than a small one.

Authoring

Internet blogs and Wikipedia have shown that many people have a desire to author—to write for a broad audience. As wiki inventor Ward Cunningham recalls, "I wanted to stroke that story-telling nature in all of us. . . . I wanted people who wouldn't normally author to find it comfortable authoring, so that there stood a chance of us discovering the structure of what they had to say."[8] Cunningham's point is not that a lot of undiscovered Shakespeares are out there, but that most people have something to contribute, whether it's knowledge, insight, experience, a comment, a fact, an edit, a link, and so on, and authorship is a way to elicit these contributions. Blogs let people author individually, and wikis enable group authorship. Content on blogs is cumulative (individual posts and responses to them accumulate over time), while on wikis it's iterative (people undo and redo each other's work). When authoring tools are deployed and used within a company, the intranet platform shifts from being the creation of a few to being the constantly updated, interlinked work of many. Evidence from Wikipedia shows that group authorship can lead to convergent, high-quality content. This seems paradoxical. How can an egalitarian, editor-free authoring environment ever yield consensus and agreement? Won't people who disagree just keep disagreeing?

Tags

The Forrester survey revealed that after better searching mechanisms, what experienced users wanted most from their companies' intranets was better categorization of content. Some sites on the Web aggregate large amounts of content, then outsource the work of categorization to their users by letting them attach tags—simple, one-word descriptions. These sites—such as Flickr for photos, Technorati for blogs, and Delicious for Web site bookmarks—don't try to impose an up-front categorization scheme; they instead let one emerge over time as a result of users' actions. The categorization system that emerges from tagging is called a folksonomy (a categorization system developed over time by folks).[9] A folksonomy is in some ways the opposite of a *taxonomy*, which is an up-front categorization scheme developed by an expert. Folksonomies have some disadvantages relative to taxonomies: They're not usually multilevel, for one thing, and they can be redundant. Their main advantage is that they reflect the information structures and relationships that people actually use, instead of the ones that were planned for them in advance. In addition to building folksonomies, tags provide a way to keep track of the platforms visited by knowledge workers. Imagine a tool like Delicious deployed within an enterprise. Employees could use it to keep track of useful intranet and Internet pages they've consulted, and to assign tags to these pages as reminders of content. They also could see which other employees are using the same tags, and what sites *they've* visited. As a result, patterns and processes in knowledge work would become more visible.

Extensions

Moderately "smart" computers take tagging one step further by automating some of the work of categorization and pattern matching. They use algorithms to say to users, "If you liked that, then by extension you'll like this." Amazon's recommendations were an early example of the use of extensions on the Web. To see another example, download the browser toolbar available from stumbleupon.com. With it, users simply select a topic they're interested in, then click the "stumble" button. They're taken to a Web site on that topic. If they like it, they click a "thumbs-up" button on the toolbar; if not, they click a "thumbsdown" button. They then "stumble" on to another site. Over time, StumbleUpon matches preferences to send users only to sites they'll like. It's surprising how quickly, and how well, this simple system works. It reasons by extension, and homes in on user tastes with great speed.

Signals

Even with powerful tools to search and categorize platform content, a user can easily feel overwhelmed. New content is added so often that it can become a full-time job just to check for updates on all sites of interest. The final element of the SLATES infrastructure is technology to signal users when new content of interest appears. Signals can come as e-mail alerts, but these contribute to overloaded inboxes and may be treated like spam. A novel technology called RSS (which usually refers to "really simple syndication") provides another solution. Authors such as bloggers use RSS to generate a short notice each time they add new content. The notice usually consists of a headline that is also a link back to the full content. User software programs called "aggregators" periodically queries sites of interest for new notices, downloads them, puts them in order and displays their headlines. With RSS, users no longer have to surf constantly to check for changes; they instead simply consult their aggregators, click on headlines of interest and are taken to the new content.

ENTERPRISE 2.0 GROUND RULES

As technologists build Enterprise 2.0 technologies that incorporate the SLATES components, they seem to be following two intelligent ground rules. First, they're making sure their offerings are easy to use. With current tools, authoring, linking, and tagging all can be done with nothing more than a Web browser, a few clicks, and some typing. No HTML skills are required. It seems reasonable to assume that anyone who can compose e-mail and search the Web can use all of the technologies described in this article with little or no training. Second, the technologists of Enterprise 2.0 are trying hard not to impose on users any preconceived notions about how work should proceed or how output should be categorized or structured. Instead, they're building tools that let these aspects of knowledge work emerge. This is a profound shift. Most current platforms, such as knowledge management systems, information portals, intranets and work-flow applications, are highly structured from the start, and users have little opportunity to influence this structure. Wiki inventor Cunningham highlights an important shortcoming of this approach: "For questions like 'What's going on in the project?' we could design a database. But whatever fields we put in the database would turn out to be what's not important about what's going on in the project. What's important about the project is the stuff that you don't anticipate."[10]

Wikis and blogs start as blank pages, and folksonomies begin when users start entering tags. After using them for a while, the degree of structure and lack of flexibility in other platforms can begin to seem strange. It also starts to seem odd that companies and technologists ever proposed highly structured KM systems to capture highly unstructured knowledge work.

Their different approaches to structure, however, do not mean that Enterprise 2.0 technologies are incompatible with older ones. They can be added to the channels and platforms already in place. In addition, existing channels and platforms can be enhanced by adding discrete SLATES components; many e-mail clients, for example, now have the ability to receive RSS signals. In other words, technologies that let users build structure over time can coexist peacefully with those that define it up front.

Enterprise 2.0 technologies have the potential to let an intranet become what the Internet already is: an online platform with a constantly changing structure built by distributed, autonomous, and largely self-interested peers. On this platform, authoring creates content; links and tags knit it together; and search, extensions, tags, and signals make emergent structures and patterns in the content visible and help people stay on top of it all.

Enterprise 2.0 technologies are subject to network effects; as more people engage in authoring, linking, and tagging, the emergent structure becomes increasingly fine grained. This suggests an intriguing possibility. It has historically been the case that as organizations grow it becomes more and more difficult for people within them to find a particular information resource—a person, a fact, a piece of knowledge, or expertise. Enterprise 2.0 technologies, however, can be a force in the opposite direction. They can make large organizations in some ways more searchable, analyzable, and navigable than smaller ones, and make it easier for people to find precisely what they're looking for. The new technologies certainly don't overcome all the dysfunctions of corporate scale, but they might be able to address some of them.

THE ROLE MANAGERS WILL PLAY

It's tempting to conclude that managers are just another group of users and have no special role to play in helping the Enterprise 2.0 platform take off within their companies. After all, they didn't need to do much to encourage use of the current channels of e-mail and instant messaging, and they can't really look over their people's shoulders all day saying, "Tag that! Make a link! Now blog about what you just did!" More fundamentally, if the new technologies are so compelling, won't people just start using them without being directed to? Indeed, the apparently spontaneous success of Wikipedia, the blogosphere, and some Web 2.0 tools could convince many companies that "if we build it, they will come." Four aspects of the DrKW case illustrate, however, that use of Enterprise 2.0 technologies is not automatic and depends greatly on decisions made and actions taken by managers:

A Receptive Culture

By most accounts, DrKW's culture was a fertile one in which to cultivate new collaboration practices. In 2005, DrKW's employees voted it the best place to work among global financial services companies,[11] and the company's managers continually strive to build a robust community and gain the trust of the work force. As DrKW CIO J. P. Rangaswami says,

"I'm not sure wikis would work in a company that *didn't* already have 360-degree performance reviews."

A Common Platform

Rangaswami and his team chose to have one large wiki at the bank instead of many unconnected ones. This common platform allowed collaborations to emerge that probably never would have happened otherwise. If a company's collaboration infrastructure consists of many mutually inaccessible "walled gardens," then search, links, tags, extensions and signals can't work across them. Rangaswami didn't want this to happen, so groups at the bank can get a private workspace only by making a special request. Other companies might make different choices about the degree of fragmentation they will allow, depending on how they evaluate the trade-offs between commonality and customization.

An Informal Rollout

The team also decided not to publicize wiki and blogging software heavily at first, or to do anything like a formal rollout of the new tools. They instead encouraged a few groups and individuals to start blogging and creating wiki pages with the hope that the content they generated would be compelling enough to draw people in. "We wanted people to come to these tools because there was something of interest already there, not because they were told to," says head of user-centered design, Myrto Lazopoulou.

Also, Rangaswami believed that by posting policies up front he'd implicitly be telling people how to use the new tools (in psychological terms he'd be *anchoring* and *framing* usage norms), and he wanted employees to define uses for themselves. He wasn't concerned when employees started using the platform for non-work purposes like setting up a poker club and asking advice on camcorder purchases. As he says, "These uses don't consume any scarce resources, and they might encourage people to use the tools more." He also felt that explicit policies about hate speech and harassment were unnecessary. Any employee familiar with the organization's culture and norms would already know that such content was forbidden, regardless of medium.

Still, for any company building a new collaborative infrastructure, online norms and culture certainly will evolve, whether or not explicit policies are in place at the start. It is likely that over time some contributions to the new infrastructure will be inappropriate—demeaning to a coworker, boss, or subordinate, or wrong on important facts. How managers deal with these contributions will be critically important, and highly visible. Wikipedia has shown that it's possible for a large group of people to interact productively and collegially, even while disagreeing, as they build a digital resource over time. It remains to be seen whether this will be true within companies.

Managerial Support

Line managers at DrKW had to do a great deal of work to make sure the new platform would be used once it was in place. Darren Lennard, DrKW's managing director, became a believer in wikis as soon as he saw a demonstration because, as he said, "I was getting 300 internal e-mail messages a day. The great majority of them were completely irrelevant to me, but I still spent hours each day going through them. I saw that wikis were a better tool for a lot of our collaborative work, and I wanted my team to start using them."

To encourage usage, Lennard put up an initial wiki page with a vague mission statement on it, e-mailed everyone to tell them about the new tool and what it could do, and encouraged them to start using it. Nothing happened. People weren't clear on what it was, what it should be used for or what its advantages were, so they stayed away. "I realized that I had to be a lot more directive if I wanted behaviors to change," says Lennard, "and I also had to put up wiki content that required users to get involved." Lennard posted the agenda and action items for an upcoming meeting, suggesting that people use the wiki for their responses to them. "I told my desk that I would no longer read e-mail on some topics," he says.

One of the most surprising aspects of Enterprise 2.0 technologies is that even though they're almost completely amorphous and egalitarian, they appear to spread most quickly when there's some initial structure and hierarchy. "Information anarchy is just that," says Lennard. "You have to give people a starting point that they can react to and modify; you can't just give them a blank workspace and say, 'Use this now.' I'm confident that we'll hit a 'tipping point' after which tool use will grow on its own, but we're not quite there yet." Blogging at DrKW, for example, has increased gradually but steadily.

Challenges and Opportunities

Even if managers and technologists do everything correctly when initiating Enterprise 2.0 technologies within their companies, two potential threats remain. The first is that busy knowledge workers won't use the new technologies, despite training and prodding. Most people who use the Internet today aren't bloggers, wikipedians, or taggers. They don't help produce the platform—they just use it. Will the situation be any different on company intranets? It's simply too soon to tell.

The second threat is that knowledge workers might use Enterprise 2.0 technologies exactly as intended, but this may lead to unintended outcomes. Intranets today reflect one viewpoint—that of management—and are not platforms for dissent or debate. After blogs, wikis, and other voice-giving technologies appear, this will change. However, the question remains: Will the change be welcomed?

Management scholar Chris Argyris has noted a distinction between people's *espoused theories* and their *theories-in-use*. An espoused theory, for example, might be, "I'm sincerely interested in learning, improvement and empowerment. I want to give the people in my organization all the tools they need to interact." Argyris found, though, that most people's theory-in-use is driven by (among other things) the need to remain in unilateral control and the desire to suppress negative feelings. When the two theories come into conflict, the theory-in-use usually wins, which helps explain why so many corporate empowerment initiatives fail, or at least disappoint.[12]

It's easy to see how these insights apply to Enterprise 2.0 technologies. These tools reduce management's ability to exert unilateral control and will be used to express some level of negativity. Do a company's leaders really want this to happen? Will they be able to resist the temptation to silence dissent? What will happen, for example, the first time someone points out in their blog that an important project is behind schedule and that corners are being cut? What will happen if the content on the new platform is uncomfortable for powerful people within a company?

Because no one's in charge of the Internet, no one can shut it down when it veers in directions they find uncomfortable. But a company's Enterprise 2.0 technologies can be shut down. They also can be influenced by people in authority—bosses can exert all kinds of subtle and not-so-subtle leverage over online content.

This means that leaders have to play a delicate role, and one that changes over time, if they want Enterprise 2.0 technologies to succeed. They have to at first encourage and stimulate use of the new tools, and then refrain from intervening too often or with too heavy a hand. If they fail at either of these roles—if they're too light at first or too heavy later on—their company is liable to wind up with only a few online newsletters and whiteboards, used for prosaic purposes.

Enterprise 2.0 technologies have the potential to usher in a new era by making both the practices of knowledge work and its outputs more visible. Because of the challenges these technologies bring with them, there will be significant differences in companies' abilities to exploit them. Because of the opportunities the technologies bring, these differences will matter a great deal.

Notes

1. DrKW's internal blogs are powered by b2evolution, its wiki-building software is Social Text, and its messaging software is Mindalign.

2. Davenport's book *Thinking for a Living* (Boston: Harvard Business School Press, 2005) is the source for all data and quotes attributed to him in this chapter.

3. M. Morris, "How Do Users Feel about Technology?" Forrester Research, April 8, 2005.

4. In *The Social Life of Information* (Boston: Harvard Business School Press, 2000), J. S. Brown and P. Duguid define practice as "the activity involved in getting work done."

5. The WIMP was developed at Xerox PARC, successfully commercialized by Apple, and adopted by Microsoft starting with its Windows operating system.

6. D. O'Reilly, "Web-User Satisfaction on the Upswing," *PC World*, May 7, 2004, http://www.pcworld.com/news/article/0,aid,116060,00.asp.

7. D. Fallows, "Search Engine Users," Pew Internet & American Life Project, January 2005.

8. B. Venners, "Exploring with Wiki: A Conversation with Ward Cunningham, Part I," October 20, 2003, http://www.artima.com/intv/wiki.html.

9. The information architect Thomas Vander Wal is usually given credit for coining this term.

10. See Note 8.

11. The vote and its results are discussed at http://news.hereisthecity.com/features/best_place_to_work/4764.cntns and http://news.hereisthecity.com/news/business_news/4764.cntns.

12. See, for example, C. Argyris, "Empowerment: The Emperor's New Clothes," *Harvard Business Review* 76 (May–June 1998): 98–105.

3

BEYOND WEB 2.0: IMPLICATIONS FOR BUSINESSES

Robert Rose

Our story starts in Hagerstown, Maryland, in September 2008. Carolyn Motz, the Hagerstown Regional Airport Director didn't say a word, but smiled slightly as she climbed up the stairs to the podium. The area of the airport where the press conference was assembled was only partially filled with uniformed airport employees, reporters, and a few local government officials. As such, her voice echoed and sounded sharper than it normally would. "Today is a big day," she announced. "This four-state area now has commercial service on Allegiant Air to Orlando, Florida."[1] Motz then invited the sales director for Allegiant Air to join her at the podium. He briefly outlined the price and schedule for the non-stop MD80 flights—and then asked the crowd to guess where they were going as he and Motz donned Mickey Mouse ears. The crowd laughed appropriately at the well-rehearsed stage craft and applauded politely. Most of the subsequent newspaper stories however, ignored that bit of comedy, and took the angle of what a "relief" it must have been that the yearlong drought of commercial air service at the airport was over. But what happened? Why was this so significant?

To understand the answers to those questions, we need to go almost 10 years back in time. Right after 2000, the city government in Hagerstown made the case to construct a longer runway at their regional airport. They did this in an effort to lure the more lucrative, regional airline jets instead of the turboprop planes that had historically been the exclusive traffic. At the time, there was an amazingly explosive growth of regional air carriers, and they were all beating the pants off of the national airlines. Hagerstown was going to be an early adopter of this hot trend and capitalize on this "new" capability. In November 2007, several years and a whopping $61 million later, Hagerstown opened its new runway. There was only one problem: Two months earlier they had lost scheduled air service altogether when Air Midwest had flown its last flight out of the airport. Airlines in general, but regional airlines in particular, were now feeling the pinch from fuel prices[2] and disappearing at an alarming rate. Around that time, the national retail average for gas prices was hovering just over the $3.00 per gallon mark,[3] and it was going up every week.

So, 10 years earlier, when the city government had put forth a plan to open this new runway and add all the space, it must have been very similar to when we first heard about Web 2.0. Surely there were calls of "we have to take advantage of this trend," and "we have to plan ahead." But then, they came stumbling into 2008 with a brand new runway and no one to land on it.

Fortunately, this story has a happy ending. Allegiant has been operating out of the airport since that announcement in September 2008. Additionally, in January 2009, a second airline joined Allegiant.[4] The more important point in the story is about why it takes $60 million and 10 years to add a new runway. But, more relevant to our discussion, this is an object lesson for us as business managers specifically in charge of our Internet strategy and how we get beyond the hype that we now know as Web 2.0. Making huge bets against only what we know today is the surest way to failure.

Let's quickly look at another story to illustrate that point—if only because this example is more relevant to our roles in our organizations. For this one we go all the way back to 1996. There was a really, really hot trend that *Wired* called "the radical future of media."[5] It was called "Push Technology."

Remember PointCast? PointCast was an online service that allowed you to download a big application to your computer. Once opened, it sat in your computer's toolbar, periodically downloading news and video from the Web in content categories that you chose. People were calling it "the new television." In fact, Jupiter Research predicted in 1997 that "perhaps a third of all electronic revenues will go to push technology products over the next three or four years."[6]

The CEO of PointCast was David Dorman. He was the Mark Zuckerberg (of Facebook fame) of his day—he was the youngest CEO of Pacific Bell, and then went on to join PointCast when it was a 260-person company. At the time, PointCast had just over 1.2 million subscribers and the business model—revolutionary for its time—was selling advertising. In 1997, Dorman was interviewed in the *Los Angeles Times* and he predicted a mass consolidation in the Internet advertising space. He said it would require a break-even of $50 million for Web sites in advertising—meaning no small company could ever hope to compete with an advertising-based business model. He was quoted in that interview as saying, "you simply won't see 400 Web sites selling advertising."[7]

Google alone is now serving ads on hundreds of thousands of Web sites that use advertising as a revenue model. Some of them are more profitable than others, but I think we can safely say that Dorman's prediction was slightly off. Neither PointCast nor Push technology as an idea would even last to see the dot-com bubble burst.

Now, in all fairness, David Dorman was (and I'm sure still is) a talented business executive. As of this writing at the beginning of 2009, Dorman is on the board of Motorola[8] after having served as the President and CEO of AT&T. In that same interview where Dorman said you'll never see 400 Web sites selling advertising; he also alluded to the rise of an Internet-based phone service delivered by IP address. Of course we all know this now as VOIP delivered by companies like Skype.

But what does all this mean?

The PointCast lesson illustrates that a fundamental assumption about how Internet technology distribution would work subsequently eliminated a complete business. In 1997, it was generally assumed that broadband to the desktop would be a premium, available to only a very few, and that experiencing rich media such as audio and video would only be accomplished by loading it while you were doing other things. The problem was that PointCast never evolved—and its fundamental architecture of downloading content (never mind the irony of the term "push" technology) to the user's desktop infuriated system administrators who subsequently blocked the application through their company networks.

So, PointCast basically built a huge runway and then when it was finished discovered that they had two fundamental problems—one was that there were fewer and fewer people to land on it, and the other was that as broadband penetration to homes and businesses grew and Web sites became more media rich, PointCast's content became increasingly irrelevant.

Web 2.0 in 2009

In 2009, Web 2.0 was everywhere. If you were in business in 2009, you couldn't get away from it. It promised to revolutionize your business, save your money, generate more revenue, bake your cake, and save the world. But what lies beyond Web 2.0? Where are we going with the "business Web" and what lies beyond the hype of building huge runways and trying to turn our Web sites into the next Google, Twitter, Facebook, or Digg? To be fair, just like every new fast assimilation of technology solutions, many aspects of the concept of Web 2.0 are real, functional, and profitable for organizations of all sizes. In some cases it *is* driving revenue, and it *is* saving money. But none of the success is built on hype. So, whether or not we've put into place a strategy to deal with Web 2.0, now is the time we can start thinking about how we go beyond Web 2.0 and position ourselves most optimally for what is coming.

To do that, let's talk through a couple of global trends in business and Internet technology and how they apply to Web 2.0. You will learn how you can use these trends to create a more effective strategy for what might lie beyond.

Trend no. 1: The Consumerization of IT

In 2005, Gartner introduced consumerization and called it "the most significant trend affecting information technology (IT) during the next 10 years."[9] This trend, which has become a hotter and hotter topic, was really pointed at internal technology managers who were going to have to learn how to manage more and more consumer-related technology devices into the workflow and processes of the enterprise. For example, network system administrators are dealing with the huge proliferation of consumer-oriented, Internet-connected devices (cameras, phones, PDAs, notebooks). Likewise, they are challenged by widespread access to Internet-based software such as Twitter, Facebook, Gmail, and YouTube. But as one starts to examine this trend, there's an expansiveness that actually leads to something more profound.

In June 2008, Linda Musthaler, principal analyst with Essential Solutions Corporation, wrote an article for *Network World*.[10] She reported that at the Altiris ManageFusion conference a few months earlier, there had been a panel on the Gartner-focused subject of the "Consumerization of IT." Appearing on that panel was Peter Varhol, the executive editor of *Redmond* magazine, who said,

> The social networking technologies are providing today's businesses with a competitive advantage. Your marketing people are using [Web 2.0] as a focus group to test new ideas with new markets. It's a fair bet your PR people are putting customer success stories up on YouTube as well. You might be able to prohibit people in your enterprise from getting to YouTube because it's a security risk and a bandwidth hog, but you're not doing your company a competitive favor by doing so.

The key takeaway here is that while the consumerization of IT is a challenge for us operationally, it's an enormous opportunity for us as well. What the consumerization of IT really boils down to is that all the wonky technology stuff that everyone screamed about during Web 1.0 now works. It really works. It's just taken longer than everyone thought. Consumers are now finally becoming a lot more technologically savvy. They are actually adopting technology and having it help their lives. The whole idea of social networks connected by Web technology, whether it's Twitter, MySpace, Facebook, or the online community on your company's Web site, is a direct result of this progress.

People are starting to be comfortable using the Web to interact with one another. As users become more technically savvy and connect to the Internet via their iPhone or their laptop or other device, then the Web technology itself becomes more and more of a commodity. Or, more simply, as a specific function of the business the Web technology becomes much less strategically important.

You can certainly see it in the surge of the iPhone App Store. As of this writing the App Store has more than 15,000 applications. Installing an iPhone application is as easy as tapping a button, waiting for it to download, and using it. With Apple products, the technology just functions. It's not "cool" anymore to see the virtual gears turning or to have to have interfaces enabled to configure infinite aspects of your software. You just need it to work—because frankly you've got too much information to deal with to care what's going on under the hood.

Looking at this from other side is of course the business. Consider that when the Apple iPhone App Store launched, the average price of an app was about $4.70. Within just the first 100 hours of opening, the average price had dropped to $4.25.[11] Then, consider that as of November 2008, that had dropped to $3.21[12] and by May 2009 it was $2.50. That's a 46 percent drop in the average price of an application in the first year of existence. Apple has no reason to worry: As of that same date, there were 50,000 applications in the App Store and Apple was making millions per day on it.[13]

Web technology applications themselves are becoming disposable. Many are free, or so nearly free as to be simple impulse buys for people. The idea that software that I run on my portable device is a "considered purchase" is now becoming anachronistic.

You can also see it happening all over the Web with social networking applications launching on Facebook and the apps themselves becoming disposable. If you've ever been poked, or superpoked, or had a pillow-fight on Facebook, you know what I'm talking about.

This is really the effect of the consumerization of IT. It's not only how consumer adoption of technology is affecting the day-to-day life of the IT Manager in the enterprise—it's how consumer adoption of technology is affecting the business-to-business adoption of Web technology. And there is huge opportunity here that hasn't existed before.

Consider the recent, rapid rise of software-as-a-service and cloud computing. Consumers took to software-as-a-service almost immediately. The adoption of Gmail, MSN (aka Hotmail), and Yahoo for the critical application of e-mail happened very quickly. Then consider the adoption of Flickr as a way for families to share and store photographs, Wikipedia as the definitive source of information, or even Twitter as a way for us follow "real-time" news such as the death of Michael Jackson or the voter turmoil in Iran. Or consider that television, as a percentage of video media watched, was down to almost half for kids between the ages of 12 and 17.

The same phenomenon is now happening in business-to-business technology as well. Salesforce.com has become a juggernaut in leading the on-demand way to handle customer relationship management (CRM). Gigantic corporations such as Microsoft, Amazon, and Google have announced huge cloud computing infrastructures where companies can "lease" server space on demand. Consider the cost and effort of launching a Web site with the ability to feed leads into a CRM System, have an e-mail newsletter, and have it all managed by a content management system. That project eight years ago would be measured in (at least) tens of thousands of dollars and months of design, programming, and effort. Today, you can just about launch it for free with a few clicks and minimal effort and start publishing content the same day.

Key Takeaways of Trend no. 1

- **Stop Revolutionizing. Start Evolving**. Stop taking 10 years to build long runways to nowhere. Consider that Web 1.0 went from approximately 1995 to 2004– and that we're talking now about Web 3.0 a mere 5 years later. Time is compressed. At a macro view start looking at smaller bite-sized experiments with your Web strategy that allow your strategy to evolve more quickly. Worry more about your ability to measure these experiments. Launch your community—but launch it small and limited. Test it. Let it grow (or not). Understand if it starts to provide benefits. If it does, then feed it—figure out how to monetize it in your business. Nurture it. If it doesn't turn into a source of revenue or cost savings, kill it and move on. Don't just launch a blog, a wiki, or a social network and leave it out there for your users to find. One rant on your Web site is not a blog. One audio file is not a podcast. Understand that you need to evolve your process, as much as you do your Web site.
- **Technology is easy—or should be easy**. We used to be concerned about having a Web team, whether outsourced or hired, to build our Web site, maintain our Web technology, and manage everything having to do with our Internet strategy. We need to get out of that mind-set. Businesses need to fundamentally change the paradigm that you have to build anything as it relates to Web technology. Whereas the lack of resources created the imperative for us to understand Web technology in the early 2000s, the Web is now merely a platform by which we leverage the applications that are already built for us. Businesses should get out of the software development business. Stop building custom functionality for your Web site.

Trend no. 2: The New "No Rules" Rule of Web Strategy

In 2005, Clay Shirky, author of *Here Comes Everybody: The Power of Organizing Without Organizations*, spoke at the Ted Conference on how more loosely affiliated networks will replace the idea of the rigid, hierarchical corporate structure.[14] One of the main themes in that talk—and his subsequent book published three years later—is that small, infrequent contributions provided by outlying members can have great impact on an effort of work. Of course, as he points out, this is anathema to many corporations—where the main idea is that it's better to have a small, expert group of people produce the greatest results. In the institutional model it is in the company's best interest to doggedly protect this rigidity in order to remain competitive—or at least competitively efficient. Clay illustrates extraordinarily well how this is really the heart of the 80/20 rule.

The 80/20 rule is better known in statistical or mathematical circles as a "Power Law Distribution" or "Pareto Distributions," or in e-commerce (made famous by *Wired* Magazine's Chris Anderson) as the "long tail."

The general idea in the institutional management model is that 80 percent of the value of work will be provided by 20 percent of the people. In other words, companies hire the few "best and brightest" and focus on a tightly heirarchical model. They can't hire a thousand people to work on a project, despite the chance that a single employee may contribute one "killer" idea. It simply isn't worth what they'd have to pay that employee to sit in a cube idle for the vast majority of time.

Shirky's point in his Ted Talk and his subsequent book is that the Internet (and today's technology more generally) is a disintermediation of this model; that a much more compelling model for effort is a loose collaboration that accepts contribution all the way down the long tail.

The rise of open-source software is certainly an indicator of this trend—where software is developed, distributed, fixed, and improved much more quickly than software in a rigid institutional (e.g., company) environment. You may have thousands of people contributing to the overall project, but in general 20 percent of the people will have the most individual contributions and 80 percent of them will only contribute one or two features or pieces of code. The important thing is that many of these small contributions can be extraordinarily important. In other words, the best feature that makes the application useful might be contributed by one person and be his only contribution. This would never happen in an institutional or company model—where that person would have been fired long ago for never making anything but the one contribution.

An example of this outside technology—and one that wasn't as self-evident in 2005 when Clay originally gave the talk—is what's happened in the music business. Major music labels have always had an inherently hierarchical "expert-based" philosophy. They hired and subsequently produced only the "best of the best," leaving the rest as amateurs who aren't "good enough" to get into the club. This is the epitome of the old joke—how do you get to Carnegie Hall? Practice, practice, practice. The television series *American Idol* is the frozen juice concentrate of this model—and produces all the subsequent drama, heartache, and mostly mediocrity in terms of ultimate output. But, because of the ultimate inverted pyramid shape of its selection process, it makes for great television. Only one person can be the American Idol.

But the reason that this model worked for the music industry for so long isn't because they had focused attention on it. It was because producing professional music was difficult, technical, and expensive. Furthermore, *distribution* of the produced music was difficult, technical, and expensive. But the explosive advancement of home studio equipment changed producing and the Internet changed distribution. In other words, the technology is easy. Suddenly it was possible for musicals artist to produce their own records, distribute them by themselves over the Internet and iTunes, and make a career of it.

Now, that's not to say that anyone with a Macbook and a copy of Garage Band will be the next Taylor Swift or Jonas Brothers. Certainly there is value in having the marketing machine of a major label financing your career. But just as the consumerization of IT brings both challenges and opportunity to the enterprise, so does the openness of loosely affiliated networks bring opportunity to the institution willing to be more open to that idea.

The music business has assuredly had its challenges with technology. Digital technology has made music easier to copy and trade, and debates rage as to whether this is good or bad for the industry. For example, a Pew Internet study found that 78 percent of teenagers don't think downloading pirated music to their hard drive is stealing.[15] Conversely, the music business is finding opportunities that they've never had before: Consider the deal that MySpace made in September 2008 with Sony BMG, Universal Music Group, and Warner Music Group to form MySpace Music.[16] In that deal, consumers are able to listen to any piece of music in the participating companies' catalogs streamed through their player—all while consuming advertising. That's a new and previously untapped business model for record companies—advertising as a revenue stream. Or consider how new phenomenal artists are found erupting out of the long tail of MySpace mediocrity. It used to be the A&R (Artists and Repertoire) people from the major labels would listen to stacks of CDs, attend thousands of local music performances, and scour the country looking for the next big act. Now, with the Internet, you can see the meteoric rise of an artist like Soulja Boy from MySpace and YouTube. He started on his own, developed his own fan base and is now a major star. After generating more than 300 million views on YouTube, he has a new album, a line of sneakers, and an animated series in the works.[17]

Music labels have definitely gotten this message. In July 2009, Universal Music Group (UMG) made a deal with an Internet start-up company called TuneCore. Independent musicians can go to TuneCore and use the marketing and other benefits of a major label (for a fee) and also retain the rights to their own songs. Artists who belong to this new site are able to take advantage of the technology that allows them to sell their music directly to their fans—and also (when applicable) pay for the services that a major label would normally provide such as expert recording sessions and marketing support. Subsequently, the label gets a window into new artists and saves opportunity costs by watching the market develop around any artist that they want to proactively invest in. But how does this apply to our business and getting beyond Web 2.0?

Key Takeaways for Trend no. 2

There are two key takeaways from this trend:

- **Wag the Long Tail**. Understanding the long tail and how you can apply it to your enterprise is essential. The Web is now the functional platform we've always wanted and from which our business model can be challenged or helped—or both. Valuable ideas can come erupting out of the long tail, and we need to be able to take advantage of those ideas when they appear. We need to ask ourselves: How can we begin to make our enterprise more open? How can we establish our customers, prospective customers, and partners as a community? Where can we leverage the great ideas that may come from the one outlier member of that community? It may be that we need to set up a Web 2.0–style community for all of these groups so that they can communicate and network with one another in order to leverage the best out of our organization. Or, if we're a smaller organization it may simply be that we can join other like-minded organizations and get the power and "wisdom of crowds."
- **Think Differently about the Web**. It's okay if we use the Web differently than we have in the past. In 2010, we need to tell ourselves that it is okay if we in marketing, or we in sales, or we in accounting use the Web differently than do other teams in our organization. It is also okay if not all the teams are involved or even know about every single Web initiative we do.

  Finding the long tail through the organization means letting departments explore the platform that is the Web in a more meaningful and open way. That means that each may have a different use for it. Just like in the record company where the new A&R process has a very different and almost inherently tense relationship with the way music is distributed, so too can our different departments find different value in the Web. Each department should be encouraged to explore (see Technology Is Easy earlier) and experiment. You don't need an e-business team or a six-week technology engagement strategy to launch a blog. You shouldn't spend six weeks on a strategic IT Engagement to understand the value of launching a micro-site with a community around a product launch. These marketing sites can be—and sometimes should be—separate and distinct from some of the other Web efforts we may be involved in.

Beyond Web 2.0: It Changes Everything
I Know—and Nothing I Do!

There's a great quote from Yogi Berra: "*I never blame myself when I'm not hitting. I just blame the bat and if it keeps up, I change bats. After all, if I know it isn't my fault that I'm not hitting, how can I get mad at myself?*"[18] It's certainly not lost on me that as 2010 gets started, many business managers are saying, "I never got my organization into Web 2.0, and now people are talking about Web 3.0?" That's okay. Just grab another bat.

It's not linear. If you get anything out of this chapter, I hope it's to understand that what's happening here is nothing new—the lessons learned from Web 1.0 to Web 2.0 was that good business sense needed to be paid to a new technology. The lessons from Web 2.0 to Web 3.0 are that the new platform is just that—a platform. And while it's revolutionizing the ease of communication, if we don't have something valuable to say, well, we still won't be heard. This is really the "no rules" rules of managing your Web strategy. Getting beyond hype, and the buzz—embracing the power of community and the ease of facilitating conversation—and letting the flow of the Web work for you.

Web 3.0 and beyond will be the same. It's starting already to get the buzz around it. Depending on your point of view, you might hear about the "Semantic Web," the "real-time Web," or "the intelligent Web." Eric Schmidt at Google said this: "Web 3.0 will ultimately be seen as applications which are pieced together. There are a number of characteristics: the applications are relatively small, the data are in the cloud, the applications can run on any device, PC or mobile phone, the applications are very fast and they're very customizable. Furthermore, the applications are distributed virally: literally by social networks, by email. You won't go to the store and purchase them. . . . That's a very different application model than we've ever seen in computing."[19]

These ideas, the intelligent Web, and how they relate to our business are just the next step in the evolution. So, regardless of whether or not you have gone into Web 2.0 yet, let's look at how to make the takeaways real. What can you do today? Here's how to make this process real for you:

1. Look to De-Geek Your Web Strategy

It's a tried-and-true consultant trick, when you want to convince a customer that they shouldn't build technology, to break out the "you don't generate your own electricity" argument. But, at the beginning of the twentieth century, individual companies were still installing their own electrical generators to provide their own supply. To operate these generators, companies employed electrical managers. Their sole job was to ensure that electricity flowed evenly through the company.

Consider that in 1980, the IBM 5120 was a $10,000 personal computer. These micro-computers (as they were called then) were about the size of a large microwave oven. And they were all designed to run very specific programs. You could run the computer for accounting systems, or database management, or word processing—but only one at a time. These micro-computers were installed by large consulting firms into businesses and they finally allowed these businesses to have computing at the desktop level without needing what (at the time) was a quite popular job—a computer operator.

When Web strategy for the enterprise took off in 1997, few people understood this technology. Companies hired consulting firms, who in turn hired the people who understood how to code and assemble Web sites and Web applications. Organizations that were large enough employed teams of technology professionals whose job it was to build software applications for the organization's Web site. In 2010, that job should and will go the way of the electrical manager and the computer operator.

Unless you are actually building an Internet-based business that is, in and of itself, trying to become something that actually becomes part of the platform, then your organization should stop developing software and start using the Web as the simple communications platform it already is.

2. Look to the Clouds for Your Infrastructure

The days of large computing infrastructure are coming to an end. Unless you are a specialized business that somehow requires a large hardware infrastructure you should stop building your "Web generators" and look to host your computing services in the cloud. Put simply, "cloud computing" means subscribing to server space and using only what you need to perform the functions you need to function. This can mean everything from hosting your Web site or housing your CRM system, to managing your records and providing your desktop productivity tools. Connectivity is becoming ubiquitous and storage is becoming more and more inexpensive, so subscribing to those services and being able to scale as you grow is a much more cost-effective method of building a computing infrastructure than buying servers and/or leasing space in a data center.

There are a few different trends in cloud computing including:

- **Software-as-a-Service**. These types of companies deliver a single computer application, usually through a browser interface. Business Web examples of this type of company include Salesforce.com for CRM and Sales Force Automation, NetSuite for Accounting and CRM, Exact-Target for e-mail campaign management, and Omniture for Web analytics and online marketing.

- **Platform-Based Services**. Another type of software-as-a-service is offered by providers that open up their entire application to let developers create new types of applications on them. For example, Salesforce.com has a subscription called AppForce. This allows creative developers to write entirely new applications based on the SalesForce.com platform. So, for example, someone could write an entire online marketing application based on the AppForce.com platform. Using this strategy, a start-up doesn't have any infrastructure costs—and can scale quickly should their new application become successful. Google has recently announced a similar type of platform
- **Grid Computing** (or utility computing). Amazon.com, IBM, and Dell have all announced offerings for this type of service, which provides customers with the ability to use virtual servers and computers for large, usually supplemental tasks. This allows organizations that need temporary server farms for large projects the ability to subscribe to a large data center for some large computing project.
- **Cloud-based Web Services**. These types of services are usually provided by larger organizations that make aspects of their applications available via a subscription service. For example, Google makes their maps application available via a Web service—meaning that if anyone wants to create a Web-based application that requires a mapping component, they don't have to build one but can simply use Google's mapping services. Other types of services include news wires for content services, social networking aggregation for community, and even credit reporting and credit card processing.

These are not strategies that you have to switch to immediately, but as your infrastructure ages consider cloud-based services to replace your infrastructure and the cost-savings it will provide.

3. Start Developing Your Own Long Tail

Anheuser-Busch's embrace of the long tail is a great example of how a company can think outside the box and take advantage of outliers. In 1997, the company offered 26 brands of beer. As of 2007, the company had more than 80 brands. And, today, the company is brewing beer that is organic, beer that is specifically targeted at women, and even a beer that is made with sorghum (i.e., no wheat or barley) and so is theoretically "non-allergenic beer."

Anheuser-Busch certainly had the resources to produce these niche beers, and the biggest challenge (how to get shelf space for them all) was solved by Anheuser-Busch's unique size and ability to distribute any product. For example, it can take local microbrews and distribute them nationally or find simple and small regional market places for beers targeted at special demographics.

How your business applies a long-tail strategy will of course differ greatly depending on the business you conduct. However, here are just a few areas for examination. Perhaps they will spur you to get creative to wag your own long tail.

- **Wag the long tail of revenue**. You probably have a primary and even secondary source of income for your business. These probably come from one or a set of products. But ask yourself how you can add multiple types of revenue, even if they're small. For example, if you have complex products—have you established a set of training courses, or online videos that you could perhaps charge for? If you sell content—have you considered new and innovative ways to package (either breaking up or aggregating) the content to make for new product?
- **Wag the long tail of knowledge**. How many times is knowledge only derived and established at the head of an organization? How can an organization establish a more free-form set of ideas being traded within the organization? Consider Wikipedia.org where the world's knowledge is being assembled by hundreds of thousands of users who get no remuneration for it other than the satisfaction of knowing they contributed. How can you create your own Wikipedia in your organization? How can you use technology to establish a more free-running and conversational style of knowledge transfer?
- **Wag the long tail of relationships**. How can we open our organization up for finding new customers, hiring more expert employees, attracting more partners? Of course some people and organizations are close to the company: the employees, the customers, and the partners. But how can our organization either utilize existing social Web networks such as LinkedIn, or Facebook, or MySpace and open ourselves up? Here's a simple example. Why not have every person in your company start a LinkedIn account—and invite their networks to join. Every person with 100+ connections has access to millions of other people. If when you're looking to fill that new, hard-to-fit position—everyone updates their "status" to say "we're hiring and looking for someone to fill XYZ position"—you've just reached millions of people.

  Now, of course it's inefficient, and it's not targeted. That's the point. It's the long tail. But, if the perfect new employee sees that notice from someone in your employees' networks, was it worth the small amount of effort to establish that long tail?
- **Wag the long tail of experimentation**. If your organization is successful, you utilize established workflow processes and methodologies to get your business conducted. These are the best practices that you utilize every day. But ask yourself if there's not a new type of practice that you can try as a small experiment. It might involve applying technology—and it might not. But, instead of establishing a huge research project to determine if it will work, take the Google way: Launch a "beta" and see if it takes off or improves things. If it does, feed that process. You may be surprised. Even if the entire process doesn't eventually replace anything you may find one or two small elements that can be applied to the existing process to make it better.

Here's an example for marketing. Let's say you buy keywords and key phrases for your search engine marketing programs. To that end, you probably buy the top 10 key words that you come up with and that are core to your business. Why not try 1,000 key words and phrases? You can certainly come up with that many even if you only have one or two products or services. You may find that one of those really odd key phrases produces only one or two searches. But, perhaps both those searches turn into customers. This is the long tail performing at its best.

GETTING BEYOND WEB 2.0

In 1960, Theodore Levitt published the classic "Marketing Myopia" in the *Harvard Business Review* when he was still a lecturer in business administration at Harvard. Even if you're not familiar with it in specifics, you will certainly know of its classic theme of asking yourself "what business are you in?"[20] The cautionary tale he used involved the railroad industry, which thought it was in the "railroad" business and not the "transportation" business. He writes brilliantly of how to succeed in marketing by thinking of customer's needs, rather than selling product.

One of the other examples that Levitt uses in the paper, and one that often goes forgotten, is his pointed critique of the Hollywood studios. In 1960, the movie business was being threatened by this new-fangled technology called television. You might even call it Movies 2.0. Levitt chastised the studios saying, "Today, TV is a bigger business than the old narrowly defined movie business ever was. Had Hollywood been customer-oriented (providing entertainment) rather than product-oriented (making movies), would it have gone through the fiscal purgatory that it did?" Replace the word "TV" with "Internet," or "Web 2.0" and we'll see that there's still much to learn from Professor Levitt. Applying new types of strategies to your business isn't, itself, new. Again, moving your business beyond Web 2.0 should change everything you know—because the Web has finally arrived. It can provide the insight we desire as business managers, and it can facilitate the conversations we want to have with our customers, our employees, and our partners.

But it should change very little, if anything, of what we do. The reason we are successful in our respective businesses is that we have a specialized expertise in a particular niche. We provide a differentiated product or service and we've asked ourselves the question "what business are we *really* in?" Assuming we still agree with that answer, the Web beyond 2.0, 3.0, or even when we stop assigning versions to it, is just another evolving communications platform that helps us become more differentiated, waste less of our resources, serve our existing customers better, and attract more new prospects. For better or worse—it's that simple.

NOTES

1. Joshua Bowman, "Hagerstown Is All Ears When It Comes to Landing Allegiant," *Herald-Mail*, September 18, 2008, http://www.herald-mail.com/?cmd=displaystory&story_id=203744&format=html.

2. Micheline Maynard, "Airlines' Cuts Making Cities No-Fly Zones," *New York Times*, May 21, 2008, http://www.nytimes.com/2008/05/21/business/21air.html?_r=1&pagewanted=print.

3. "U.S. Gas Prices—November 26, 2007," *Consumer Reports*, November 26, 2007, http://blogs.consumerreports.org/cars/2007/11/us-gas-prices-3.html.

4. "New & Gallery: Recent News," Hagerstown Regional Airport, 2009, http://www.flyhagerstown.com/airport_info/news/newsRecent.html.

5. Kevin Kelly and Gary Wolf, "PUSH! Kiss Your Browser Goodbye: The Radical Future of Media Beyond the Web," *Wired*, 2004, http://www.wired.com/wired/archive/5.03/ff_push_pr.html.

6. Terry Schwadron, "The Push for Push and What It Says About New Media," *Los Angeles Times*, March 24, 1997, http://articles.latimes.com/1997-03-24/business/fi-41669_1_push-technology.

7. John Geirland and Eva Sonesh-Kedar, "PointCash Chief Describes The Pull of 'Push' Media," *Los Angeles Times*, April 6, 1998, http://articles.latimes.com/1998/apr/06/business/fi-36524.

8. Ibid.

9. "Gartner Says Consumerization Will Be Most Significant Trend Affecting IT during Next 10 Years," Gartner, October 20, 2005, http://www.gartner.com/press_releases/asset_138285_11.html.

10. Linda Musthaler, "What the Consumerization of IT Means to You: The Security Risks Involved in the Consumerization of IT," *NetworkWorld*, June 9, 2008, http://www.networkworld.com/newsletters/techexec/2008/060908techexec1.html.

11. David Hill, "App Store Day 4: Observations Coming out of the Smoke," Medialets, July 14, 2008, http://www.medialets.com/blog/2008/07/14/app-store-day-4-observations-coming-out-of-the-smoke.

12. Charles Teague, "5 Months and 9,000 Applications Later," DragonStyle, November 25, 2008, http://blog.charlesteague.com/links/2008/11/5-months-and-9000-applications-later.html.

13. Sara Haley, "Happy Birthday, App Store! Apple's App Store Turns One Year Old Today, with Over 50,000 Apps!," *Examiner*, July 11, 2009, http://www.examiner.com/x-14813-iPhone-Apps-Examiner~y2009m7d11-Happy-birthday-App-Store—Apples-App-Store-turns-one-year-old-today-with-over-50000-apps.

14. "Talks Clay Shirky on Institutions vs. Collaboration," TED: Ideas Worth Spreading, July 2005, http://www.ted.com/index.php/talks/clay_shirky_on_institutions_versus_collaboration.html.

15. "78% of Those Who Download Music Online Don't Think They Are Stealing," Pew Internet & American Life Project, Press Release, September 29, 2000, http://www.pewinternet.org/Press-Releases/2000/78-of-those-who-download-music-online-dont-think-they-are-stealing.aspx.

16. Mike Steere, "Rocking or Reeling? Record Labels Adapt to a World of Online Music," CNN, September 22, 2008, http://www.cnn.com/2008/TECH/09/22/music.future/.

17. Melissa Arseniuk, "Teen Rap Sensation Outlines Success to CES Crowd," *Las Vegas Sun*, January 7, 2009, http://www.lasvegassun.com/news/2009/jan/07/teen-rap-sensation-outlines-success-ces-crowd/.

18. Yogi Berra Quotes, Brainy Quote, http://www.brainyquote.com/quotes/quotes/y/yogiberra139940.html.

19. Richard MacManus, "Eric Schmidt Defines Web 3.0," ReadWriteWeb, August 7, 2007, http://www.readwriteweb.com/archives/eric_schmidt_defines_web_30.php.

20. Theodore Levitt, "Marketing Myopia," *Harvard Business Review*, July–August 1960: 24–42.

4

How to Adapt and Prosper in the Web 2.0 Marketspace

Anne Giles Clelland and Iain J. Clelland

Only connect!

—*E. M. Forster*, Howard's End

WEB 2.0 FOR ENTERPRISE 2.0

Four fundamental principles underpin the business use of Web 2.0, regardless of whether you are a solo start-up or a multinational corporation.

- It's you doing it.
- How you do it will change.
- The end leads the means.
- People seek connection.

It's You Doing It

Whatever term you use—Web 2.0 technologies, social networks, social media, new media, digital marketing, Web 3.0 and beyond—and regardless of how complex it is or becomes—Web 2.0 is used by individuals. It is "you" offering words, images, videos, audio, and interactivity to another "you."

The implications are awing, inspiring, and daunting. The behavior of your "you" online determines the quality of your business results. In order to get the best results from your use of Web 2.0 for your Enterprise 2.0, "you" must show up in Web 2.0 as your best self.

How You Do It Will Change

This is not the only personal demand Web 2.0 places on us. In addition to being our best selves online, we have to be flexible. Web 2.0 technology changes so quickly that "best practices" one day are dandelion seeds puffed into the breeze the next.

At the writing of this—the winter of 2009—our examples of Web 2.0 technologies for enterprises seem timely, even cutting edge. At your reading of this—sometime in the future—our examples will be dated, even quaint.

The lesson to be learned from the constantly changing nature of technology is this: Means will change. But many different means can achieve the same end.

Focusing on the mission, goals, and objectives of your enterprise—the end in mind—keeps the means used to achieve them dispensable. You can use the Web 2.0 technology at hand. When it becomes limited or is surpassed by a new technology, you can let it go and let your mission guide your selection and use of the next technology, i.e., your next means to achieve your end.

The End Leads the Means

Ah, the end in mind. What result do you want for your enterprise from your use of Web 2.0? We've heard answers about results phrased like this:

- We want to get the word out.
- We want more exposure.
- We want to brand our company.
- We want more traffic to our site.

And, simply:

- More

Each of these examples begs a repeat of the question. As a result of getting the word out, more exposure, branding your company, getting more traffic to your site, or just more of anything, what do you want to have happen?

Cash. Whatever enterprises do with Web 2.0 has to result in sales of products, services, or processes by retaining existing customers, attracting new ones, and increasing sales per customer.

Here are examples of results-based, profit-based ends in mind that align with missions, goals, and/or objectives.

- We want buyers or clients to generate $X amount of additional revenue per month, right here, right now.
- We have in development a _____ (fill in the blank with your high-end product, service, or complex process) that will require

a great deal of understanding before purchase. We need to create a market of potential customers or clients.

- We want X more recruits to place in these named, specific, revenue-generating positions.
- As recruiters, we want X more candidates per quarter to place in positions for referral fees.
- We are writing a book, want to sell it, and want to create a following now to serve as a potential market for the book later.

Specific ends in mind, such as the examples above, must lead the way for any business strategy, particularly for Web 2.0.

Web 2.0 technologies are, simply put, cool. But no matter how cool they are, they must be used as a means to achieve a specific end rather than serve as ends in themselves. Being a company that uses the latest Web 2.0 technologies is of little value if the use of those Web 2.0 technologies doesn't result in mission-supporting cash.

People Seek Connection

Everything you need to know about the fourth and final fundamental principle of using Web 2.0 for Enterprise 2.0 you learned waiting in the checkout line at a superstore. If you weren't talking to the person next to you in line, two, even three, even more people were talking to each other in the line farther back. Complete strangers, in proximity to each other, are drawn to connect.

Web 2.0 gives us a virtual sense of proximity to each other and the tools to act on that nearness. What we do naturally in the physical world—connect—we find ourselves drawn to do and capable of doing in the virtual world.

IMPLEMENTATION

The four fundamental principles of using Web 2.0 for Enterprise 2.0 provide companies with a foundation upon which to build a Web 2.0 strategy. We now offer foundational principles for implementing that strategy.

- It's who you are.
- It's what you know.
- It's who you know.
- It's what you say.
- It's how you say it.

It's Who You Are

The paradox of the business use of Web 2.0 is that a company is an entity and Web 2.0 is used by individuals. This necessitates that a company disentangle itself from its collective identity and select distinct individuals to lead its Web 2.0 strategy. As we mentioned, for the best business results, those individuals must, online, be their best selves.

Why? People do business with people they know. They particularly do business with people with whom they have relationships. Relationships are based on intuition, experience, and trust.

Humans have an intuitive sense about the authenticity and genuineness of the people with whom they interact. In the checkout line at the superstore, we start by reading body language. Online, we read words. We almost always know a fraud when we meet one in person. In reading someone's words, fraudulence is a little harder to detect. So Web 2.0 users scrutinize words relentlessly for any hints of phoniness. A company risks its business results if it's not prepared to be authentic and candid online.

Just as it works in the physical world, if we have good experiences with others, we begin to trust them. If we have bad experiences, we distrust them. Patterns of behavior matter.

The individuals in your company who design and execute your Web 2.0 strategy need to be courageously frank, authentic, transparent, and, simply put, worth knowing. Otherwise, those who connect with them through Web 2.0 won't intuit good things, have good experiences, develop relationships, or do business with you. Result? No cash.

If that mandate is followed—that your Web 2.0 people must be your best people—the exciting part of implementing a Web 2.0 strategy with the "It's who you are" principle is that a company is entering a competitive market with a unique product that can never, ever be duplicated.

You heard it from your mother or your science teacher—and if you didn't hear it, we're telling you now—there's no one like you. It is your "you" you have to offer the world, especially the world of Web 2.0.

Every type of experience, knowledge, perspective, or synthesis has been offered online—except yours. The more deeply you know your product—yourself—the more genuine originality you offer to Web 2.0.

It's What You Know

Whether Internet users go online as bargain hunters, job seekers, movie buffs, classmate finders, background checkers, game players, market intelligence gatherers—for whatever reason—the basic unit of construction for what they seek is information. Whether put together in words, images, videos, audio, or a multimedia software-enabled extravaganza, online users interact with what someone else knows.

Implementing a Web 2.0 Enterprise 2.0 strategy, therefore, necessitates information expertise.

To claim your company's star in the universe of Web 2.0, you must establish yourself as a knowledgeable, credible, authoritative, citable, evidence-based, impeccable source of information. Otherwise, you become forgettable, or worse, a source of amusement.

Implementing a highly competitive Web 2.0 Enterprise strategy requires a value-added feature.

Offer from your company and your Web 2.0 team generous information, then use that information to generate insights into your field, market, or industry. You become a thought leader. You become a bright light of inspiration and creativity.

Success in the world of Web 2.0 is about being a star evolving into a constellation. Online stars generate advertising revenue for themselves. Online constellations generate revenues for their companies.

A competitive Web 2.0 business strategy combines "It's who you are" with "It's what you know." You and what you know are always a unique, incomparable, irreproducible product. In Web 2.0, you and what you know are your intellectual property, your patent, trademark, copyright, mindshare, your formula for Coca-Cola, your 11 Kentucky Fried Chicken herbs and spices.

It's Who You Know

No matter how many tomes, journal articles, white papers, blog entries, and Twitter tweets are written about how to make money in business, tradespeople from the Roman Forum selling sandals two millennia ago to the convention hall trade show selling iPhone apps two days ago know the one business truth: It's who you know. And, of course, who they know.

You need contacts. Without people to buy the products and services of your business, there is no business. Savvy businesses know their contact-to-sales conversion rate. If from 10 contacts, I get one sale, then from 100 contacts, I should get 10 sales. To increase my sales, I, therefore, need to increase my contacts.

"It's who you know" reigns supreme in the physical world. Word-of-mouth referrals are the top source of contacts in multiple industries.

Using this principle applies exponentially in Web 2.0. Any level of participation in Web 2.0, from commenting on a blog to running your own company's social networking site, increases your contacts. You get known.

Players dominate the business world of your locale and "who you know" falls into a hierarchy determined by quantity and quality of contacts. In your town, you're history-bound and geography-limited. In that established network, it's hard to get in and it's hard to get known.

Unlike arriving at your local networking meeting where a rigid hierarchy of who's who in what line of business was established long ago, when you begin your Web 2.0 strategy, you enter a flexible hierarchy with three unique assets: (1) who you are, (2) what you know, (3) your own list of "who you know."

How you leverage these assets—i.e., showing up as your best self as a thought leader in mutually supportive ways with your "It's who you know" network—will determine the quantity and quality of the contacts you attract using Web 2.0. That determines your contacts to sales conversion rate and ultimately determines whether you even have an Enterprise 2.0 with which to implement a Web 2.0 strategy.

It's What You Say

Content matters. Regardless of the Web 2.0 tools you use for your enterprise, the content you create, regardless of the medium, must be:

- Mission-driven
- Link-worthy

Common wisdom is that, in the physical world, we are known and judged, not by our words, but by our actions. In contrast, our words—the foundation of our content—are the virtual actions by which we are known and judged in Web 2.0. Behavior, emotion, and thought are condensed and synthesized into what we write. Images, video, and interaction simulations continue to play a very small role in creating who we are online.

For what and how does your Enterprise 2.0 want to be known? As an Enterprise 2.0, a deep and probing discussion of your mission needs to occur prior to implementation of a Web 2.0 strategy. What you put online will be taken seriously and personally by your current and potential customers, clients, employees, and partners.

One way to think of a Web 2.0 strategy is to consider how an online dating service or a personal ad works. If you create a profile or description that sounds good to you, but doesn't really describe you, you will attract those interested in the phony profile rather than in you. A Web 2.0 strategy expands your contacts. The contacts you attract with your Web 2.0 content need to be ones with whom you and your mission are compatible.

A note of caution is in order here. While Web 2.0 tools feel personal, they're global. One of the author's mothers told her as a child, "Never write anything on paper you can't have the whole world read." We extend that advice to Web 2.0 and point to the example of the individual brought to a city to consult with a top company.[1] He used the microblogging tool Twitter to express disdain for that city. The top company's employees, residents of the town, also Twitter-users, read the consultant's "tweet." The result was a Web 2.0–style, public, globally available reprimand of the consultant by the company's CEO. One of the authors of this paper learned about the incident, yes, via Twitter.

Content matters. If in doubt about what your Enterprise 2.0 wants to be known for, err with your content selection on the side of goodwill.

The primary way your clients, customers, and all members of your target market find information online is through search engines. Search results show up in a list. The results at the top of the list get clicked on more readily than those farther down the list. Logically, then, a business would want to be at the top of the list.

A company cannot buy its way into organic search results. A company can, however, buy Pay-Per-Click (PPC) ads that run next to the actual search results, and even on other Web sites. The Google AdWords program works this way. Ads appear "near" the search results, but not in the results. The Cost Per Click (CPC) bids for AdWords keywords does determine where your ad might appear among the other ads for that keyword, but this is unrelated to what is listed in the actual search results.

A company, for example, could buy Pay-Per-Click ads that run next to actual search results for "cellphone." According to the Google AdWords Traffic Estimator on February 16, 2008, the average Cost Per Click (CPC) a company would have to pay for that to happen is $1.64[2] each time.

One hundred clicks per day would cost $164.00 per day. Because that's pricier than many wish to pay to simply appear in an ad "near" a business-crucial search term, the only other way to influence a company's position in organic search results is simply to be excellent.

All the search engine optimization (SEO) and alchemy you may try cannot convert leaden, mediocre text into golden nuggets of wisdom that your site's readers and users will treasure and, more importantly, forward to others.

The "Introduction to Google Ranking" from *The Official Google Blog* on the first philosophy behind Google ranking, states "Best locally relevant results served globally."[3] It doesn't say, "Content jimmied to trick our algorithms to make us list your site even though what you offer isn't what our users want." To us, "relevant results" offers a mission statement to Google's vendors, i.e., to those who create Web 2.0 content. Here's our version: "Join Google in serving Google's clients. Create relevant content."

Translation? Be good. Be an excellent writer on topics of value to others.

Google uses a complex system to determine PageRank defined simply by Google as "our view of the importance of web pages."[4] This importance is determined partially by the quantity and quality of links leading to a site.

Daryl Scott, creator of competitive intelligence software AttaainCI, explains "importance" further: "One other phrase sometimes used to describe the whole PageRank/linking aspect is 'shared reputation,' i.e. when a highly ranked site or blog links to you, it is in essence 'sharing its reputation' with your site, and therefore drives up the reputation of your own site. Kind of an interesting way to think about it, as well, and the implication is that getting links from low ranked/'poor reputation' sites doesn't really help you—something that people often overlook in the quest to get links into their sites."[5]

Translation? Your Web 2.0 content needs to be really good, good enough to link to, considered link-worthy by the most reputable sites.

How do you be good? Use the first three principles of implementing a Web 2.0 strategy.

- It's who you are.
- It's what you know.
- It's who you know.

You must share a deep, authentic identity that extends beyond profit-making. You offer the best of who you are, what you know, and your mutually beneficial assistance to your social network.

Continuing with the online dating metaphor may be helpful here: You make linking to your Web 2.0 content by the most reputable sites irresistible.

It's How You Say It

When we introduced the four principles of the use of Web 2.0 for business, we stated "Web 2.0 is used by individuals. It is 'you' offering words, images, videos, audio, and interactivity to another 'you.'"

You-to-you. That's a relationship. Whether it's personal or professional, fiber-optic-cable distant or nose-to-nose close, how one—each of the "you's"—communicates in a relationship determines the depth and longevity of that relationship. Depth and longevity in relationships between companies and their customers and clients equals the ability of the company to offer multiple products and services, expanded and upgraded, to a loyal customer base over time. For a company, it is a difficult and costly-to-imitate form of competitive advantage. That makes it priceless.

How a company expresses itself online, regardless of the Web 2.0 tool used, therefore, is crucial.

In "How to Adapt and Prosper in the Web 2.0 Marketspace," we have in mind the highly improbable but well-intentioned desire to offer readers timeless principles that can serve them well as online strategists in the ever-changing online world. With regard to "It's how you say it," we attempt to provide the same. Regardless of the tool, technique, or medium, we believe these guidelines for communicating online are of value. We mention the written word often—the basic unit by which online information in Web 2.0 is conveyed and measured—but the principles apply as well to images, video, audio, and interactivity with a variety of media.

Create from Within

Although diversity defines us, common humanity joins us. The more profoundly you can connect with the essence of who you are and write or create from there, the more you will connect with your users.

Create for the User

From all of who you are and all of what you know, select the portion that will be of most value to your users. The paradox of Web 2.0 is that the source mined for creativity and content is you and your Web 2.0 team, but it's all about your user. In a Web 2.0 business strategy, the focus must be on the user.

Use One-to-One Experience to Think One-to-Many

Business-building in the physical world involves developing one-to-one relationships with potential clients and customers. Use the same skills you use offline in the online world—relating to your prospects and their lives and telling real stories about the positive results of your company—to reach and engage both the "one" and the "many."

Make 'em Laugh

People buy feelings, not features. Use your Web 2.0 strategy to relate to your users' emotions. Let the reader do the thinking. In the feel-think-act continuum of human behavior, if people are genuinely moved—whether to laughter or to tears—they are more likely to then think about how to take action to make a purchase or become a client.

Use Your Vocabulary Words

Your English teacher taught you to write for Web 2.0 when he or she made you write sentences using vocabulary words. Enrich your content with specific terms related to your mission so (a) you deepen the level of your content from abstract to concrete, and (b) search engine users can find you based on keywords central to your mission.

Support with Sources

Linking key points in your online content to authoritative, credible sources such as well-regarded blogs in your field, the latest research, or timely news in media channels, increases the weight of your content. Links to reliable sources are considered "value adds," and users are likely to return to your site trustingly for more. If search engines continue to evaluate links when determining site rankings, this can assist your placement in search engine results as well.

Less Is More

Shakespeare wrote 14-line sonnets as well as multi-act plays. For greater appeal to time-challenged online users, think of Web 2.0 content as a sonnet. Attempt an opening that says "you-will-engage-with-me," tell or show a story, convey a universal truth, and end with an emotional and mental uppercut. For text, instead of 14 lines, think 250 words, the equivalent of an offline "one-pager." For video, think minutes, not hours, a one act play, not *Macbeth*.

Include an Image

In the online competition for readers' attention, long blocks of text are second string players. Use the wisdom of "a picture is worth a thousand words" to let an image or a video do a thousand words of work on behalf of your company.

Edit

Just as serious job candidates wear business suits to interviews to display their seriousness, so must Web 2.0 content be presented impeccably to your potential users—the entire globe's citizenry. Error-free Web 2.0 content speaks well of your organization and its customers and clients. Poor editing casts doubt on the organization's leaders, its employees, and its associates.

A CASE STUDY: HANDSHAKE 2.0

Handshake 2.0 is an enterprise of Handshake Media, Incorporated, founded by one of the authors of this chapter under the auspices of VT KnowledgeWorks, the business acceleration center located at the Virginia Tech Corporate Research Center in Blacksburg, Virginia.

Launched in July 2008, Handshake 2.0 is a business news and public relations blog offering Web 2.0/new media public relations and marketing services to its clients. Handshake 2.0's business model is based on multiple revenue streams including fees for posting content on the site, advertising, and Web 2.0/new media consulting.

These Handshake 2.0 revenue streams depend on what Pat Matthews, founder of Mailtrust, a division of Rackspace, termed in an e-mail to one of the authors, building "a large, loyal readership."[6]

We reiterate our fundamental principles underpinning the business use of Web 2.0:

- It's you doing it.
- How you do it will change.
- The end leads the means.
- People seek connection.

and our foundational principles for implementing a Web 2.0 strategy:

- It's who you are.
- It's what you know.
- It's who you know.
- It's what you say.
- It's how you say it.

The following excerpts, adapted from a Handshake 2.0 blog post, "Handshake 2.0 in the *Huffington Post*,"[7] demonstrate our fundamental principles underpinning the business use of Web 2.0 and our foundational principles for implementing a Web 2.0 strategy. *The Huffington Post* is the top-rated Technorati blog. Patricia Handschiegel has written a series for the *Huffington Post* on women entrepreneurs entitled "The New Power Girls." She quoted Handshake 2.0's CEO on January 16, 2009 in "The New Power Girls: How to Strike Balance in Business." In a congratulatory e-mail, regionalism advocate Stuart Mease asked, "How did that happen?" We've answered the question below. It's a somewhat lengthy story and involves a lot of people. The short answer to "How did that happen?"—and the instructive one—is this: It's still who you know.

Z. Kelly Queijo, a freelance writer who crafts excellent posts for Handshake 2.0, sent me a query from Peter Shankman's HARO—Help a Reporter Out. Journalists submit queries via HARO for sources on stories. Subscribers to the service—over 45,000, according to the site—receive three e-mail newsletters per day with a dozen or more queries. Ms. Queijo spotted a request from Patricia Handshchiegel and e-mailed it to me on December 23, 2008.

"Seeking women entrepreneurs who have started companies within the last 3–5 years for a series I've been doing on my Huffington Post blog. The series is published 2x a week for ten weeks total (we're on week 5). Sources should send a short email describing company, blog, and background. Please be sure to include any relevant website addresses. Thanks!"

Handshake 2.0's CEO is also a subscriber to HARO but missed that query. In September 2008, she had a brief e-mail correspondence with Peter Shankman to receive his permission to quote one of his newsletters about Twitter for Handshake 2.0. Peter Shankman established Web 2.0 credibility with Handshake 2.0's CEO, as all of us online are advised to do, by offering a genuine, informed, distinctive, consistent voice that is shared reliably, i.e., day after day after day.

Handshake's CEO was also referred to HARO by another credible source, Robert Geller, senior vice president with Fusion Public Relations in New York. He, too, had established Web 2.0 credibility with the company because his online presence in his blog, Flack's Revenge, is knowledgeable, thoughtful, and thought-provoking. He mentioned HARO in a Flack's Revenge blog post. How does Handshake's CEO "know" Robert Geller? They have never met. One of his colleagues was using Google to research a company mentioned in a Handshake 2.0 post. She forwarded the link to Geller. He looked at the site, then mentioned Handshake 2.0 on Flack's Revenge.

Geller was the first person Handshake's CEO didn't know directly in the physical world who linked to Handshake 2.0. Since then, they have had an ongoing conversation via blog comments, e-mail, and Twitter, @handshake20 and @rgeller.

Our point? Passionate, highly engaged entrepreneurs must choose wisely what they do with their time. Because Handshake's CEO had "It's still who you know" referrals, she knew the query [from the *Huffington Post*] was legitimate, so she gave it her time. She responded to Patricia Handschiegel and received a reply the very next day. Was she open to being placed on an e-mail list to receive requests for answers and anecdotes? Yes. Very yes.

Twice per week, Handshake's CEO received Patricia Handschiegel's questions, wrote answers and submitted them, and received an e-mailed link to her new entry in "The New Power Girls" series—but each time she checked found no mention of Handshake 2.0 there.

Near the end of the twice-weekly correspondence, Handschiegel asked women entrepreneurs to contemplate how they achieve balance in their lives. Handshake's CEO told her husband, "I have trouble with balance." He replied that he thought she worked very hard on balance. They both laughed. Then he described some of the ways he'd seen her attempt to achieve balance in her life. He mentioned her cat, and that mention of the cat inspired the insight that was expressed in words and e-mailed to Patricia Handschiegel—and she chose some of those words to quote.

So, Stuart Mease, that's how Handshake 2.0 got mentioned in the *Huffington Post*.

Oh, one more "It's still who you know."

How did Handshake's CEO find out about the mention? An e-mail alert sent to her through a subscription to AttaainCI, the competitive intelligence service.

In pondering this remarkable experience, one conclusion is that it takes a lot of "who you knows" for things to happen.

CONCLUSION

The Handshake 2.0 case study of the use of Web 2.0 for Enterprise 2.0 shows the founder as the "who you are" and the "you doing it." With the end in mind of "a large, loyal readership," the founder accepted a content creation opportunity as a means to achieve that end. The founder would not have known of this opportunity, however, without both an online and offline network of "It's who you know" seeking connection with each other. And the founder was required to change and adapt to the demands of the medium, shaping what she knew to the "what" and "how" of her expression in order to ultimately connect with the "customer," the *Huffington Post*.

The question we posed in our section on "The end leads the means" remains. Can the fundamental longing of people for connection, and the myriad ways Web 2.0 offers to address that longing, convert for businesses to cash?

Will the use of Web 2.0 for an Enterprise 2.0 like Handshake 2.0 ultimately result in entity-sustaining profit? Handshake 2.0—and an ever-increasing number of enterprises—is banking on it.

NOTES

1. Peter Shankman, "Be Careful What You Post," *Peter Shankman: CEO, Entrepreneur, Adventurist*, http://shankman.com/be-careful-what-you-post.

2. *Google AdWords Traffic Estimator*, https://adwords.google.com/select/Traffic EstimatorSandbox.

3. Amit Singhal, "Introduction to Google Ranking," *The Official Google Blog*, http://googleblog.blogspot.com/2008/07/introduction-to-google-ranking.html.

4. "Corporate Information: Technology Overview," *Google*, http://www.google.com/corporate/tech.html.

5. Daryl Scott, "AttaainCI Reports PageRank," *Inside VT KnowledgeWorks*, http://www.insidevtknowledgeworks.com/2009/02/attaainci-pagerank.html.

6. Pat Matthews, "What's the Value of a Blog Post?" July 16, 2008, personal e-mail (July 17, 2008).

7. Anne Giles Clelland, "Handshake 2.0 in the Huffington Post," *Handshake 2.0*, http://www.handshake20.com/2009/01/huffington.html.

SUGGESTED READING

Battelle, John. *The Search: How Google and Its Rivals Rewrote the Rules of Business and Transformed Our Culture*. New York: Portfolio, 2005.

Li, Charlene, and Josh Bernoff. *Groundswell: Winning in a World Transformed by Social Technologies*. Boston: Harvard Business School Press, 2008.

Scoble, Robert, and Shel Israel. *Naked Conversations: How Blogs Are Changing the Way Businesses Talk with Customers*. Hoboken, New Jersey: John Wiley & Sons, Inc., 2006.

5

E2.0 LAW: LEGAL CONCERNS FOR THE WEB 2.0 BUSINESS

Ken Maready, J.D.

This chapter examines legal issues that a Web 2.0 Business should be aware of, including federal requirements, federal protections, and general legal issues particular to an online business. This chapter is not legal advice but rather a summary of certain laws and common practices. You should seek individual legal guidance, as the facts and circumstances of your business may differ, and the law in this area is rapidly evolving.

Your Web 2.0 Business traffics in content, links, and interaction provided by and among its users. This means that you act as a forum and conduit for the interaction of potentially millions of people with whom you have no prior contact or control. And because you operate on the Internet, you are providing this information and opportunity over the most public and widespread forum in the history of man. You must generally give your users great freedom in providing content, because if you were to impose significant legal restrictions or regularly remove or edit user content your business would likely fail.

All of this you know. We restate it here because these facts create a particular set of legal concerns that face a Web 2.0 Business and that we examine here as an attempt to familiarize you with some of your obligations and some things you can do to mitigate certain types of liability for your site.

A large part of the potential for liability for a Web 2.0 Business is that you publish and distribute content generated, in whole or in part, by your users (referred to herein as user-generated content or UGC) over which you may have little control or ability to monitor. Fortunately, in the United States, Congress has provided two very important protections for you in this regard, which are discussed in this chapter. It is important to remember while reading this chapter that these federally provided protections may not apply to content that you yourself have had some part in developing (including through your employees, contractors, or other agents), but may only apply to content provided purely by a user.

Finally, many of the protections provided and potential liability for online businesses will differ to the extent that the content contains pornography or obscenity (or sometimes merely sexually suggestive materials), or incites criminal or violent activity. Additionally, certain types of businesses (e.g., banks or financial institutions, healthcare providers) or activity (e.g., gambling, sweepstakes, adult materials) will be subject to additional regulation. Except where specifically mentioned, this chapter does not cover additional laws that apply to these materials. If your business or site contains any types of regulated or restricted activity, you should engage legal professionals experienced in these areas.

YOUR TERMS OF USE AND USER AGREEMENTS

Throughout this chapter, we discuss certain requirements or recommendations that you should have in your "Terms of Use" and "user agreements." Here, we use the term "Terms of Use" to mean the terms and conditions that you list on your Web site on a "Terms" or "Terms of Use" page, often linked via hypertext link from the home page of your Web site. We include in this term any related policies you might post separately (for example, some sites separate out their privacy policy, or copyright and intellectual property policy). We use the term "user agreements" to include any such terms, conditions and other provisions to which you require your user to affirmatively indicate his or her agreement by checking a box, clicking a button, replying to an e-mail, or taking any other affirmative step.

Typically, a site's Terms of Use are indicated to visitors simply by a hypertext link (labeled "Terms" or "Terms of Use" or something to that effect) at the bottom of the home page and possibly other pages on the Web site. Within the main Terms of Use (or accessible by hypertext links in the main Terms of Use page) are other related policies and guidelines, such as a privacy policy or intellectual property policy, if they are not included in the body of the Terms of Use.

Terms of Use, by themselves, may or may not be binding on visitors to your site. There is case law on both sides of the issue—some cases holding that a separate page with Terms of Use and a simple unremarkable hypertext link at the bottom of the Web site's pages (i.e., a "Browse-Wrap Agreement") does not bind the user.[1] On the other hand, some cases indicate that even a simple hypertext link may be enough to put the visitor on constructive notice that he or she is subject to your terms, and his or her further use of your Web site is agreement to be bound by them.[2]

Given the varying outcomes of these cases, you should assume that the simple Terms of Use, without an affirmative agreement by the user, may not govern your user in the way that a standard contract would. However, it is still important that you include a Terms of Use page as it helps you to comply with certain notice provisions and to fulfill disclosure requirements as to certain policies, and having the provisions available in some form is better than not.

If you want to be more certain that legal terms and protections are binding on your user, you must get a user to take an affirmative step to indicate he or she is aware of the terms and agrees to them (i.e., a "Click-Wrap Agreement"), such as checking a box ("I have read and agree to the Terms & Conditions . . . .") or by including language ON a click-through button that their actions are subject to the terms ("By Clicking This Button I agree to the Terms & Conditions . . . ."). For a Web 2.0 Business some kind of Click-Wrap Agreement is typically included any time a user affirmatively interacts with your site, such as when they submit a blog entry, reply, or comment to an article; sign up to be a member; make a purchase; or download a file. In addition, when the user is making a purchase or download, or signing up as a member, the Click-Wrap Agreement typically includes both (i) the specific terms and conditions applicable to that purchase or download (i.e., the license and payment terms) and (ii) a statement that they are agreeing to the site's overall Terms of Use, with a link or reference.

Terms of Use vary widely in style and substance for online businesses. Some businesses, such as Facebook, have a very conversational, plain-English approach and fairly liberal, user-friendly policies governing their use of the material.[3] Others, such as the WSJ.com site of Dow Jones & Co., Inc., read more like a traditional legal contract and take a more conservative approach.[4] Some have very limited Terms of Use applicable to casual viewers, and only include the more substantive provisions when a viewer attempts to provide content or otherwise interacts with the site. There's no right or wrong approach, but you'll probably want your Terms of Use to cover at least the specific areas mentioned in this chapter. It is also important that you accurately describe your practices and policies to the extent they are disclosed. Often businesses get into trouble for taking actions that wouldn't be illegal or problematic for any reason other than they're not complying with their own stated policies.

Some of these basic terms are likely to be included:

- A statement that your user, by submitting or linking to any content, is representing to you that he or she has the full ownership or right to provide or link to such content, and to give you the right to publish or link to any and all such materials on the terms herein, without the need for disclaimer, payment of royalty, or license fee, and without the need of consent of or notice to any third party

- A statement that your user, by submitting any such material, is granting your business the non-exclusive, perpetual, worldwide, fully paid, and royalty-free right to reproduce, publish, and distribute such materials on your Web site and any mirror, foreign-language, or affiliate sites you or your affiliate may operate now or in the future
- A representation by your user that he or she will not submit any false or misleading, defamatory, obscene, or otherwise illegal content, that he or she will not commit any illegal activity on or with the assistance of your site, and that he will not submit any materials in violation of any contractual obligations he or she may have, or in violation of the confidentiality or privacy rights (whether by law or contract) of another
- A statement, and an acknowledgment by your user, that you are not guaranteeing the truth or completeness of content on your site, that some or all of the materials may be submitted by users or advertisers, and that you have no responsibility for such materials whatsoever, including without limitation, whether such materials are true, false, complete, up-to-date, defamatory, infringing, obscene, or otherwise illegal
- A similar agreement by the user that he or she is taking the risk that user-provided content (whether or not so labeled) may be false, misleading, or otherwise damaging, and that he or she will not hold you responsible for any damages arising out of his or her reliance on such materials or communications and interactions with such persons, and that this is in addition to any rights or protections afforded to you by Section 230 of the Communications Decency Act[5]
- A statement that you reserve the right (but do not take on the obligation) to reject, remove, edit, replace, block, or condition access to any user-submitted material, in whole or in part for any reason or no reason whatsoever, including without limitation, your determination in your sole discretion that such material is infringing, defamatory, obscene, harassing, or otherwise illegal or objectionable, but that your decision in any one instance to take action is not an indication of an obligation to take similar actions and you may selectively monitor, review, edit, and/or remove content, in whole or in part, without taking on the obligation to do so over the entire site or from that point forward
- Unless your business is specifically for children, you will probably want to prohibit use of your site by anyone under 13 years of age, and include a representation by the user that he or she is at least 13 years of age[6] (you may want to change this to over 18 years of age if your site contains questionable material)
- A notice regarding parental controls required by Section 230 of the Communications Decency Act[7]
- Your privacy policy, clearly set forth either within the terms of the Terms of Use or linked to as a separate policy[8], and a statement that any content submitted for publication, including that submitted through a reply, comment or blog function on your site, will not be considered private information and, therefore, not subject to the privacy policies
- Designation of a person (i.e., "Copyright Officer" or "DMCA Officer") responsible for receiving notices of copyright infringement for materials on your site, including the current address and other contact

information (and you may want to include instructions for submitting a notice of infringement that complies with the Digital Millennium Copyright Act notification requirements[9])

- A choice-of-law provision stating that the laws of your state (or another state, if you prefer) apply to all matters arising out of or relating to the Terms of Use, your Web site, or the use thereof[10]
- A choice-of-venue provision stating that all lawsuits, proceedings or legal actions relating to or arising out of the Terms of Use, your Web site, or the use thereof will take place in state or federal courts located in a specified location (typically a county where you or your main law firm are located if a federal court is located there), and that the user agrees to such exclusive jurisdiction, is hereby consenting to personal jurisdiction of such courts, and is waiving all objections based on lack of personal jurisdiction, forum non conveniens and the like
- A reservation of your right to modify, alter, delete, or add to these Terms of Use from time to time hereafter, that such changes will become effective upon publication online, and a statement that the user agrees to check the Terms of Use before submitting additional materials or using the site in the future as the revised Terms of Use will apply as soon as effective.

This is by no means the entire list of terms and conditions you will include, and there may be other specific provisions you'll want to include for specific types of Web sites (i.e., such as matching or complex social networking sites, sites with adult material, sites specifically targeting users in other countries). This gives you a good idea of provisions your basic Terms of Use should contain to address some flexibility to operate your Web site, while meeting some important legal requirements and reserving the right for certain important federal protections. As stated above, it is good practice to include your Terms of Use on your site in both Browse-Wrap and Click-Wrap forms.

LIABILITY FOR CONTENT AND ACTIONS OF YOUR USERS

In the United States, both online and off, we enjoy a freedom of speech that is constitutionally protected and very near and dear to our way of life. This is important to you as an online operator in this country as it generally allows you to publish content of almost any type without fear of government action or illegality, subject to some exceptions. The most common areas where your freedom of speech may be limited by law are: (i) infringement of another's copyright, (ii) obscenity, (iii) fighting words or words inciting immediately lawless action, (iv) defamation (libel or slander), (v) certain communications with regard to children, (vi) certain types of materially misleading (false) speech, and (vii) disclosure of certain types of private data (i.e., financial or medical) or trade secrets. In addition, both online and off, if your words (or your actions in helping the speaker of the words) have contributed in some way to the physical, financial, reputational, or in some cases psychological damage of a person or group, or the breach of a contractual requirement, you could find yourself liable to the victim in a civil lawsuit.

The above is true for all speech, whether applied to an Internet business, a publisher of a traditional newspaper, a town crier on the street corner, or a friend e-mailing or whispering to a friend. And online, the same is generally true for any content that you yourself create or contribute to significantly (including through employees, contractors, and other agents). However, given that a Web 2.0 Business is in large part driven by content and interaction of your users, and given that the universe of potential liability for their activity is unlimited, it is important to be aware of some legal protections available to you as the Web 2.0 Business for the content and actions of your users.

Limitation of Liability for Copyright Violations by Your Users—the Digital Millennium Copyright Act

The author (creator) of a work fixed in a tangible medium has copyright protection in his or work immediately upon creation, regardless of whether the work is registered with any state or federal authority. This includes books, articles, songs, recorded performances of songs, software, photographs, drawings, movies, you name it. Subject to certain exceptions, that copyright holder has the exclusive right to reproduce, distribute, and, in most cases, publicly display his or her work. Any unlicensed reproduction or public display of the work (or a derivative work) is therefore a violation of the author's copyright, unless it falls within one of the exceptions.

Copyright infringement on the Internet is ubiquitous. Widespread publication of someone else's copyrighted work is now as simple as highlighting the picture, text or video, pressing Ctrl+C to copy, and then pasting (Ctrl+V) to another site. It likely happens millions of times per day, often by people who don't have a clear concept of what copyrights are and don't know that with a few keystrokes they are breaking laws and infringing on someone else's intellectual property rights. Because the basic federal copyright law prohibits one from reproducing, distributing, or, in many cases, displaying publicly a copyrighted work,[11] this action by your users could potentially cause you, as a Web 2.0 Business owner, to regularly be in violation of copyright laws for materials you don't create, when your site displays or reproduces these works publicly.[12]

Fortunately, recognizing this potential liability and the overwhelming burden it would place on Internet businesses to attempt to monitor any potential copyright infringement on their sites, in 1998 Congress passed the Digital Millennium Copyright Act (DMCA), which allows you, by participating in a notice regime set up under the statute, to enjoy very serious limitations on the liability you might otherwise have for copyright infringement in UGC on your site. In addition to providing the limitations on liability, the effect of the law is to shift the burden of monitoring for possible copyright violations from you, as the Web 2.0 Business, to the holder of the copyright being infringed.

This protection is not automatic, however. In order to avail yourself of the limitations on liability under the DMCA, you must comply with various technical requirements, including implementing a policy to take down infringing materials, designating an agent to receive notifications of copyright infringement and complying with certain "takedown notices" from copyright holders. The law is more detailed and nuanced than presented here, but you should have in place the following basic requirements to limit liability from copyright holders:

- In general, you should have a policy for taking down, or disabling access to, any items posted on your site that you become aware are in violation of someone's copyrights or that raise a "red flag" of such violation.[13]
- You must adopt and reasonably implement a policy "providing for the termination in appropriate circumstances of subscribers and account holders of [your] network who are repeat infringers."[14]
- You must designate an agent to receive notifications (and "counter-notifications") under the DMCA, and make the agent's contact information available on a publicly accessible location of your Web site as well as filing it with the U.S. Copyright Office.[15]
- Upon receipt of a valid notification under the DMCA,[16] you must "expeditiously" remove or disable access to the allegedly infringing material.[17]

DMCA Limitation of Liability for Takedowns Based on Copyright Concerns

The DMCA also allows you to limit your liability from those whose material you take down in concern over possible copyright infringement, whether your takedown was in response to a notification or otherwise. In general, your Terms of Use and any user agreements you have should be drafted to give you wide latitude to take down information from your site for any reason or no reason in your complete discretion, and further stating that the user agrees that your business will not be liable under any legal or equitable theory for taking down such information, whether in whole or in part. However, the DMCA protection can provide you more assurance in copyright cases.

In cases where your takedown is in response to a DMCA notification regarding materials posted by a "subscriber," the DMCA sets up a procedure you should follow to limit liability for the takedown (as well as for the put-back that may be required in certain circumstances). The process is as follows:

- When you originally take the material down in response to a notification, you should "take reasonable steps to promptly notify" the subscriber of the takedown.[18]
- Upon receipt of a counter-notification from the subscriber,[19] you must promptly provide the person from whom you received the original notification with (a) a copy of the Counter-Notification and (b) notice that you will replace the material, or re-allow access to it, within ten (10) business days.[20]
- Unless you receive evidence that the original complainant has filed a lawsuit against the alleged infringer to restrain him from the infringing activity on your network, you must put back (or re-allow access to) the materials you took down, with such put-back occurring not less than ten (10) business days, but not more than fourteen (14) business days following the day you received the counter-notification.[21]
- If you do receive evidence of a filing of such court action within the time limit, you may of course refrain from putting back the materials and await the determination of the court.

On the other hand, in cases where your takedown was not in response to a valid DMCA notification with regard to allegedly infringing material posted by a "subscriber," the DMCA generally provides that you would not be liable to "any person" (including subscribers and nonsubscribers) for your good faith takedown of materials because you either received a claim that the material was infringing, or because facts and circumstances make the infringing activity apparent. This allows you to respond to claims of infringement by immediately taking down material if you wish, without fear of lawsuit by your user for taking down the material. This provision of the DMCA appears to protect you from the spectrum of lawsuits that could range from a simple breach of your contract to a more complicated claim that you have interrupted the user's business, sullied their reputation, or placed any remaining material in a false light, etc. You should, however, document your decision and any claims you received that the information was infringing and/or the facts and circumstances that made the infringement apparent to you.

The DMCA statutory procedure provides great incentive for an online provider to reflexively and mechanically remove materials upon receipt of a valid DMCA Notification (and to reflexively and mechanically put back materials upon receipt of a valid DMCA counter-notification). To prevent people from abusing either the notification or counter-notification procedures, the DMCA provides specifically for liability for persons making knowing material misrepresentations in either of these notices, including recovery of attorneys' fees.[22]

Note that the DMCA appears not to apply to individual, natural persons —so if you are operating your business as a sole proprietorship, this may give you added incentive to incorporate or organize as a corporation, LLC, or some other business entity. As stated above, details and nuances of this law require investigation of the facts and circumstances of each case, and knowledge of developing case law under the DMCA. Also note that you cannot rely on the limitations provided by the DMCA for materials that you have posted yourself (including through your employees or agents), or if you have a financial interest in, and ability to control, the infringing activity.[23]

Finally, it is completely in your discretion whether to participate in the DMCA procedures, and there is no direct penalty for not following them. However, if you do not follow the DMCA, you remove yourself from the statute's limitations on liability and place yourself into the stream of "normal" copyright law, including the potential for violation yourself directly, as a "publisher" of the materials of your users, or on a contributory basis. Because of the relative certainty of the DMCA, most well-known Web 2.0 Businesses utilize its provisions. In fact, if you receive a notice alleging something on your site is violating copyright law, but that notice doesn't comply with the DMCA requirements for a valid notification, it is often advisable to immediately communicate with the sender of the notice to assist him in correcting their notice, to make it a valid DMCA notification, thus bringing the particular complaint clearly into the DMCA regime (some providers, such as Facebook, even provide an online notification generator to ensure that notices of copyright infringement would meet the DMCA requirements, and thus remove the uncertainty of whether they're operating under a DMCA complaint or not).[24]

Limitation on Liability for Crimes or Torts Committed by Your Users on Your Site or with the Help of Your Site: Section 230 of the Communications Decency Act

Although copyright infringement is likely the most ubiquitous legal violation occurring on Internet sites, it is by no means the only type of activity that will occur within UGC on your site that could cause you legal concerns. For example, similar to copyright law, the law of defamation (i.e., libel) applies to anyone who publishes libelous information about another party. Without the specific legal protection discussed in this section, your Web 2.0 Business would almost certainly be considered to be a publisher of the information on your site, regardless of your involvement in creating the material, and thus your business would be subject to lawsuits for defamation in your UGC.

Similarly, lawsuits have been brought against Web sites or ISPs for involvement in more heinous crimes committed by one user against another. This includes situations in which the actual crime is committed over the Internet, such as the cyber-bullying case in which a mother used a social network to bully one of her daughter's schoolmates, eventually resulting in the girl's suicide. It also includes crimes in which someone has used a Web 2.0 Business (most often, a social networking or dating site) to meet and talk with a victim before arranging a meeting in the real world where the criminal committed acts ranging from sexual assault to rape and murder.

Based on case law from analogous non-Internet cases, it seems very likely that, without the protection of Section 230, the Web 2.0 Businesses involved in these activities would be sued quite regularly, and would lose some of these cases for large verdicts. A large number of these cases would at least proceed beyond the summary judgment stage, thus vastly increasing settlement costs for the Internet businesses—all of which would probably result in severe restrictions and changes in the way that these sites (and you) could conduct business.

However, Congress passed Section 230 of the Communications Decency Act to provide what has been a very effective shield against such liability. Section 230 provides, among other things:

> No provider or user of an interactive computer service shall be treated as the publisher or speaker of any information provided by another information content provider.[25]

This section was intended to be (and it has been) applied broadly, resulting in a very effective protection for ISPs, blogs, social networks, and other online businesses against lawsuits based upon the actions of their users. Note that Section 230 expressly does not apply in criminal cases, it does not limit or expand intellectual property law, and it does not limit the application of the Electronic Communications Privacy Act of 1986 (or similar state laws).[26] Importantly, Section 230 does preempt state laws that are inconsistent with it.[27]

Outside these specific exceptions, Section 230's application is very broad, and can protect you from a wide variety of lawsuits and proceedings. For example, it has been applied to protect online businesses from claims of libel (defamation),[28] discrimination in housing advertisements,[29] publication of a false profile (impersonation by another user),[30] negligence and gross negligence in monitoring age of users (in case involving sexual assault on a minor),[31] negligent misrepresentation,[32] tortious interference,[33] breach of contract,[34] and negligence in failing to remove false or defamatory materials.[35] It is very important to note that Section 230 often results in a dismissal of the claims at the summary judgment stage, before the case even proceeds to trial or heavy discovery. Therefore it can substantially limit your litigation costs, and it often dissuades a potential plaintiff from bringing a claim at all.

Unlike the DMCA regime, you do not have to adopt specific policies, appoint an agent, or take other actions for the Section 230 protection to apply. However, you should be mindful of the boundary of Section 230's application, so that you can alter the ways in which you interact with your users' content if you decide you want to be more sure of Section 230 protection.

Section 230 provides protection for you so long as the information is "provided by another information content provider." This means that the protection does not apply if you or your business is found to be "responsible, in whole or in part, for the creation or development of" the material or information that is the subject of the claim.[36] Predictably, lawsuits involving online businesses in which Section 230 is raised all tend to focus on this issue—so there is some case law on the topic of what can cause you to become "responsible . . . for the creation or development of" material on your site.

If your site merely provides a comment entry form at the bottom of an article or blog through which a user can post his or her thoughts and replies, then it is fairly clear that you are not responsible for the creation of any information that the user may enter and post on your site. According to current case law, your ability and contractual right to reject, remove, or edit UGC does not render you responsible for the material's creation or development.[37] In fact, it is fairly well settled that even if you proactively select which UGC to post and even actually edit the material to some extent, you will not thereby become responsible for its creation or development.[38]

The trickier question arises when your site takes actions to solicit very specific information from the user, and/or categorizes or organizes the user information before presenting it—for example, a guided questionnaire leading to the creation of a "profile" on a social networking site. Although most case law has indicated that even this activity would not cause the Web site to be responsible for the creation of the resulting profile (so you would still be protected by Section 230), there is some case law to the contrary[39].

The only major decision to hold a Web 2.0 Business liable for UGC in the face of Section 230 appears to be *Fair Housing Council of San Fernando Valley v. Roommates.com, LLC.*[40] In this case, a local housing council sued an online business that helped roommates find matches for purposes of sharing housing. The housing council alleged that Roommates.com violated the Fair Housing Act because of some of the statements in user profiles. The operator of Roommates.com raised Section 230, but in this case the court found that Section 230 did not protect the site with regard to statements in the portion of a user's profile which were generated based on answers elicited by the Web site through its online questionnaire.[41] In trying to distinguish this case from other cases in which Section 230 did protect the online business, commenters have pointed to specific language of the opinion, which stated that the test for whether an online business is responsible for the creation or development of the information is (1) whether the site "categorizes, channels and limits the distribution of information, thus creating another layer (meta-layer) of information and (2) whether it actively prompts, encourages, or solicits the unlawful information."[42]

However, other cases seem to contradict the holding.[43] For instance, in *Doe v. MySpace*,[44] a minor and her mother sued MySpace after the girl (who had misrepresented her age as 18 on her MySpace profile) was sexually assaulted during a real-life meeting with a man she had initially met and communicated with on MySpace. The plaintiffs claimed that MySpace was liable for negligence and gross negligence for failing to implement basic safety measures to protect minors.[45] The plaintiffs attempted to argue that Section 230 was not applicable because they were not suing MySpace as a publisher, but rather they were suing for its negligence in its own actions, i.e., not policing sexual predators. However, the court found that their claims essentially related to MySpace's business of publishing the user-generated information, which is the intended protected activity of Section 230, and that therefore Section 230 would protect MySpace from liability. Therefore, the case was dismissed.

Given the incredible protection afforded by Section 230 and the resulting exposure you could face if you fall outside its protections, you should seriously consider the additional risk you take for potentially becoming "responsible for the creation and development" of UGC on your site, and consider the ramifications of including such features as:

- Heavy editing of or collaborating in creation of UGC on your site
- Offering "professional" development or editing of UGC, including services to help users on social network sites write more effective profiles
- Setting up your site so that people can collaborate or make inline changes or comments to others' works, especially if you (or your staff or hired contractors) are going to be participating in such changes and comments
- Online guided questionnaires, based on which you will create metadata based upon that user's responses, categorize the users, or potentially be seen as eliciting illegal or defamatory statements

Section 230 Limitation on Liability for Takedown of Offensive User Content

As described above in the section on copyright law, the DMCA provides protection for taking down UGC based on allegations or "red flags" of potential copyright violations. Outside copyright law, Section 230 provides a limitation on your liability for taking down or restricting access to UGC that either you or your user considers to be "obscene, lewd, lascivious, filthy, excessively violent, harassing, or otherwise objectionable, whether or not such material is constitutionally protected."[46] This provision—often called the "Good Samaritan" provision—is an important protection and should protect you from a wide range of lawsuits from the affected user (or from others, for that matter) based on your taking down or restricting objectionable user information.

As stated above, we advise you to broaden your rights even further, by including a provision in your Terms of Use and user agreements that allow you the complete discretion to take down, in whole or in part, any information for any reason you deem appropriate or for no reason, whether based on complaints of others or on your own initiative. However, the Section 230 Good Samaritan protection is important in situations where your contract terms might be found not to apply, and may result in dismissal of lawsuits at a summary judgment stage. In any cases where you remove objectionable user material, you should document your decision, so that you can provide such documentation immediately in support a claim for a Section 230 dismissal, if needed.

Liability for Trademark Infringement on Your Site

The DMCA above only applies with respect to copyright violations, not trademark violations, and there is no equivalent Digital Millennium Trademark Act. Section 230 above specifically does not "limit or expand any law pertaining to intellectual property,"[47] which would mean it does not come into play for trademark violations. This means that you are without these types of protections if your Web site infringes on another party's trademarks, including through trademark violations in UGC.

That is the bad news. The good news is that the threshold for proving contributory trademark infringement (which is what you would be charged with as the operator of the Web site for trademark infringement contained in UGC) is very high, and you should be able to avoid liability unless you have very direct and specific information that user content contains a trademark violation. As a reminder, here we are talking about trademark violations contained in your UGC, not trademark violations you may commit directly (i.e., if your company or domain name is already trademarked or confusingly similar to an existing trademark, or if you use others' trademarks in a confusing way within content that you create yourself).

Trademark violations in your UGC could come about in a couple of situations. This would mainly be where a user is attempting to pass off their goods, services, or remarks as someone else's through the use of names, logos, and other trademarks that are the same or are confusingly similar as a legitimate company's marks—i.e., a knock-off product on eBay. Additionally, trademark liability could arise if a user included a name, logo, or other trademark of someone else in commentary where it could be confusing as to whether the actual company whose mark was mentioned was providing the commentary or had approved or sanctioned it in some way. In these cases, you would likely receive a letter or complaint from the owner of the trademark telling you, among other things, to remove the content that contained the unauthorized use of their marks.

In such cases, where you receive a letter pointing out specific trademark violations and the letter appears on its face to have some merit, you should react by taking down or altering the content containing the unauthorized use of the marks. If the letter relates to commentary where the user was simply talking about the company who owns the mark, and not attempting to pass himself off as that company, then you can typically fix the problem with a very clear disclaimer at the beginning of the content and/or near the use of the mark to the effect that "DISCLAIMER: This article is not written, sanctioned or approved by [Company X], and it does not represent its views or beliefs in any way." If it is a situation where a user is apparently trying to pass himself off as another company, you would be better advised to remove the content altogether. In addition, to the extent possible, you can implement steps to avoid such user from submitting additional infringing content.

As you might guess, companies owning trademarks (and their lawyers) can be very aggressive about protecting their marks and often send out threatening letters even where there is an exception or non-violative use of the mark. So if you remove material in reaction, it is possible that you are taking down material that is not in fact a violation of trademark law, exposing yourself to a counter-reaction from your user. In order to protect yourself against a claim by your user upon such takedowns, your Terms of Use and user agreements should include a provision giving you broad flexibility to reject, remove, edit, or alter content.

However, you should be comforted that in contributory trademark infringement law, as in the policy behind the DMCA and Section 230, there is an apparent policy choice to place the burden of monitoring trademark violations on the owner of the mark, and not on you as the online business operator—the intermediary. Therefore, cases have typically required that before you could actually be liable in a lawsuit, you would have to be on specific actual notice (i.e., not implied notice, or constructive notice) as to specific instances of trademark violations.[48] On the other hand, without a law like the DMCA or Section 230 covering the area clearly, you should consider some type of anti-piracy efforts if your business allows users to sell goods and services, or if you regularly receive content containing actual trademark violations.

Privacy of Data and User Identity

Data Privacy and Security Policies

Almost all online businesses collect some personal data of its users, whether proactively or inadvertently. A user visiting your site may leave behind an IP address and, in many cases, a cookie indicating that his or her computer has visited your site. In addition, depending on your business you may collect basic personal information about your users, including name, address, age, and sex. If you require log-in, you collect user names and passwords that could be used to access their accounts (both on your site and elsewhere if they commonly use the same log-in information). Your site may also collect shopping preferences, hobbies, interests, and other information that advertisers would love to have access to, or which could be embarrassing for the user if disclosed publicly. And if your business collects payments over the Internet, you (or your third-party payment system) gather financial information from users, including bank account or credit card numbers, along with expiration dates and security validation codes.

Privacy of this data is of paramount importance to your users, and most sites have a specific privacy policy outlining the types of information that will be collected, what purposes it may be used for, whether or not it will be provided to third parties, and how long it will be retained. It is important to have such policies, but you should be prepared to comply completely with your own policies, which requires a technical understanding of what occurs with the data on your server and transmission systems, how you can secure the data and whether the data are completely removed from (and "written over" on) all servers when your policy says it will be discarded. For some types of data, particularly financial data, sites will often team up with a trusted third-party (e.g., www.TRUSTe .org) in order to develop privacy policies and receive independent certification of trustworthiness.

There are some basic legal requirements in this area.[49] The laws can be vague with regard to both what types of information is covered by the law and what level of security is required. And as an online business, you will have to simultaneously comply with many overlapping and varied requirements at once, including the Federal Trade Commission's stance that an insufficient data security and privacy system is an unfair and deceptive trade practice,[50] the laws of various states affecting the privacy of data of their citizens,[51] and the European Union's Data Protection Directive (the "EU Directive").[52]

Given that all of these laws vary in purpose and scope, that new state laws are likely to be passed regularly in the future, and that in many cases the laws themselves are vague and subject to wide interpretation by the officials charged with enforcing them, it becomes very difficult to ensure that you are complying with all of these laws. However, in general and taken as a whole, it is important to understand that these laws attempt to ensure: (1) that certain very sensitive information (particularly financial information, such as bank account or bank card information) is kept secure, (2) that you disclose to your users what those policies are, including what uses might be made of any information they provide to you, and (3) that you comply with your own stated privacy policies.

So rather than simply cutting-and-pasting a form privacy policy as part of your site's Terms of Use, you should spend some time really thinking about data privacy and security issues with regard to your site, including:

- Performing a technical assessment of all the types of data you're collecting from your users (including information you collect inadvertently, where all of the information may be stored and copied, how long it is retained in each of these places, how it is discarded (i.e., is it simply deleted? or is it also "written over" with a data-wiping application?)
- As part of this assessment, understand what third parties (i.e., your outsourced server, your domain provider, your ISP, your third party programmers, or others) touch or have access to your user's data, and understand their privacy polices and technical security processes
- Make sure that you have binding agreements in place with your employees, consultants, and any third parties who may have access to your user data, which confidentiality agreements should include proper confidentiality clauses specifically identifying the user data
- Restricting access to particularly sensitive data (i.e., financial or highly personal information) to as few employees or consultants as absolutely necessary whom you remind and educate about the need to maintain confidentiality and take care with data (i.e., keep sensitive data encrypted if feasible, use secure transmission over potentially insecure networks, don't use portable drives to transport, and keep unattended computers "locked")
- Make a determination as to how you would likely respond to requests or subpoenas for user information from the government, or from a plaintiff in a lawsuit (unmasking of users in these situations is discussed below), and state the policy in a way that gives you maximum flexibility
- Put some real thought into your privacy policy; make sure that it gives you the flexibility you may need as your business develops and grows but accurately describes the types of information you may collect, the uses you may make of the data, any controls or limitations you may allow the users to place on the data and state whether or not you share the data with third parties, either individually or in the aggregate

The EU Directive

You should be aware that the EU Directive is broader and more involved than U.S. laws. It applies to "personal data," which is interpreted extremely broadly, covering a lot of data you might not otherwise believe to be private. Unlike U.S. laws, the EU Directive has specific security requirements, and it applies to you not only if you are located in the European Union, but also if you use any equipment situated in the European Union to process data—which certainly means if you have customers in the European Union (because they would be interacting with servers located in the European Union). This can be read very broadly to apply if you have users in the European Union providing any kind of UGC.

The EU Directive makes it illegal to transfer any personal data outside of the European Union to any country that does not provide an adequate level of protection, subject to certain exceptions if you as a company can self-certify that your business meet certain requirements. In general, the United States is not considered a country providing an adequate level of protection; however, the European Union and the Unite States have worked out a streamlined process for U.S. companies to be able to meet the certification requirements. This is referred to as the "U.S.-E.U. Safe Harbor" and you can find the requirements and contact information on the U.S. Department of Commerce's export Web site: http://www.export .gov/safeharbor/eu/eg_main_018483.asp.

User Anonymity

From time to time you may receive a letter or subpoena demanding that you turn over the identity of a user. Typically this is because someone is unhappy with something your user has posted and is suing or contemplating suing the user but doesn't yet know the identity. There have been cases where the lawsuit is a pretext for finding out the identity of the user—such as where a user is posting anonymous criticism of a company, where the user appears to be an employee of the company, and the company would like to find out his or her identity so that it can terminate employment. In other cases, the letter or subpoena may come from a government agency believing that your user is involved in criminal activity.

You may have the name and other contact information for the user, but more likely in these cases the user has posted anonymously or pseudony-mously and you only have an IP address or possibly information from cookies. It is common practice in these cases for the plaintiff to file the lawsuit against "John Doe," then seek the IP address from you by subpoena, locate the ISP to whom that IP address is registered, and then issue a second subpoena to the ISP, finally uncovering the user's real identity. Once the request gets to the ISP stage, the ISP will often notify their customer John Doe (if it has correct contact information) and give him a very limited time to respond to attempt to quash the subpoena or request letter.

Whether or not a user's name or identifying information must be revealed is an evolving area of law, and differs from case to case, with the standards differing from court to court.[53] It implicates First Amendment Freedom of Speech concerns (because many believe that the right to speak anonymously is an important component of free speech). Similarly, it is also unclear whether the law providing some protection to journalists from revealing their sources would apply to bloggers or similar online information providers, which would be another argument for anonymity of contributors to a Web 2.0 Business in some situations.[54] Subpoenas and identity request letters, even letters from government authorities, are issued all the time without a court having first determined whether the request is legally enforceable. So when you receive such a letter or request, it is far from certain whether you would be "legally required" to turn over the information.

Here it is important to consider in advance what steps you would be willing to take in response to an initial request letter or subpoena and, more specifically, what legal fees you would be willing to spend on behalf of a user. If you elect not to provide the identity information requested, you would likely spend at least some legal fees with your attorney to help you determine the next steps (whether to formally reject the request or just to ignore until a court order is issued), and you may spend some legal fees in court while a final determination is made as to whether the request is enforceable. Whatever you determine you will likely do, you should make sure that your Terms of Use and user agreements (particularly your privacy policy) describe your options accurately, while giving you the flexibility to take actions you might want to in any given case.

In this regard, the precise wording of your policy is important. Some Terms of Use state that the information will be turned over if "legally required." As stated above, a subpoena or letter requesting the information is far from an absolute legal requirement—the issue must be decided in a court which would then issue you a court order. So if you were to decide in a particular case that you would turn over the information to comply with a subpoena (without court order), it is possible that you would open yourself up to charges from your user that you violated the terms of your policy.

So you may decide to include broader language in your privacy policy alerting your users that you may turn over identification information within your control upon receipt of such things as "legal process, requests from governmental agencies, or as otherwise legally required." This would probably mean that you couldn't turn over the information simply in response to a threatening letter from a private person who wants to sue the user, but you would instead wait for him to issue a subpoena in a filed lawsuit, which would be legal process. This provides some protection against easy access to information by private parties but still gives you relative flexibility to provide the information without much legal expense.

If you do not have such a provision in your Terms of Use or user agreement, then you should seek advice from an attorney well-versed in this area before responding (or not responding) to any such requests.

Some Additional Federal Requirements and Restrictions

E-mail Restrictions on Spam and Other Commercial E-mails

If your business sends electronic communications either to potential customers or to your users, subscribers, or any group of people (whether to the e-mail addresses they've provided to you, or to any individual electronic mail addresses you may provide them within your site), you should be aware of the "Controlling the Assault of Non-Solicited Pornography and Marketing Act of 2003" (the CAN-SPAM Act) and its regulation of any types of commercial e-mail messages you might send. Generally speaking, the requirements for such e-mails are:

- First, the "header" information (the source of the e-mail, including the domain address of the sender, etc.) must not be materially false or misleading
- Second, the subject line of the e-mail must not be misleading
- Third, unless consent to send the e-mail has been obtained (if you send these communications to anyone who has not affirmatively consented to them, e.g., by way of a Click-Wrap Agreement containing such consent), you must clearly identify the e-mail as an advertisement or solicitation
- Fourth, you must include a valid physical postal address of the sender (may include a postal office box registered in the sender's name)
- Fifth, you must provide a clear and conspicuous notice to all recipients of their right to opt out of future mailings, providing an e-mail address or other mechanism for opting out that remains operative for at least 30 days after the sending of the message
- Sixth, you must honor any opt-out requests within 10 business days of receipt, and you can't charge any fee or impose any other requirements on recipients attempting to opt out
- There are additional requirements for e-mails containing sexually oriented material

Note that this regulation does not only apply to e-mails traditionally considered as "spam" (i.e., bulk e-mails or unsolicited advertisements), but it covers any commercial e-mails you send, which are defined as "any electronic message the primary purpose of which is the commercial advertisement or promotion of a commercial product or service (including content on an Internet Web site operated for a commercial purpose)."[55]

The only e-mails relating to your business to which the Act does not impose the above requirements are called "transactional or relationship messages" and include e-mails for such things as:

- The actual delivery of a good or service to which the customer is entitled under an agreement the customer has entered into with you, including product updates or upgrades to which they are entitled
- Notification of change in terms and conditions for a subscriber or member
- Notification of account balance to a subscriber or member
- Providing warranty, safety, or recall information for a product or service purchased by the recipient
- Information to facilitate, complete, or confirm a commercial transaction the recipient has agreed to enter into with you

In other words, the CAN-SPAM restrictions listed above don't apply to communications that are customary or necessary for the completion of a valid commercial transaction or voluntary, substantive, ongoing commercial relationship with the recipient. It is not advised to try to "fit" any type of advertisement within one of the above exceptions because the FTC has the authority to review messages in the light of how a recipient might reasonably view them.

As with all laws, there are a number of nuances and applications to specific instances of which you or your legal counsel should be aware if you are regularly sending out e-mail communications to potential clients, users, or members. In order to comply with CAN-SPAM and any updates, most businesses sending out e-mails now engage the services of third-parties (such as Constant Contact® or iContact®) to produce and distribute e-mails, as their software and processes automatically assist you in conforming to up-to-date legal requirements (although you are still responsible if the e-mail fails to comply in some way).

Protection of Children

The Children's Online Privacy Protection Act of 1998 (COPPA)[56] imposes certain requirements on Web sites collecting personal information from children under the age of 13 (which would include allowing such children to post comments to blogs, chat in chat rooms, or otherwise provide UGC). The requirements include:

- Obtaining "verifiable parental consent" by a method reasonably calculated to determine that the person providing consent is, in fact, the child's parent. Remember that whether the method you use is reasonable or not will often be determined in hindsight (after you have failed in some respect), so this is not an area to tread lightly.
- Disclosing online your collection and use practices with respect to children's information
- Providing parents with the opportunity to review personal information collected from their children

As a result, the Terms of Use of most Web sites will contain prohibitions against anyone under 13 using any interactive functions of their Web sites, including posting a comment or response. If your business does collect information from children under 13, you need to spend some time and attention to making sure your site is COPPA-compliant.[57]

In addition, under Section 230 of the Communications Decency Act, the Terms of Use and/or any user agreements of any Web 2.0 Business should a notice "that parental control protections (such as computer hardware, software, or filtering services) are commercially available that may assist the customer in limiting access to material that is harmful to minors."[58] In addition, the notice must "identify, or provide the customer with access to information identifying, current providers of such protections."[59] For example, here is a common form of the notice:

> Child Online Protection Act Notification. Pursuant to 47 USC Section 230(d) as amended, we hereby notify you that parental control protections (such as computer hardware, software or filtering service) are commercially available that may assist you in limiting access to material that is harmful to minors. Visit safetysurf.com for more info.

Political Speech

Fortunately, blogs and other Web sites are not subject to the types of election restrictions that broadcast news and others are—such as "equal time" requirements and the like. Generally speaking, a blogger is free to weigh in heavily on one side or the other of an election (subject of course to defamation and other laws), and you may allow your users to do the same.

The only areas of regulation thus far impact paid advertisements by a political campaign.[60] These are subject to campaign spending limits and similar restrictions. There is also a disclosure requirement ("This ad paid for by ... ") for paid advertisements (including pop-up ads, banner ads, directed search results, and streaming video). However, the disclosure requirement does not likely apply to paid-for positive mentions in blogs, etc. (although the campaign would have to disclose the spending for the paid-for blogging).

In addition, the "press exemption" for spending while covering a campaign (i.e., if you blog about a campaign or candidate and spend money traveling or otherwise covering the campaign), applies to online activities. This means that you do not have to report as a campaign contribution expenses you incur in coverage of a campaign or candidate if these expenses would be covered by the "press exemption" for traditional media reporters.

SOME CONCERNS BASED ON YOUR STATUS (EMPLOYEE, EX-EMPLOYEE, STUDENT, ETC.)

Employees and Ex-Employees

In addition to legal concerns that affect Web 2.0 Businesses generally, often additional legal concerns will apply based on your individual status if you are, for example, an employee or ex-employee of a company and operating a blog aimed at that particular company. We touch on these briefly here to highlight the main issues that you should consider.

If you are an employee or ex-employee of a company and you are blogging, whether overtly or anonymously, about your company, coworkers, or your company's business partners, you may be operating in violation of your employment agreements and other confidentiality protections that the business has. If you are revealing information that the business considers confidential and that you obtained on the job, you could be in violation of an agreement that you signed with the company or, in some cases, trade secret law. Many employees forget that they signed such an agreement, and many no longer have copies of all the policies or agreements they signed when they initially joining the company. But if your blog covers these areas, you will likely receive a cease and desist letter from your (former) employer's law firm and/or a lawsuit for these violations.

In addition, these blogs are typically derogatory by nature, and you may be subject to claims of defamation by your (former) employer and by coworkers identified in the comments. Because these cases typically involve a blog more or less intentionally eliciting derogatory comments about the company or coworkers, you may also find yourself unprotected by Section 230 for derogatory comments appearing on your Web site. You should also take care when setting up the domain and including any logos, trade names, or trade symbols on your site, that you do not make it appear that you are representing the company or are sanctioned by or affiliated with the company. A good, visible disclaimer ("We are NOT affiliated with or sanctioned by Company X") will likely avoid this issue.

These concerns are somewhat different when you are the employee or former employee of a government agency. In these cases, the First Amendment may give you a little more freedom because the government is subject to Freedom of Speech limitations. However, your Freedom of Speech as a government employee with regard to employment matters is somewhat different from, say, Freedom of Speech in general (i.e., the antiwar protester on the corner) or even Freedom of Speech of students in public schools. You should still be mindful of revealing confidential information and defamation issues when your blog addresses normal employment-type concerns.

In addition, if you are the employee or former employee of a publicly traded corporation, there is an additional layer of legal issues related to the disclosure of material non-public information. These stems from "insider trading" regulations under the securities laws. In general, you should not disclose any information, which isn't already public, that you became aware of as part of your employment (including things you learn from others with access to confidential information).

Students

If you are a student operating a blog that touches on matters involving your school, the local department of education, or other students, then you may be sanctioned by the school in certain cases even if you operate the Web site completely outside the school and without any use of school facilities or equipment. Although this implicates important First Amendment concerns, courts have long recognized that public schools have a right to take actions against students even in Free Speech cases, when that speech threatens to disrupt the school's ability to carry out its functions.[61] In the Internet age, courts have applied this reasoning to student blogging so that in order for a school to sanction a student for a Web site created and maintained completely outside school property without any use of school facilities, the school must be able to show that the speech creates a foreseeable risk of material and substantial disruption of the work and discipline of the school.

Although this is believed to be a very restrictive test against the schools, different courts have applied it liberally from time to time.[62] And there have been recent cases where the Supreme Court has indicated the "foreseeable risk of material disruption" is not necessarily the only reason a school might be able to sanction a student for free speech.[63] Practically speaking, if you are operating a blog of this type, you should be prepared for sanctions and potential court fights even if you do not believe you have crossed the line of material disruption.

The Dangers of Operating Worldwide: Which Laws Apply and Where Can You Be Hauled into Court?

Whose Laws Apply?

Throughout this chapter we have dealt primarily with federal U.S. laws and, even though the laws of each state vary in important ways, we have also used a general working assumption about the basic state laws generally. However, any Internet business naturally crosses state and national lines and will have a global presence from the moment you go live. You will be publishing to citizens of every country in the world and, depending on your business model, will likely be interacting with them in various ways. So which laws do you have to comply with?

This can be tricky to determine for any Internet-based business, even a small one. In fact, you are certainly operating simultaneously under the laws of many jurisdictions. You should attempt to control the issue as much as possible with a "choice-of-law provision" in your site's Terms of Use and again in any user agreement that you have your users assent to.[64] However, you should know that such a provision will not always control the matter and will certainly not impact the choice of law when it comes to laws that are criminal in nature. And consider that some countries criminalize actions that we take for granted here in the United States (most notably, freedom of speech and freedom of the press).

So although you may have a choice-of-law provision in your Terms of Use, you should also strongly consider familiarizing yourself with foreign laws (and hiring an expert) if your site begins to deal regularly with citizens of another jurisdiction, particularly if: (1) you intentionally solicit or encourage that participation specifically, (2) if you derive, or plan to derive, substantial revenue from that jurisdiction, or (3) you or your business has substantial assets in that jurisdiction. With regard to international laws, lawyers and other consultants from the foreign country who deal with international businesses will usually know from experience which types of laws you may be violating and the types of changes businesses in your situation typically make in order to comply.

Where Can You Be Sued or Prosecuted?

A related matter that presents similar concerns for a Web 2.0 Business owner is the question of where geographically you can be sued or prosecuted. Unfortunately, this question remains particularly open and unanswered for Web 2.0 Businesses. This is true even among states in the United States, and even more so internationally. Regardless of whether it will save you in every case, you should include a "choice of venue clause" in your Terms of Use and again in any "click-wrap" agreement stating that any litigation will be brought in a court that is local to your business headquarters.[65]

Within the United States

Under the U.S. Constitution and the laws of the 50 states, before you can be sued in any court, the court must have "personal jurisdiction" over you. The determination will be based upon whether you or your business has "minimum contacts" with that state (or its citizens) and whether you have "purposefully availed" yourself of doing business there.[66] Because a Web 2.0 Business can be said to encourage participation by users located anywhere, the terms "purposefully availed" and "minimum contacts" in this context are difficult to apply in a meaningful way without guidance by the courts. There are several court cases dealing with personal jurisdiction for online businesses, and some cases involving non-Internet businesses that are still analogous (particularly cases involving online publications).[67] However, the courts of each state will make their own decisions and interpretation, and each case will be heavily fact specific, so it is difficult to discern a rule that you can rely upon in trying to anticipate in which states you might be subject to lawsuits for your business.

For a general idea, the general principles that would likely guide a U.S. court in making a decision regarding personal jurisdiction are well-stated in the 1997 opinion from a case titled *Zippo Manufacturing Company v. Zippo Dot Com, Inc.*,[68] which discussed a "sliding scale" of contacts with a state that a court would consider in making the decision of personal jurisdiction:

This sliding scale is consistent with well developed personal jurisdiction principles. At one end of the spectrum are situations where a defendant clearly does business over the Internet. If the defendant enters into contracts with residents of a foreign jurisdiction that involve the knowing and repeated transmission of computer files over the Internet, personal jurisdiction is proper. E.g. *CompuServe, Inc. v. Patterson*, 89 F.2d 1257 (6th Cir. 1996). At the opposite end are situations where a defendant has simply posted information on an Internet Web site which is accessible to users in foreign jurisdictions. A passive Web site that does little more than make information available to those who are interested in it is not grounds for the exercise personal jurisdiction. E.g. *Bensusan Restaurant Corp., v. King*, 937 F.Supp. 296 (S.N.D.Y. 1996). The middle ground is occupied by interactive Web sites where a user can exchange information with the host computer. In these cases, the exercise of jurisdiction is determined by examining the level of interactivity and commercial nature of the exchange of information that occurs on the Web site. E.g. *Maritz, Inc. v. Cybergold, Inc.*, 1996 U.S. Dist. Lexis 14976 (E.D.Mo. Aug. 19, 1996).[69]

Internationally

Internationally, the question is even more wide open. Online businesses that felt that they were safe in their home countries were shaken by a 2002 decision of an Australian court,[70] which decided that Dow Jones & Co. could be sued in Australia for defamation stemming from an article about an Australian businessman in *Barron's* even though Dow Jones & Co. delivered only seven copies of the print edition of *Barron's* to Australia and only had around 1,700 paid online subscribers located in Australia (which was only 00.3 percent of Dow Jones' total online subscribership). The opinion stated that a "publication" of the article occurred every time and in every place that a user logged in and a copy of the article was sent to the user's server,[71] so that the defendant would theoretically be subject to personal jurisdiction in any location where a user views the site.

This principle, sometimes called the "law of the server," would mean that your business could be called into court in any country in which a user calls up an allegedly offending Web page—at least in defamation cases. Of course, practically, it doesn't necessarily mean a completely wide-open field—typically cases will only be brought in venues where someone is harmed (i.e., in a defamation case, the alleged victim's country of residence or other places where they have significant personal or business dealings) or a country where you have substantial assets.

However, consider that it is unlikely that a U.S. court would enforce certain penal orders issued by foreign courts, and may not recognize the foreign court orders at all if either (1) the foreign court's assertion of jurisdiction over you or your business did not meet the same types of "minimum contacts" and "purposeful availment" tests that are constitutionally required for states to assert jurisdiction or (2) the application of laws in the court order violate U.S. constitutional rights (typically, this would be a Freedom of Speech question). As a result it is possible that if you don't have assets in a foreign country in which you are sued or prosecuted (and you don't plan to travel to that country), you may decide not to respond to the foreign legal action at all, but rather let it proceed to its conclusion without your participation. You should get legal advice before making that kind of decision.

Yahoo! v. LICRA: **Some Lessons**

One real-world example showing how these concepts interact and how differing laws of various jurisdictions can impact an online business, involves actions by nonprofit organizations in France seeking to stop Yahoo! from allowing the sale of Nazi-related items on the auction portion of its Web site (or to at least make that part of its Web site inaccessible in France), based on a French law banning trafficking in Nazi or Third Reich paraphernalia.

Yahoo! operates its main site www.yahoo.com, and through subsidiaries incorporated under the laws of other countries, it operates sites in other countries under the general yahoo.com domain, but including a two-letter country code in the domain address (i.e., fr.yahoo.com in France). It is the policy of Yahoo! and its subsidiaries that each of the specific country sites will comply with the laws of that particular country. However, any citizen in any country can easily access Yahoo!'s main site or that of any other country.

In this case, the nonprofit organizations sent Yahoo! and Yahoo! France a letter demanding that it remove the offending Nazi items and certain "negationist" links or information from its sites—or at least that it completely prevent access to these items from any user located in France. The letter was followed in short order by a lawsuit in a French court. After an initial court order, Yahoo! or its French subsidiary removed the offending items on its fr.yahoo.com Web site and took other actions required by the court with respect to its French Web site. However, the items were still available on www.yahoo.com (and other Yahoo! country sites), which was still easily accessible by French citizens. The plaintiffs went back to court where the judge issued a second order clarifying that Yahoo! must block access to the items from computers in France on its main site in addition to the French subsidiary site. Although Yahoo! claimed that it would be technically impossible to comply because it would be impossible to determine definitively which users were located in France, the court commissioned a report from three experts indicating that Yahoo! could identify up to 90 percent of French users through a combined use of IP addresses plus an "honor system" questionnaire that could be required of visitors to the offending portion of the auction site, and reiterated the requirements.

Instead of appealing the French decision, Yahoo! went to court in San Jose, California, to obtain a declaratory judgment that the French ruling lacked authority over Yahoo!, that it violated First Amendment principals, and that it was otherwise unenforceable against Yahoo!.[72] Although the district court initially awarded Yahoo! a judgment that the French order was unenforceable, an appeals court overturned this ruling.[73] The basis of the finding and much of the opinions of the courts in this case are procedural and based on the "posture of the case," and thus don't necessarily answer substantive questions of free speech protection or the jurisdiction of the French court over Yahoo!'s actions on the Internet. However, some discussions in the U.S. and French cases bring up interesting guidelines:

- If there are aspects of your Web 2.0 Business that are illegal in a foreign country, a foreign court may determine that it has jurisdiction over your business by looking at aspects of your site that "target" or show your recognition that you have a user base in that country—this may include even such things as the presence of advertising in that country's language when users in that country pull up your site (although it is unclear whether this would be true if such geographic-based advertising occurred automatically through a third-party's contextual advertising software over which you have no control).
- There is probably not an "extraterritorial" right of Free Speech that expands beyond the U.S. borders. In other words, if a foreign country's courts require that you cease speech activities only in that country, it is unlikely that a U.S. court will find that this violates your First Amendment rights.
- If you are faced with a foreign law or court order requiring you to disable access to parts of your site in a foreign country, and you intend to make a Free Speech argument that you can't technically do so without also curtailing your free speech activities in the United States (and therefore your U.S. free speech rights would be violated by the order), you should be prepared with technical proof that it would be impossible or at least cost-prohibitive to do so, and should be ready for the court or opposing party to have experts showing that it is technically possible, and therefore not a violation of your Free Speech rights in the United States.
- Even if a foreign government or party is able to get an order against you under foreign laws, a U.S. court would be unlikely to enforce that order against you here in the United States, if it can be found that the order is a penalty in nature (which was indicated to be the case with the monetary penalties threatened by the French court in the Yahoo! case).

On the Internet, it is probably impossible, and certainly impractical, to avoid violating the laws of every jurisdiction in the world (e.g., Iran may determine that your relatively innocent blog violates religious or authoritarian principles)—but by keeping track of the laws applicable to the jurisdictions with which you interact the most (particularly with any from which you are deriving revenue), you should at least keep out of trouble with authorities who could substantially impact your business or, in the extreme case, seek to extradite you for a criminal proceeding.[74]

NOTES

1. See, for example, *Ticketmaster Corp. v. Tickets.com, Inc.*, 2000 WL 525390 (C.D.Cal. March 27, 2000) (a browse-wrap license situated in small type at the bottom of the Web page was *not* binding without more facts showing the customer was aware of the terms); *Specht v. Netscape Communications Corp.*, 306 F.3d 17 (2nd Cir.2002) (customers downloading software from a Web site were *not* bound to terms of license that were not apparent at the point at which customer clicked to download).

2. *Hubbert v. Dell Corp.*, 835 N.E. 2d 113 (Ill. App. Ct. 2005) (a browse-wrap license *was* effective and binding when the hypertext link was conspicuous and located on various pages).

3. Facebook's main Terms of Use page is here: http://www.facebook.com/terms.php?ref=pf. Facebook separates out other related policies, which are referred and linked to in the body of the main terms page.

4. The WSJ.com Subscriber Agreement and Terms of Use is located here: http://online.wsj.com/public/page/subscriber_agreement.html. Note that the WSJ.com Web site now has several user-interactive components and so the site's terms of use contains many Web 2.0 type provisions. UGC is dealt with specifically in Section 7 of the Subscriber Agreement.

5. 47 U.S.C. § 230. See the discussion in this chapter regarding protections of your Web 2.0 Business arising out of Section 230.

6. See the discussion in this chapter about the Children's Online Privacy Protection Act of 1998 (COPPA).

7. 47 U.S.C. § 230(d). See the discussion in this chapter regarding this and other aspects of Section 230.

8. See the discussion in this chapter regarding privacy requirements and your privacy policy.

9. See discussions in this chapter regarding copyright notifications, takedowns and other related matters under the Digital Millennium Copyright Act.

10. See the discussion in this chapter regarding which law applies to your site. Note that this provision is not going to be binding in all cases, but it is a good idea to include anyway.

11. 17 U.S.C. § 106. The federal copyright law (the Copyright Act of 1976 and subsequent amendments) is contained in Title 17 of the United States Code, Chapters 1–8 and 10–12.

12. In fact, ISPs and any server along the chain of transmission or publication could have technically been liable for "publication" of copyrighted material by someone else, as was demonstrated in cases such as *MAI Systems Corp. v. Peak Computer, Inc.*, 991 F.2d 511 (9th Cir. 1993), *cert. dismissed*, 510 U.S. 1033 (1994).

These kinds of cases led to the passage of the Digital Millennium Copyright Act, discussed in this chapter.

13. 17 U.S.C. § 512(c)(1). The statute requires that, in order to be eligible for its protections, you can't allow materials for which you have "actual knowledge" that they infringe on someone else's copyrights, or for which you are "aware of facts and circumstances from which infringing activity is apparent" (i.e., a "red flag"). And that, upon gaining such actual knowledge of infringement or awareness of red flags, you act "expeditiously" to remove or disable access to the material. The good news for you here is that courts have been very hesitant to impose any burden on online service providers to investigate red flags in light of the DMCA's apparent policy of shifting the burden of monitoring copyright violations from the site operator to the copyright holder. For your protection from your users whose material you might take down, your policy should go further than the basic requirements of the DMCA and establish your ability to remove or disable access to, partially or in full, to materials that you determine in your complete discretion to be actually, or potentially, offensive or in violation of the law. For example, the *WSJ Terms of Use* provides the broadest latitude by stating: "We may also remove any User Content for any reason and without notice to you. This includes all materials related to your use of the Services or membership, including email accounts, postings, profiles or other personalized information you have created while on the Services."

14. 17 U.S.C. § 512(i)(1). Note that the written policy can be very simple, a fact which has been affirmed by case law. For example, see the sentence in the *WSJ Copyright & IP Policy* reading: "For our sites that have subscriber, membership or similar account holder privileges, we reserve the right, in appropriate circumstances and at our discretion, to terminate the privileges of any account holder who repeatedly infringes the copyrights or other intellectual property rights of Dow Jones or others." This is a sufficient policy to meet the statutory requirements as long as it is "reasonably implemented." Because terms such as "repeat infringer" and even "subscriber" are not defined in the DCMA, it may seem more difficult to know whether you are "reasonably implementing" your policy. However, this is likely a very common-sense test with a fairly low threshold on your part, but you should document any efforts you make to determine whether a person is or is not a "repeat infringer," so that you could produce these efforts should the question ever arise. On the far end of the spectrum, it is clear that if your business actively encourages people to violate copyright law, you will not be found to have reasonably implemented the policy and wouldn't be eligible for the DMCA liability limitations. For example, see *In re: Aimster Copyright Litig.*, 252 F.Supp. 2d 634 (N.D. Ill. 2002), *aff'd* 334 F.3d 643 (7th Cit. 2003).

15. 17 U.S.C. § 512(c)(2). The U.S. Copyright Office does not provide a form for designating an agent under the DMCA, but the fairly simple requirements for the filing have been set forth at 31 C.F.R. § 201.38 (online at http://www.loc.gov/cgi-bin/formprocessor/copyright/cfr.pl?&urlmiddle=1.0.2.6.1.0.174.35&part=201&section=38&prev=34&next=39), and you can see forms that other companies have used successfully by browsing through the online agent registry at http://www.copyright.gov/onlinesp/list/index.html.

16. You or your attorney should be familiar with the requirements of what constitutes a valid notification under the DMCA. Among others, it should be

"written" (including by e-mail), and signed or authenticated by the copyright holder or someone authorized to act on its behalf.

17. 17 U.S.C. § 512(c)(1)(C).

18. 17 U.S.C. § 512(g)(2)(A).

19. Similar to the rules regarding notifications, it is important to understand the statutory requirements that a counter-notification must meet to be valid under the DMCA. These requirements are set forth at 17 U.S.C. § 512(g)(3), and some familiarity with case law is helpful in making the determination of whether a particular counter-notification is valid to trigger your put-back requirements. Otherwise, a put-back in response to an invalid counter-notification might open you to liability from the copyright holder.

20. 17 U.S.C. § 512(g)(2)(B).

21. 17 U.S.C. § 512(g)(C). Note that your put-back time (between 10 and 14 business days) is based on the date on which *you received the counter-notification*, not on when the original complainant receives your notice that a counter-notification has been issued. This gives the original complainant a fairly limited time to file such a lawsuit and provide you with evidence of the filing in order to prevent your put-back of the information.

22. 17 U.S.C. § 512(f).

23. 17 U.S.C. § 512(c)(1)(B). Typically, you won't be found to have "financial interest" and "control" in infringing activity absent some special arrangement with the particular poster of the material. Courts deciding these issues have generally determined that a "financial interest" in the activity does not mean merely standard fees you may collect from subscribers, and that "control" means more than just your technical ability to disable or remove the infringing material or your policies giving you the legal right to do so. For example, see *Tur v. YouTube, Inc.*, No. VC 064436 FMC AJWX, 2007 WL 1893635 (C.D. Cal. June 20, 2007).

24. Facebook's form can be found at http://www.facebook.com/copyright.php?copyright_notice=1.

25. 47 U.S.C. § 230(c)(1).

26. 47 U.S.C. § 230(e). In cases involving intellectual property law violation (i.e., copyright infringement) you would look elsewhere, such as 17 U.S.C. § 512 as discussed earlier in this chapter.

27. 47 U.S.C. § 230(e)(3).

28. *DiMeo, III, v. Max*, 433 F.Supp.2d 523 (E.D. Pa. 2006) (operator of blog site not liable for defamation in several entries even though operator selected the entries for publication and even edited them); *Batzel v. Smith*, 333 F.3d 1018 (9th Cir. 2003) (editor of listserv published excerpts from e-mail claiming another user owned paintings looted during WWII); *Ben Ezra, Weinstein & Co., Inc. v. America Online, Inc.*, 206 F.3d 980 (10th Cir. 2000) (AOL not liable for publication of continuous stock data even though AOL was aware of erroneous information and had notified the provider several times); *Blumenthal v. Drudge*, 992 F.Supp. 44 (D.D.C. 1998) (AOL not liable for Drudge Report article that was published over AOL).

29. *Chicago Lawyers' Committee for Civil Rights Under Law, Inc. v. Craigslist, Inc.*, 519 F.3d 666 (7th Cir. 2008) (Craigslist not liable for discriminatory preferences indicated in user solicitations); But see *Housing Council of San Fernando Valley v. Roommates.com, LLC*, 489 F.3d 921 (9th Cir. 2007) (discussed in the text in this chapter).

30. *Carafano v. Metrosplash.com, Inc.*, 339 F.3d 1119 (9th Cir. 2003) (Metrosplash not liable for one of its users submitting a false profile impersonating Carafano, which contained very derogatory and sexually suggestive information).

31. *Doe v. MySpace, Inc.*, 474 F.Supp.2d 843 (W.D. Tex. 2007) (discussed in text; MySpace not liable to victim of sexual assault who misrepresented her age as 18 and met another user who sexually assaulted her); *Doe v. SexSearch.com*, 502 F.Supp.2d 719 (N.D. Ohio 2007) (plaintiff sued SexSearch.com after he was prosecuted for unlawful sex with a minor for encounter with another SexSearch.com user who was a minor, but had misrepresented herself as being 18 years old).

32. *Schneider v. Amazon.com, Inc.*, 108 Wash.App. 454 (2001) (Amazon.com not liable for failing to remove allegedly defamatory reviews of author's books, even though Amazon.com retained right to remove or edit these postings).

33. Ibid.

34. Ibid.

35. *Zeran v. America Online, Inc.*, 129 F.3d 327 (4th Cir. 1997) (AOL not liable for failing to remove false advertisements for clothing containing offensive slogans related to Oklahoma City bombings; Section 230 also protected AOL from liability for "unreasonably" delaying to remove the defamatory messages, refusing to post retractions and failing to screen for similar postings thereafter).

36. 47 U.S.C. § 230(f)(3) (the definition of "information content provider").

37. For example, see *Schneider v. Amazon.com, Inc.*, 108 Wash.App. 454 (2001).

38. For example, see *DiMeo, III, v. Max*, 433 F.Supp.2d 523 (E.D. Pa. 2006); *Batzel v. Smith*, 333 F.3d 1018 (9th Cir. 2003). Although these cases indicate that the selection and editing of the materials did not result in the Web site's responsibility for creation and development, you should exercise extreme caution in editing UGC. It is likely that different courts may come to different conclusions, and it would be highly dependent on the facts and circumstances of every specific case. If you edit any content for substance and/or if your edits "touch" the statements or material that turn out to be the subject of a lawsuit or crime, you run a substantial risk of being found to be responsible in part for its creation or development, particularly for any language that is yours.

39. *Fair Housing Council of San Fernando Valley v. Roommates.com, LLC*, 489 F.3d 921 (9th Cir. 2007).

40. 489 F.3d 921 (9th Cir. 2007).

41. Note that the court stated that statements in the "Additional Comments" section of a profile—which were completely created at the discretion of the user without prompts from the Web site—would remain covered by Section 230 protection.

42. *Blogging and Social Networking: Current Legal Issues*, Cydney Tune and Marley Degner (pp. 113–137), included in course materials for *Information Technology Law Institute 2009: Web 2.0 and the Future of Mobile Computing: Privacy, Blogs, Data Breaches, Advertising, and Portable Information Systems*, Peter T. Brown and Leonard T. Nuara, cochairs (© 2009 Practising Law Institute), available from Practising Law Institute at (800) 260-4PLI or www.pli.edu.

43. *Carafano v. Metrosplash.com, Inc.*, 339 F.3d 1119 (9th Cir. 2003); *Doe v. MySpace, Inc.*, 474 F.Supp.2d 843 (W.D. Tex. 2007) (discussed in text; however, note that in this case the plaintiff's claims that MySpace become involved in the creation of the profile because of their questionnaire weren't raised until the appeal and

therefore the court declined to consider them but did indicate that Section 230 was meant to be applied very broadly).

44. *Doe v. MySpace*, 528 F.3d 413 (5th Cir. 2007), *cert. denied*, 129 S. Ct. 600 (2008).

45. Initially, the charges also included fraud and negligent misrepresentation, but these were dropped as it was clear that these cases would be barred by Section 230 of the CDA or other law.

46. 47 U.S.C. § 230(c)(2)(A).

47. 47 U.S.C. § 230(e)(2).

48. See, e.g., *Inwood Laboratories, Inc. v. Ives Laboratories, Inc.*, 546 U.S. 844 (1982); *Tiffany (NJ) Inc. v. eBay, Inc.*, No. 04 4607 (S.D.N.Y. July 14, 2008).

49. On a related current hot topic, note that the Obama administration has remained notably silent about privacy rules proposed by the Federal Trade Commission, among others, because of its support of social networking and other Web 2.0 Businesses, which are opposed to privacy controls, http://bits.blogs.nytimes.com/2009/06/02/the-obama-adminstrations-silence-on-privacy/. These types of rules, if passed, may affect your site's ability to use context-based advertising, which is a potentially big source of revenue for some Web 2.0 Businesses.

50. See, e.g., the *Prepared Statement of the Federal Trade Commission Before the Committee on Commerce, Science, and Transportation, U.S. Senate on Data Breaches and Identity Theft*, June 16, 2005. Available online at http://www.ftc.gov/os/2005/06/050616 databreaches.pdf.

51. See, e.g., California (Cal. Civ. Code §§ 1798.80, .81, .81.5 & .82 and Cal. Bus. & Prof. Code §§ 22575–22578); Conn. H.B. 5658 (signed into law in 2008; only applies to willful [intentional] violations); Massachusetts (201 CMR § 17.00); Minnesota (Minn. Stat. §§ 325M.01 to .09); ; Nevada (Nev. Rev. Stat. §§ 205.498 & 597.970); Oregon comprehensive information security and data breach act; R.I. Gen. Laws §§ 11–49.2(2) and (3); Tex. Bus. & Com. Code § 48.102(a).

52. Directive 95/46/EC of the European Parliament.

53. See, e.g., *Doe v. Cahill*, 884A.2d 451 (Del. 2005) (requiring plaintiff to meet a higher "summary judgment" standard before unmasking of the blogger is required); *Krinsky v. Doe 6*, 159 Cal.App.4th 1154 (2008) (court quashed a subpoena requesting an unmasking, requiring that the plaintiff first make a prima facie case of the claims (here, libel) before unmasking of the user was required).

54. See, e.g., *Wolf v. U.S.*, 201 Fed.Appx. 430 (9th Cir. 2006) (Court found that freelance journalist and video blogger was *not* protected by state shield law because he was not connected with a traditional news source); *O'Grady v. Superior Court*, 139 Cal.App.4th 1423 (2006) (Court found that state shield law *did* apply to Web sites and blogs providing information to the public).

55. 15 U.S.C. § 7702(A).

56. 15 U.S.C. §§ 6501 et seq.; 16 C.F.R. § 312.

57. The Federal Trade Commission Web site includes an interactive checklist you can use to assess whether your privacy policies and Web site are in compliance with COPPA: http://www.ftc.gov/coppa/checklist.htm.

58. 47 U.S.C. 230(d).

59. Ibid.

60. See the Federal Election Commission's new rules published in the Federal Register, Vol. 71, No. 71 (April 12, 2006) p.18589. Online at http://www.fec.gov/law/cfr/ej_compilation/2006/notice_2006-8.pdf.

61. See, for example, *Tinker v. Des Moines Independent Community School District*, 393 U.S. 503 (1969).

62. Of current interest, in a case in which Supreme Court nominee Sonia Soto-mayor agreed as part of an appellate court panel (*Doninger v. Niehoff*, 514 F. Supp. 2d 199 (D. Conn. 2007) (also known as "the D-Bag case"), the sanctions of the school were upheld when the school refused to allow a student to run for student government after she posted a comment on her blog referring to the school super-intendent and other school officials as a derogatory term because they cancelled a battle of the bands that the student had helped to organize.

63. *Morse v. Frederick*, 551 U.S. 393 (2007) (also known as "the bong hits 4 Jesus case"). In this case, the court indicated that in addition to traditional sanctions allowed only for foreseeable risk of material disruption of education or discipline, a school could also sanction for free speech if the speech was against a compelling interest of the school, at least where the speech was at a school-sponsored activity and the compelling interest was prevention of drug abuse. It is hard to tell whether this case will be limited specifically to cases where the speech is seen to promote drug abuse, or will open the door to sanctions related to many kinds of speech related to other "compelling interests" of schools, or whether it would be extended to purely off-campus speech.

64. For example, see the sentence in Section 10 of the *WSJ Terms of Use*, which states: "You agree that this Agreement, as well as any and all claims arising from this Agreement will be governed by and construed in accordance with the laws of the State of New York, United States of America applicable to contracts made entirely within New York and wholly performed in New York, without regard to any conflict or choice of law principles."

65. For example, see the sentence in Section 10 of the *WSJ Terms of Use*, which states: "The sole jurisdiction and venue for any litigation arising out of this Agree-ment will be an appropriate federal or state court located in New York." In fact, you may go further and try to lock down the issue by adding something such as "By using this Web site [by agreeing to these terms], you are agreeing that you are subject to the personal jurisdiction of the courts of such venue for matters arising out of this Agreement, and you hereby waive and agree not to contest the personal jurisdictions of such courts for any such matters and to waive any challenge or objection to such venue for *forum non conveniens* or other grounds."

66. This is based on a long and well-established line of cases starting with *International Shoe Co. v. Washington,* 326 U.S. 310, 66 S.Ct. 154, 90 L.Ed. 95 (1945); *Pennoyer v. Neff,* 95 U.S. 714, 24 L. Ed. 565 (1877); *World-Wide Volkswagen Corp. v. Woodson,* 444 U.S. 286 (1980). Each state has now adopted a "long-arm" jurisdiction statute that defines the specific ways in which a court in that state can get personal jurisdiction over you or your business; however, these statutes can't require *less* contact with the state than the constitutional principles of "minimum contacts" and "purposeful availment."

67. For example, see *Young v. New Haven Advocate* 318 F.3d 86 (2002), in which a Virginia citizen sued an online publication based in Connecticut for libel of the Virginia resident. The court found that because the Connecticut publication did not take specific actions to attract Virginia subscribers, it would not be subject to personal jurisdiction in a Virginia court, even though the publication was accessible online in Virginia and even had several Virginia subscribers. See also *Toys "R" Us, Inc., v. Step Two,* 318 F.3d 446 (2003), in which a New Jersey court

determined that a Spanish company that sold products online was not susceptible to personal jurisdiction in New Jersey, even though it had sold and shipped products to at least two customers in New Jersey. But consider that this last case was influenced by other facts, such as the Spanish company had no bank account, employees, or other assets in the United States, its Web site was entirely in Spanish, only quoted prices in pesetas and Euros, and there were e-mails indicating that it had difficulty shipping to the United States because its computer programs didn't properly accept U.S. addresses. However, there is an influential non-Internet Supreme Court case that could easily provide grounds for the opposite result in many cases, *Jones v. Calder*, 465 U.S. 783 (1984). In that case, the actress Shirley Jones sued a Florida publication called the *National Inquirer* for defamation, and the Supreme Court ruled that the *National Inquirer* could be sued in California because the story involved a California citizen (Jones), was based on sources called in California, and the magazine had a substantial readership in California.

68. 952 F Supp 1119 (WD Pa, 1997).

69. Ibid., 1124.

70. *Dow Jones & Company, Inc v. Gutnick,* 2002 High Court of Australia 56.

71. When and where a publication occurs is important not only for purposes of personal jurisdiction but may also be important to which copyright, trademark, or defamation laws apply.

72. *Yahoo!, Inc. v. La Ligue Contra Le Racisme et L'Antisemitisme,* 169 F.Supp. 2d 1181 (N.D. Cal. 2001).

73. *Yahoo!, Inc. v. La Ligue Contra Le Racisme et L'Antisemitisme,* 433 F.3d 1199 (9th Cir.2006).

74. Extradition to another country is governed by bilateral treaties between the United States and respective foreign countries (with about 50 countries currently having no treaty in place with the United States). In addition to the many opportunities you would have to be heard and reheard in U.S. courts (making even an attempt to extradite *extremely* unlikely for anything other than heinous or financially devastating crimes), typically treaties entered into (or rewritten) after 1980 contain a "dual criminality" requirement so that you could only be extradited if, among other requirements, your act was a crime in both the United States and the foreign country (with "crime" typically meaning a breach of law punishable by at least a year imprisonment in both the United States and the foreign country), which is almost certainly not applicable to the topics we're covering here. Prior to 1980, most treaties contained a list of extraditable offenses which, similarly, would almost certainly not contain the types of actions we are discussing here.

6

Content Management Beyond a Web 2.0–Overwhelmed World

Robert Rose

On September 8, 2008, United Airlines Stock (UAL) lost tens of millions of dollars in value over a span of 10 minutes. The stock, which opened that day at $12.45, crashed to $3.00 before trading was finally halted. Many of the major carriers were struggling with the weak economy and higher fuel prices. Like the others, United Airlines had a history of financial turbulence. But that morning the turbulence spun out of control. An employee of a Florida-based investor information service, browsing Google news, saw a headline published from the *Florida Sun-Sentinel*'s Web site. Clicking through, he went to the *Sun-Sentinel* site and saw that the story had actually been syndicated from the *Chicago Tribune*'s Web site (UAL is based in Chicago). The news stated that United Airlines was declaring bankruptcy.

The investor, realizing the enormous importance of such a story to his subscribers, quickly wrote up a headline relaying the bankruptcy and summarized the subsequent point of the story that the airline was attempting to cut costs by 20 percent. He then published it using his content management system. It was not only transmitted immediately to the subscribers of the investor's information system, but also through the Bloomberg news service; meaning his content would hit the national wires as well.

As soon as the news hit the national wires and other investors saw it, the results were crushing. More than 20 million shares were traded in the span of less than 10 minutes, and the NASDAQ finally halted trading on UAL at 11:06 A.M. But the question is "why?" If the airline was indeed going bankrupt, why halt trading on a valuable piece of news? Well, the problem was—it wasn't true. The story that had appeared in the *Florida Sun-Sentinel* was six years old—and was accurately reporting on United Airlines' chapter 11 bankruptcy in 2002.

Indeed, *The Chicago Tribune* was actually the originator of the story and it had appeared on December 10, 2002. It had been subsequently picked up by the *Florida Sun-Sentinel*—where it also ran on December 10, 2002 and, apparently, then had been archived by the newspaper until this unfortunate day six years later[1] when it had unwittingly appeared again as a top story.

Fingers were pointed, and the "blame game" was played with fury. The *Sun-Sentinel* blamed Google for pulling the headline of the archived story erroneously. Google blamed the *Sun-Sentinel*, saying that its content robot correctly looked at the date on the page, and saw that it was current— and therefore saw the story as current. Some blamed the information service employee for not recognizing that the story was six years old by its context (which was clear) and for basically screaming fire in a crowded theater. Ultimately the source of the issue came down to a semantics argument over look and feel—specifically where, if, and how a date should be placed on an article to make sure its date is understood in context. That's right, it came down to a fight over the design of the Web site.

What is the moral of this story? One might think given the name of this chapter that the focus would be on the *Sun-Sentinel*, how it managed its content, and how something like releasing a six-year-old story could ever happen. Certainly there are questions about how archived content should be released back into the wild. Further, there are lessons that lie squarely at the feet of the investor information service—and how snippets of content that live in multiple places, and are displayed through multiple interfaces, can quickly lose meaning. When this kind of content spurs rash action, it becomes like that childhood game of "telephone." At its heart, the UAL story is simply a growing pain in an evolving World Wide Web. Content is growing explosively. It's easy to hit the publish button in today's world and disseminate content widely. Our Web 2.0–overwhelmed, socially networked thirst for 24/7/365 access to information just encourages us to act faster than we should.

How do we manage our content in and beyond a Web 2.0 world where our content is aggregated from various atomic bits through different Web sites? How do we manage this content when speed is often much more important than accuracy? How do we manage our content when the context (e.g., the look and feel) is becoming less important than the "mobility" of that content? Is it simply something we can't trust machines to do? As Chris McNeilly, vice president of technology at SmartBrief.com—one of the services that *did not* pick up the UAL story that fateful September day—was quoted as saying, "Technology gets you so far, but then our human editors make the final decisions for publication."[2]

In short—how do we manage our content in and beyond the Web 2.0 world? To address that, we should look at three distinct phases of how content is evolving on the Web and how it is affecting the way we access it over the Internet. These three phases themselves are not equal, nor are they all-inclusive. Rather, think of them as two of the smaller, perhaps more important, cobblestones leading to a much larger open garden.

THE FIRST COBBLESTONE: THE ATOMIC AGE OF CONTENT

When the UAL Story first appeared on that fateful day, it was a headline and abstract on Google News, from a story that appeared in full on the *Sun-Sentinel* Web site, syndicated from a larger story on the *Chicago Tribune* Web site. This is an explosive trend in Web content and Web-content management—and that trend is that content is being broken up into smaller and smaller bits—so that it can be aggregated and consumed in an ever-more filtered manner.

Very few of us manage newspapers or other such high-velocity content vehicles. And few of us have to worry about an erroneous piece of news like the UAL fable. But consider how that same process might be taking place with your brand or your product information. Consider the headline of the press release announcing your new product; the one you're about to spend a thousand dollars sending over the National Wire Services. Did you assume that the context would be derived from the sub-headline or the press release detail? If you read it alone does it even make sense? Your risk is not only that erroneous information could be syndicated but also that breaking up your content can remove contextual meaning and result in a waste of your marketing dollars as well.

In Web 1.0, our Web sites were the sole source of our marketing and product and customer service information. In fact, many still are. But the world beyond Web 2.0 allows us to syndicate this content out in innumerable ways. Today we can publish our product marketing and press releases in RSS Feeds. Done with some skill, our press releases will be automatically picked up by global news organizations such as CNN and CBS. Google News will pick up our RSS Feeds. Blogging strategies help us communicate more effectively with our constituencies, and the index of that blog might get scraped into Google Blogs, or picked up on other social media like Digg.com or Slashdot.org. Our last 10 blog entries will appear as "related content" on industry Web sites. Or, other people may consciously break it down into even smaller bits by using Twitter or other microblogging strategies.

This is a key strategy for us today as business managers. It is now so much easier for us to communicate with large groups of our constituents —and easier for our constituents to "subscribe" to what we are saying. While the UAL story is a cautionary tale, and there is (as we'll see) a dark side to this trend, the real story here is the unique opportunity that this breakdown of content provides. This is really the heart of Web 2.0—it's the conversation that begins with the subscription to a small piece of content and leads to a lead in your sales organization, a more satisfied and well-informed customer, or a better partner.

Consider that as many business managers experiment with social media, and the ultimate breakdown of content into headlines, abstracts, and blurbs, we must be aware of new trends that break down the content even further. Think of Facebook—where content is literally broken into descriptive field levels so that it can be aggregated—and re-aggregated—and of course targeted for advertising.

The Web is inviting us to segment our content into smaller and smaller chunks so that we can provide the flexibility of other interfaces to display filtered versions of it. But how does the Web know which versions—which chunks—to display? That brings us to our second cobblestone.

The Second Cobblestone: Content about Content

When reporters interview legendary artists, one question is used quite frequently—usually toward the end of an interview, where the interviewer is trying to sum it all up and wants his subject to become philosophical. They ask "what would you like your epitaph to be?" Or, sometimes they'll ask "how would you like to be remembered?" This is the quintessential example of what is happening with content. It's being tagged with an epitaph. How would you like your blog post to be remembered? Please write its epitaph.

Within nearly every piece of content we produce these days—whether it is a photo uploaded to our Facebook profile, a blog post we put on our corporate Web site, or the general search engine description we put on our marketing white paper—we are asked to sum up in a few words what this content is about. This is the metadata. Search engines use this metadata to find our content—not necessarily in every case, but it is one of the primary ways of aggregating and filtering that content. This content about the content can, itself, be broken into smaller and smaller bits: description, keywords, tag—breaking down the content into one word or label. All 150 million of you with Facebook accounts have received the message that you've been "tagged" in a photo. Guess what? Unless you untag it, that photo now lives with you on the Internet. So, if someone has tagged the photo as "Sam" and "Drunk," someone can put up a Web page of all the drunk Sams on Facebook. Pretty powerful and pretty scary isn't it? I'll pause here while you all go untag your photos in Facebook.

Companies like CrownPeak, a company for which I once worked, help organizations to manage their Web content. The software the company sells manages thousands of Web sites for hundreds of customers. Consider that on average a business Web site focused on selling a product or service (i.e., not e-commerce or a magazine site) might have approximately

300 pages.[3] The metadata about that content would fill 10,000 pages. Every piece of content stored in a content management tool has metadata around it. How much metadata is determined largely by the tool you use. Some of it is explicit, including the content that helps to categorize it, but metadata is also implicit. For example, there may have been 42 versions of that content before it went live, so each date and timestamp (as well as the changes themselves) reside as metadata. There may have been multiple authors in its life, so each author and their changes are stored as metadata. You can see how quickly these elements can be taken to a dizzying level of detail.

This fine detail is key in our strategy to take advantage of the opportunity. By breaking our content up into smaller and smaller bits, and by describing the content accurately and with a level of depth appropriate for our organization, we are preparing to take the next step—into the garden beyond Web 2.0.

THE GARDEN—WEB 3.0 OR THE SEMANTIC WEB

Think about the experience you have with content on the Web today. You go to Google, type in a search phrase, and, assuming you've constructed your search phrase accurately, your answer may be right at your fingertips. Chances are, however, that you'll either perform that search with other key phrases in order to find the answer you're looking for, or you will click through several sites looking for the most relevant answer. Then, assuming you find a link that looks relevant, you click on it. We all (and Google is included in this by the way) think of the World Wide Web as a series of interconnected pages that really have no relationship to one another *unless* they are linked. In fact, at a high level, this is how Google determines relevance and rank of the links you see when you perform a search. The Google search robot examines each page, and also how many other pages link to the page at which you are looking. Because you found it on the first page of Google, you can safely assume that it was a high number. You can see how this might be manipulated by unscrupulous consultants with a lot of time on their hands trying to artificially raise their Google search ranking. Indeed, Google will demote sites that they deem inappropriately linked from sites that are primarily "link farms." But still this manipulation can produce some humorous and prankish results. These are called Google Bombs. One of the most famous of these is the phrase "miserable failure." Until very recently, when you typed that into Google the first page result was a link to George W. Bush's White House page. Google has since manipulated the search results to eliminate this occurrence.[4] In essence a large number of people got together and linked the words "miserable failure" to the home page of the White House—and voilá, Google determined that the most relevant page for "miserable failure" was the White House home page and returned that as the top result.

However, you can immediately see the flaw in that thinking. Despite what you think of our 43rd President, this is not a true relationship of content to content. Google had to "fix" this linking in order for the new White House to not be associated with it. So, think of all the other "mistakes" that are out there—intentional or otherwise. Think of what you're currently linking in your own Web site, and how Google sees that.

Let's go back to our page view. When accessing the Web, we think in pages. You access a Web "page." And that document is presented to you on one screen, and you read that document much as you would any—typically scrolling through the document or clicking hyperlinks that take you to something the author has decided should be linked for additional or relevant expansion of that document's idea.

But as shown in the Google Bomb example, this is really an inefficient and potentially inaccurate process. The Web is an ever-evolving organism—and with billions and billions of "pages" added every year, filtering that information and making it easier to access relevant information is critical. The idea of Web 3.0, from a content perspective, is that as content becomes more atomic and as metadata and schemes for assigning relationships to content become more sophisticated, content will not be presented as a singular document but as a series of related ideas that can be assembled in any number of ways.

To be sure, this is not a new idea; the Semantic Web was something that the originators of the Internet envisioned. In fact, in 1999, Sir Tim Berners-Lee, one of the original inventors of the protocols for the World Wide Web said:

> I have a dream for the Web [in which computers] become capable of analyzing all the data on the Web—the content, links, and transactions between people and computers. A "Semantic Web," which should make this possible, has yet to emerge, but when it does, the day-to-day mechanisms of trade, bureaucracy and our daily lives will be handled by machines talking to machines. The intelligent agents people have touted for ages will finally materialize.[5]

The entire realization of that vision may be a bit science fiction, but pieces of this idea of a Semantic Web are closer to reality. At least conceptually near realization is the idea that content can be assembled based on relationships with other content and the interconnection of these ideas automatically without having to think about them at time of authorship or reading. Think back to our embarrassing Web page example of all the drunk Sams—that's a very manual, simplistic way to begin to think about it. All of the content is aggregated by relationship of one field or one piece of metadata.

In fact, an example of just this kind of application was launched in May 2009. Wolfram Alpha (www.wolframalpha.com) is being called an "answer engine."[6] It was developed by Stephen Wolfram, a British physicist and the original developer of the popular (and very sophisticated) Mathematica application. Other than being the creator of Mathematica, Wolfram is mostly known for his work in theoretical particle physics. The Wolfram Alpha "answer engine" is more than just a search engine because it returns more than just page-based results against a search query. Rather, users submit questions or key phrases into the engine, and the "answer engine" then computes, aggregates, infers (yes infers), and produces interesting and meaningful visual representations of those results.

So, for example, let's say you want to know what the circulation numbers are for *National Geographic* magazine. If you were to type "circulation of National Geographic Magazine" into Google, you'll get all the pages where that phrase appears, or where those key words appear. The first links are for Wikipedia articles, and then links for the National Geographic Society and then the magazine's Web site and so on. Perhaps on one of those pages lies your answer—but you will need to click through and read all those pages to find out.

Typing that query into Wolfram Alpha, on the other hand, generates a single page of results that pulls information in from disparate sources. It tells you the current circulation number, confirms the full name of the magazine, lets you know that it's a monthly magazine, and provides a link to the Web site. Additionally, it provides the source information for that data as ProQuest LLC, Publist, and Wikipedia, and provides links to those source Web sites as well.

To be sure, this is just the beginning stages. Currently only a few types of queries work in Wolfram Alpha, and the "answer engine" can be confounding as it doesn't quite "understand" the myriad ways you might type in a particular search query. But, this is only a matter of time and learning. Certainly, the idea of deeper machine understanding of the relationship of content is here to stay.

As a deeper example, let's pretend that you were searching me, Rob Rose. It's a very common name—and you'll get more than 25 million search results if you search Google for it today. Thankfully (I think), I'm now on the front page. But if you didn't identify me from any of those links that are provided, and you also happen to know that I'm associated with CrownPeak, you might retry your search and use that as an additional descriptor in your search query. Or, if you knew me from high school, you might use it as your descriptor. Or, perhaps you might use my wife Elizabeth as a descriptor. Whatever your relationship to me you'd continue to add descriptors until you actually got a list (of at least a few front page results) that looked like it had something to do with me.

Unfortunately, that still may not answer your question. Maybe you're trying to find a particular blog post or something I'd written. That's where the Semantic Web comes in. Now pretend you do that same search for Rob Rose on the Semantic Web. Let's say it's on a site called Shmooglehoo.com. You Shmooglehoo (see it's already a verb) and what comes back is a nicely formatted page asking which Rob Rose you're looking for—the jeweler who resides in New York City, the realtor who lives in Salt Lake City, or the Internet Marketing guy who lives in Los Angeles. Then, if you choose the last one, you get another page—assembled automatically—that pulls information from my LinkedIn Profile, my Facebook profile, the list of articles that I've written on iMedia Connection, a summary of my last six months of blog posts, and possibly other information. None of these results is content that resides in Shmooglehoo. It's content that's pulled semantically from various Web properties because Shmooglehoo recognizes that the relationships between all of these things have one thing in common—"Rob Rose"—and the content and the metadata that surround Rob Rose are what draw the complete picture around the profile and give the machine even deeper understanding until it develops the accurate profile it provides you.

The true realization of this Semantic Web depends on an ever-evolving set of technologies and is probably much further off than we think. When it does arrive, the Semantic Web is going to fundamentally change the way the Web is accessed and exponentially increase its usefulness for those organizations that can get their arms around how to make it work for them.

What does Shmooglehoo mean to me? The implications, of course, are just like any Web or technology innovation—it will differ depending on what kind of business you are in. But whether you are managing content for a nonprofit, a government agency, an online retailer, or a media publisher it will have broad implications on your Web strategy. Business leaders need to understand and begin to think about a plan to consider these implications. Ultimately, content management is a process—and the transformation of your content management process is key to being able to take advantage of this innovation if and when it arrives.

And just like Web 2.0 didn't end up being all that it was billed as—its impact was just as profound. Consider that Facebook alone now has the equivalent of half the population of the United States as members. So, this innovation may ultimately not be called Web 3.0 or the Semantic Web, or have everything Berners-Lee described. But the implications will be profound nevertheless. Your customers will not care what this is called—they will just know that it exists—and how you deal with it will be the indicator of whether it helps you or doesn't.

Now to be clear, this isn't something that you have to go out and tackle tomorrow. You may not even have the Web site redesigned for Web 2.0 yet, and now you have to start thinking about how to manage your content in a Web 3.0 world. But as you do begin to strategize about your roadmap toward the Semantic Web and your content management processes, consider a few guideposts that will help you today.

The Importance of Content Mobility

When the subject of content "mobility" arises, most of the time the discussion turns to publishing content for mobile technologies such as cell phones and PDAs. The expansion of broadband connectivity over cellular networks, along with the proliferation of mobile phones and especially the phenomenal success of Apple's iPhone, is quickly driving more and more content to mobile technologies. However, from a content perspective, smart phone technology is outpacing the need to tailor content to mobile technologies. Publishing content in specialized formats such as Wireless Markup Language (WML) or designing special Web Sites that can be displayed on smaller screens is becoming anachronistic. The third guidepost ("The End of Look and Feel") notwithstanding, the Web browsers on the current generation of iPhones and BlackBerries can now view Web Sites as any other computer-based browser does.

While this aspect of content mobility is really interesting—and definitely the fodder for yet another book of its own—by "content mobility," I mean something quite different. If you have ever gone through the process of migrating content from one content management tool to another, you know it is one of the most painful slogs this side of an audit. In 2009 having "content mobility" is a critical factor in making your content flexible enough to move at any time and having the right system in place to be able to scale your content management process to address whatever trend may come along.

This flexibility and scalability really comes down to two elements. First, flexibility is needed for the *content we have*, meaning as an organization we have content and we need to publish it to many different devices. This capability means publishing our content to our Web site, our intranet, and, yes, mobile phones and BlackBerries. But it also means being able to publish content into different types of interfaces that may present themselves to us, including kiosks, televisions, cars, Microsoft Xbox, Facebook. As content breaks into smaller bits, and more and more devices become connected, opportunities will present themselves to display our content in more and more interfaces. Our ability to publish and format our content to meet these opportunities is critical.

Second, scalability is needed for *content we don't yet have*. This means we need to support needs in an ever-expanding content-management world. As user-generated content becomes more or less important, as metadata becomes more or less important, or as external content that we don't control becomes more or less important, we need to have systems in place to manage it. We don't even know all the content we're going to need to manage; much less where we will need to manage it. Therefore, we need a strategy that will evolve with us, rather than require us to recreate it every time something new comes along.

To address flexibility, we need an effective way to manage, publish, and reuse our content. A capable online content management tool that is devoted to that purpose is essential here. Now, whether that tool is Bill, or Jane, or a commercial software product, it not only needs to be easy so that your content experts can use it; it also needs to be flexible and fast so that it facilitates all those changes we just outlined. Let's say tomorrow Web 2.0 changes drastically and Web sites go out of style. The hot new trend for your industry is the capability to publish your marketing content to some hot new search engine. Shmooglehoo is calling. You need a method to manage your content that can facilitate that change—not be a hindrance to it. You shouldn't have to reinvent your content management process or tool every time there's a new online format.

Not All Your Content Should Be Managed Equally

Managing content beyond Web 2.0 also means recognizing that there are varying degrees of value to your content—and that the appropriate processes should be put into place accordingly. Let's take a technology company for example. Generally speaking, it has the following basic categories of content (see, I'm already applying metadata).

- Marketing and Sales Content; meant for as wide an audience as possible
- Customer/Partner Related Content; meant for or relevant only to existing customers or perhaps partners
- Internal Content; meant for or relevant only to employees or contractors

You could certainly make different buckets—or even reduce it to two (public vs. private content). You may have already looked at this list and subdivided it into deeper and deeper hierarchies. Just for the sake of simplicity, let's look at these three as the general categories. If these buckets will have such different needs why would we manage them with same set of rigor?

Here's an example. I've left the name of the bank anonymous, but the example is real. First Wonder Bank is a financial services company with its headquarters in St. Louis, Missouri. It has over $7.8 billion in assets. It is the largest bank headquartered in Missouri, with more than 100 banks throughout Missouri, Kansas, and Kentucky. For many years, First Wonder's Web site was its online banking application. Basically there was no distinction between marketing content and the online banking software application data. The online banking application was controlled by the internal technical team at First Wonder, and it (quite rightly) had an extraordinarily rigorous workflow, security, and release cycle for adding new content to the site. If marketing wanted to change content for any reason or add new pages it was a two-week process for any change.

Unfortunately for the marketing team, this long lead time made reacting to the online marketing programs and optimizing the site for search engines quite difficult. The team wanted to manage sales and marketing content separately from the online banking application.

First Wonder then changed the process for how it managed online marketing content. Bank personnel separated it from the IT Group and empowered the marketing team to deploy their own tools and processes. They acquired a content management system (CMS) tool that complied with all the legal and auditing that they required from the marketing content—but the key was that the technology group had nothing to do with the selection of the tool or its ongoing management. The marketing group completely outsourced this function to another company.

The result was that the marketing team doubled the speed at which they could iterate content on the Web site. The marketing content on the site was now optimized for search engines, thereby giving it more visibility to new online consumers, and business improved. First Wonder changed its process (and subsequently its content management tool) for managing the online marketing content in a different way, using a different tool, and provided huge benefit for the organization.

The End of Look and Feel

In the first guidepost, we looked at making our content more mobile so that it has the flexibility to be displayed through multiple interfaces. Ultimately, it will be much more important for you to manage your content and be able to "publish" it to any format in which it will be consumed. As you think about content management processes, start to think about your content less as a hierarchical structured set of file and folders that live in major sections and subsections on your Web site and instead think of your content repository as a wellspring of content that is well described with metadata and can be assembled into any type of construct.

In other words, very soon, you're going to get out of the look-and-feel business—and start depending on display of your content through interfaces that are designed and provided by other mechanisms that you do not control. Think back to our UAL story. The content was produced by the *Chicago Tribune*, and then sucked automatically into an interface controlled by the *Florida Sun Sentinel*, which was then syndicated out to Google News. Additionally, you can see it happening with portals such as Yahoo!, and your ability to assemble your MyYahoo page with any particular set of content you like. Then, if you roll over a particular headline, you may get at least the lead of the story, if not the whole thing—without ever having to leave that page.

To put that into real perspective, think of it this way: your content (at least the pieces that are appropriate for syndication), without extra effort, should ultimately be enabled to be consumed by any device or interface whether that interface is a Web site, a mobile phone, a Facebook application, a search engine, a car, or any other interface that may develop in the future.

There are legal considerations as well for this strategy. Consider a lawsuit that was just settled in January 2009 between GateHouse, a community newspaper chain based in Fairport, New York, and The New York Times Company—which owns (among many other newspapers) the *Boston Globe* and Boston.com.[7] GateHouse's lawsuit is the direct corollary to the UAL story. GateHouse charged that the Times was scraping the GateHouse local community papers for headlines and snippets of content—and placing those snippets on their own newspaper sites as "local" content. They linked through to GateHouse Web properties when they used the content and credited GateHouse as the originator of the content. But GateHouse charged that despite this, pulling atomic bits of content was copyright infringement. The lawsuit brings into question just how much content can be pulled as a "link" to an external site. So, for example, if your competitor pulls your RSS feed of press releases and displays that on a content Web site that extols itself as an independent online portal with expertise in your industry is that copyright infringement?

Because the lawsuit was settled, there was no precedent set as of this writing, but certainly this will come up again as content becomes much more mobile around the Internet. As you develop your own internal strategies for how you'll address a roadmap for managing content beyond the Web 2.0 world, real life comes crashing in. You're faced with selecting a tool that can handle the job today and help you prepare for tomorrow.

What will your content management strategy be? The overarching strategy will be far more important than any specific tool you may select. All content is not managed equally and all tools must be scrutinized to determine their value to meeting your strategy. Too many times when trying to decide on a simple Web content management solution for the marketing group, the committee assembled to approach that project looks like the economics team going to the G8 conference.

Content management systems (or more accurately tools) have earned a bad reputation since they came onto the scene in the late 1990s and early 2000s. Two main reasons account for this bad reputation: First , the products themselves were so large and unwieldy that they took months and months to implement—and even then were so inflexible that they were impossible to really use in any fluid organization. Second, organizations still see the idea of content management as a project that has a start, a middle, and an end. Many content management systems are deployed and launched with a flurry. Then over time, because (as we've learned) the process for content management changes so frequently, the tool becomes stale, and it eventually goes unused and fails.

In the case of the Web site, someone typically decides that the site design needs a refresh. So, interviews are conducted and requirements are listed. An agency or designers are hired and the project kicks off. It's usually at this point that someone points out that the current technology solution used to manage the content on the Web site will need to be rewritten/revamped/replaced in order to accommodate the new design.

The committee then sets itself to adding to and/or replacing the content management tool along with the new Web site redesign.

That's when the trouble begins. Creating a new look and feel for the Web site along with functionality for that Web site is a project. As has been established, content management is a process. In short, the Web site redesign is a date and your new CMS (the process and the tool) is getting married. It's an agreement to be a part of an ongoing process—and one that should, over time, make your life easier and more productive. But this relationship has the inherent risk of consuming you and your team in an endless stream of misery. Is it any wonder that about half of all marriages end in divorce[8] and that almost the exact same percentage of CMS implementations end in failure.[9]

I've been happily married for 17 years, and something I fundamentally believe is that neither marriage nor the process of selecting, implementing, and managing a content management tool has to be difficult. Just like the give and take and process for every successful marriage, avoiding "divorce" from your content management tool has a similar process.

SELECTING A TECHNOLOGY TOOL FOR THE JOB

Selecting and implementing a content management tool is a project within the larger process. It, indeed, has a beginning, a middle, and an end. Selecting your CMS tool starts with a set of fun, fresh ideas for the types of new services, new capabilities or other desired outcomes from your new solution. The challenge will be to keep these new ideas in line with your more comprehensive content management system—your strategy, process, people, and tools. Considerations of how you'll break down your content and manage it beyond Web 2.0 will come up, and this mandate should be communicated and understood by your project sponsors. Then, your selection project will typically fall into the following four-step process:

- Decide and Buy
- Implement and Integrate
- Manage and Maintain
- Upgrade and Enhance

Each step has its own challenges, deliverables, and requirements.

Decide and Buy

The Decide and Buy step includes defining the project, identifying likely vendors, and developing a request for proposals. Project definition takes place once you've decided on your process and your mandate is understood. At that point develop an official document that will explain the CMS implementation project and its desired outcome in detail. This Project Definition will be your requirements document as you gather all of the desired outcomes and new capabilities and start to map them against a set of features, functions, and services you require.

Many larger organizations choose to outsource the Project Definition phase to consultants with either vertical expertise and/or previous CMS Tool implementation experience.

In general, the goal of this Project Definition is to outline:

- The scope of the project: What this project will entail (which divisions, which Web sites, intranets, etc.)
- The business goals of the project: What the business will achieve from a business point of view and how it will measure the success of the selection and management of the tool
- The key assumptions being made: The basic premises and dependencies that need to be outlined so that all involved agree on the deliverables
- The key people involved: The integral people and their roles on the project
- The functional business requirements of the project: The key benefits not specific features (e.g., easier to publish content more atomically to different formats or publish search engine friendly content—*NOT* "XHTML-compliant" output)
- Functional technical requirements of the project: Critical but high-level needs (e.g., must be Microsoft based or must be able to scale as site and content management needs grow)
- Cost and Duration of the Project: Your budget and time line

Once you have developed the Project Definition, there will typically be a natural prioritization in terms of the features, functions, and services that your organization will require. Separate these, both in the document and in your selection process, into "product features" and "services/vendor" requirements. For example, you may have a strong need for implementation services because your technology team has limited bandwidth or, in the case of some smaller organization, is nonexistent. Or, you may have strong product feature requirements such as workflow and auditing needs because you are in a regulated industry.

You will also develop a short list of potential solution providers, and develop a Request for Proposal (RFP). A number of analysts and resource Web sites are available to you online to develop a short list of vendor candidates for your content management tool. When considering the short list, try not to get too focused on granular sets of capabilities in a feature/function matrix. Unless you have very specific feature needs, you are unlikely to get actionable information from these feature-by-feature comparisons. Most likely at this point all the vendors will check the "yes" box. Instead, develop "groupings" of features from the general business requirements you defined in your Project Definition, and have the vendor comment (in a paragraph or two) on their ability to meet these specific set of prioritized features or benefits. In addition, have the vendor demo these sets of features to you during a product demonstration.

Once you have your short list of solutions, consider developing a One-Month Review Cycle for the top solutions. Following is a sample schedule for a vendor review cycle:

- Week 1: RFP goes to 4 or 5 vendors on a short list. That RFP should include any set of particular features you'd like to see demonstrated during a meeting, which will be scheduled that week.
- Week 2 or 3: Online or in-person demonstrations with all vendors on the short list. If possible all stakeholders should see all demos. At this point you may start eliminating vendors based on capabilities shown in the demo.
- Week 3: Proposals due from all remaining vendors. Keeping the proposals mercifully short is a key instruction. Remember, a 20-page proposal from four vendors is 80 pages of reading for you and all your team members.
- Week 4: Decision and contract negotiations with chosen vendor. If that sounds too simple, it's because this step is often made far too complex. In general, if you do your homework on the front end—and make sure that your short list of vendors are qualified—any of them should be able to handle the "technical functional" requirements of your project. The decision will (and should) come down to the following business intangibles:

  a. Which solution will meet all my business needs the best?
  b. Which solution will be easiest to use, assuring high adoption? Keep in mind our audience of contributors, reviewers, and approvers.
  c. Which solution will enable me to get up and running the fastest?
  d. Which solution provides the best support and ongoing service?
  e. Which solution provides the flexibility for content management that I need to move forward
  f. Which solution will scale as my needs grow and change—facilitating change instead of impeding it?
  g. Which solution promises to provide the best return on investment?

Implement and Integrate

Entire books have been written about this next phase so I certainly won't try to capture all the detail here. Additionally, the implementation and integration will differ greatly depending on the type of solution that you have chosen (e.g., installed vs. hosted or commercial vs. open source). As you put together your project plan, consider the following helpful safety tips:

- Check your time before you send the check: Depending on the solution you choose and the size of your project it can take anywhere from 30 days to 12 months to implement. *Before* you choose a vendor, get an estimate and/or commitment on the implementation time line and make sure it meets your business need.
- It's a process—don't try to boil the ocean: In case it hasn't been communicated frequently enough, here it is again—content management is

a process. You will assuredly not get it exactly right on your first launch. There are always unforeseen obstacles and more often than not something will be left out. So, accept that now, and don't spend weeks and weeks trying to capture every little feature, workflow step, approval process, and/or template that you're going to need. Phase your launches and get the key functions up first. Your CMS tool should be flexible enough for you to make easy and fast corrections along the way and, of course, after you've launched.

- Take inventory—know where the content is and who's got it: Early in the implementation (or even before) conduct a content audit. The biggest challenge you will face during this project will be the migration of the existing content into the new content management system, with one goal of this plan that this will be the last time you'll have to take on such a project. Create a list or a spreadsheet that documents the entire content inventory. For example, in a Web content management project, the audit should list all the pages on the Web site, whether they will be included in the new site, where they will live in the new site (assuming a redesign), and whether any of them need to be edited prior to moving. Then, you can use that as a checklist when migrating the content.

  When you determine the strategy for content migration, consider that you will likely never want to do this again. Take the time now (if you can) to re-calibrate, re-categorize, and take care in how you migrate your content. This is the time to start breaking the content down into its atomic bits that will later be used for re-purposing and reusing that content. For example, if the "Title," "Author," "Date," and "Body" of a page are all in one field today, take the extra time to manually import those into three separate fields in the new CMS. This way, you are taking a big step down the road of content reuse.

  In addition, go back to the previous checkpoint. Find out the "critical mass" of content needed to relaunch your Web site and draw a line there. You can always go back and migrate your "archive" site when you have the time.

- Assign all content an owner: There should always be someone responsible for the quality and placement of all the content. These can be different people for different articles, assets, sections, or pages on the Web site, but they all need to have an assigned owner responsible for making sure it is up to date and correct.

- Simplify your life, your workflow, and your approvals: When designing your workflow and approval processes for your new CMS, resist the urge to use the technology to "herd the cats." If your workflow process is too complex or cumbersome, be prepared for resistance to adoption of the CMS. The main goal is to get the new CMS adopted throughout the organization. Keep it simple to begin with, and then add restrictions as people either violate something or need to be managed. When you're through with the content migration process and have successfully launched your new Web site with the CMS integrated, you're ready for Step 3.

Manage and Maintain

Choosing the right CMS tool is important, but along with your more comprehensive strategy, developing the right plan for services and support of that application is even more important. For some reason, services often take a back seat to product selection during the early phases of a CMS project, when budgets are often set. This may have something to do with the difficulty for software vendors to differentiate their services, and thus their desire to focus on product features and platform choices.

The two pieces of successful services are implementation and ongoing support and maintenance. Getting them both right is a requirement; but the more neglected of the two is, of course, support and maintenance. The consequences of failing to implement correctly are clear—the software doesn't work, is clunky, or has bugs—or all three. The consequences of failing to manage and update the system are much less clear but over time are just as severe.

A well-chosen and well-implemented but poorly maintained content management tool will always lead to failure. It's sadly ironic that the software system put into place to enable a Web site to be managed can also be that site's eventual degradation. Imagine an IT department that has a dedicated group of CMS experts; always ready to respond to any request by a Web site manager to adjust the content management tool. Unfortunately, in most cases, this simply isn't possible. Having an expert integration firm at your beck and call to make system changes can be untenable as well—even if you can find one willing and available to work on a system over many years.

Usually, the internal IT group is chosen as the answer to this challenge, but it can certainly be a problematic to develop and maintain expertise in the software application and find free developer time, especially when rapid changes are required over and over again.

But didn't we just state that it's a requirement to have good support and maintenance? Hence the dilemma. These problems are solved to a great extent by the software-as-a-service (SaaS) model, but most organizations haven't moved in that direction yet and need to find a balance between internal service levels and cost/resource availability.

The other half of the ongoing management of a content management implementation, and just as important as having developers working to adjust the application over time, is the application "owner." Often this is the same person who manages the project implementation, who later trains new users, plans application changes, works with vendors, and supports system users. Owning the CMS tool is typically only a part of this person's job. They often own all of the other Web functional pieces—search, e-mail campaigns, analytics, and so on. They also may own responsibility for the site's content. Whether the application owner relies on an external team, an internal team, or a combination, that team needs to exist and be responsive. A service level agreement, even if it is just a simple, internally created document, is a great document to work from. It will set expectations for everybody's responsibility.

The bottom line is this: don't skimp on building post-launch services into the project plan and budget as you start your next CMS selection and implementation. Define the players and responsibilities in the immediate post-launch "tweaking blitz" and for the multiyear maintenance, upgrade, and modification program. It's not the glamorous part of the project, but if you've picked a tool that will be flexible and scale with you, the success in the support and maintenance phase will determine how long the tool lives and how successful it is in the months and years post launch.

Upgrade and Enhance

At this step, you've launched your new CMS and your project. You've trained your end users and you have a hold on your maintenance challenge. The content management solution you've chosen is flexible enough to handle ongoing system enhancements and changes, and now you can think about upgrades and enhancements to your project. This is where the process really begins all over again—and where putting good thought and work into your more comprehensive process really starts to pay off.

Remember one of the core questions any CMS vendor should be able to answer is how their solution will facilitate change to your ongoing strategy and not make it difficult to redesign, tweak, or enhance your strategy for managing content.

A good answer at that stage will be key during this phase. Inevitably you will want to add new sections to your Web sites, you will want to add new micro-sites, new landing pages, new integrations with analytics and reporting. You'll want to break down your content for publishing to social networks; you'll want to take that next step into Web 3.0. This means developing new templates, new workflows, new enhancements to your tool.

The key here is to approach upgrades or enhancements in the same way you approached the initial project. Start the process all over . Create an addendum to your Project Definition document—and move on from there. Let's hope you can skip the selection of a CMS tool because you've chosen one that will grow with you. But implementing the changes otherwise fall in line with the process.

Choosing the right CMS tool will truly strengthen your business. It will not only create efficiency for the Content Management process but also (depending on your business) provide you with a number of opportunities to create competitive advantages, revenue opportunities, and new avenues for customers and partners to communicate with you.

You're an expert in your business, and you shouldn't have to become an expert in content management in order to be successful. Consider working with a content management vendor who will become a core part of your team as your content management expert.

PUTTING IT ALL TOGETHER

The Web is evolving. Whether we place a version number after it to give ourselves a frame of reference or whether it just evolves doesn't matter. From a content management perspective, this evolving Web is inviting us to segment our content into smaller and smaller chunks—and to describe that content much more fully. By taking steps to do this as we evolve our own content management strategy, we are preparing for the Semantic Web—or quite frankly for whatever opportunities present themselves. There will be tremendous business opportunities for those who embrace this capability in their content management strategy.

The implications and opportunities will differ greatly depending on the business that you're in. But whether you're avoiding being a cautionary tale, taking advantage of a new business opportunity, or just making the content management processes in your business more efficient, these new capabilities will have great impact. As a business leader, you've got to consider these implications and create a plan to address them. To be sure, the steps you take today are the first ones. As a process, there is room for missteps. Of course, the earlier you start, and the smaller steps you take, the more room you'll have to make many mistakes. As you formulate strategies and select tools, you should start at best practices but don't end there. Develop your own measuring devices—your own tools for what works in your business—and remember that all content shouldn't be managed equally.

Your customers won't care what you call your system, how you manage the content, or the specifics of your internal capabilities. They will just know that your content management system is working and your company is better able to serve their needs as customers because of it.

As Yogi Berra once said, "You have to be careful if you don't know where you're going, because you might not get there." In managing our content beyond Web 2.0, we may not know where we're going, but if we prepare—establish a strategy and a process—it doesn't matter because we'll know we're ready to be there.

NOTES

1. James Erik Abels, "Inside the UAL Story Debacle," *Forbes*, September 8, 2008, http://www.forbes.com/2008/09/08/ual-tribune-bankruptcy-biz-media-cz_ja _0908ualstory2.html.

2. Ibid.

3. "WWW FAQS: How Many Websites Are There?" Boutell, 2008, http://www .boutell.com/newfaq/misc/sizeofweb.html.

4. Noam Cohen, "Google Halts 'Miserable Failure' Link to President Bush," *New York Times*, January 29, 2007, http://www.nytimes.com/2007/01/29/technology/29 google.html?_r=1.

5. Aaron Strout and John Cass, "The Semantic Web: A Treasure Trove for Marketers," ReadWriteWeb, March 12, 2009, http://www.readwriteweb.com/ enterprise/2009/03/semantic-web-treasure-trove-for-marketers.php.

6. Tom Krazit, "Bing Strikes Licensing Deal with Wolfram Alpha," CNET News, August 21, 2009, http://news.cnet.com/8301-30684_3-10315117-265.html.

7. Robert Weisman, "Media Chains Settle Lawsuit: Times Co. and GateHouse Avert Trial over Linking," *Boston Globe*, January 27, 2009, http://www.boston.com/business/articles/2009/01/27/media_chains_settle_lawsuit/.

8. "Divorce Rate," Divorce Rate, http://www.divorcerate.org/.

9. "The CMS Myth: What Is the CMS Myth?" Isite Design, 2008, http://www.cmsmyth.com/what-is-the-myth/.

7

TRANSPARENCY*

Lauren McKay

Imagine looking in a mirror. What you find yourself looking at may not be what you were looking for. But isn't seeing what's real better than seeing an illusion? Aren't we better off knowing what's true? When skin-, body-, and hair-care company Dove, a branch of global brand Unilever,[1] released its "Campaign for Real Beauty" in September 2004—featuring women whose body types fell outside the stereotypical marketing norms—the message was that real women aren't the ones you usually see gracing billboards and centerfolds. The ad directed viewers to www.CampaignForReal Beauty.com to foster conversation about what beauty is.

The second phase of Dove's campaign introduced an ad with another six real women—shapely, non–model-like bodies—and again funneled people back to its site for discussion. A year later, a Dove-sponsored viral video began circulating. "Evolution,"[2] a short clip showing the effort (and trickery) that goes into prepping a model for a photo shoot. "Evolution" won awards and received accolades from viewers—male and female alike. Dove took a step away from the norms with its campaign—hoping to convey to young girls that what you see isn't reality. Real beauty isn't just what you see on a magazine cover.

Coincidentally, as Dove was praised for its efforts, the company faced backlash for being hypocritical. Unilever, the parent company of Dove, also owns Axe/Lynx, the male-grooming-product company known for its scandalous, sexual commercials that show women in a less-than-wholesome light. To the criticisms, the company responds: "The chosen vehicle for Axe/Lynx is a series of light-hearted and tongue-in-cheek

*Based on the article "Transparency," which first appeared in *CRM* magazine, published by Information Today, Inc., www.InfoToday.com. Used with permission.

adverts. They are . . . not meant to be taken seriously." How can a company promote inner beauty on one hand and degrade women on the other?

Accusations of hypocrisy did not end there, however. Halfway around the globe, in India, Unilever owns a cosmetics company that markets a product called "Fair & Lovely"—essentially a skin-lightening cream, hardly the kind of product that champions the natural beauty you might see in the mirror. (Unilever did not respond to questions regarding Fair & Lovely.)

"Seeing is believing"[3] may be an age-old mantra, but it's as visceral today as it's ever been, and perhaps even more so in terms of customer relationships.

Unilever and its various brands capture the struggle in customer relationship management (CRM) today—a battle for what's real and what's not, for the line between marketing and message, for the heart and soul and mind of the relationship between company and consumer. It's all about transparency, a growing concept in today's world. As used in the humanities, transparency implies openness, communication, and accountability, the pillars of which are the stuff of consumer dreams—and often corporate nightmares.

But today, enterprises face heightened expectations from said consumers. They are expected to provide multiple channels and to cater to the customer's ever-growing want, need, desire. Days of simply ringing up a company and immediately speaking about an issue, concern, or complaint are long gone. Interactive voice responders, offshore contact centers, and automated agents work as enablers—and barriers—in linking customers with corporations. It's easy to take the consumer's side in harping about the ever-complex corporate landscape. Is there such a thing as speaking with a *human* anymore, people often harp. But on the same side of the coin are businesses, desperately trying to keep up with the always-on, always-connected consumer—the ones who are demanding that their purchases be made easier, that they can contact whomever they like via chat, text message, social networking post, or coconut shell. Consumers are a tricky bunch, especially when they respond to surveys saying they trust and value opinions of their peers more than marketers or corporate brands. Then where does that leave enterprises? Web 2.0[4] does a fantastic job of uniting communities, bringing two sides of the world together all in the name of joint interest. At the same time, Web 2.0—or Enterprise 2.0[5]—is fabulously complicated, with greater attention, responsibility, and ownership on behalf of an enterprise.

The irony is that Enterprise 2.0, as advanced as it sounds, has brought us back to basics in more ways than one. Human interaction is more important than ever. It's bringing the cornerstone ideas of communication, conversation, and courtesy back into the limelight—albeit at a much greater speed than before. Some talk about the Web removing human interactions, but, in reality, it enables more interaction than before.

Given the amount of information at the fingertips of any given Web visitor, consumers now have options to supersede a corporation and seek information above and beyond what the enterprise is providing. A consumer can say, "You aren't going to give me an answer? That's okay; I have 396 other portals to search for it. Oh, and by the way, I just might share with my 496 Facebook friends—and your potential customers—the inconvenience you caused me." That's why and how transparency enters the picture.

It happened in a matter of hours. On social networking, microblogging Web site Twitter, it was marked with the hash tag and phrase, "Motrin Mom." (Twitter.com asks the question to users, "What are you doing?" In 140 characters, users post to the site, made visible to "followers" and those who opt in to the site.) Twitter posts linked to blogs and those blogs linked to other posts and articles—within hours, an anti-Motrin revolution was on the rise. The root? The pain reliever released a new campaign geared toward moms who "wear their babies"—using slings such as the Baby Bjorn.[6] The campaign, outcriers thought, was derogatory to such mothers. To illustrate, one Twitter wrote that Motrin offended moms everywhere—that a baby is not a fashion statement. Voices of dissenters popped up all over the Web, and once the controversy broke out it was easier to stumble upon hundreds of blog posts and Twitter microblog posts on the topic than a statement or apology from Motrin. Had Motrin been monitoring its Twitter stream or entered the conversation sooner, perhaps the backlash would have been less powerful. "There was an immediate, an instant negative impact on the Motrin brand," says Suresh Vittal, Forrester analyst and researcher of brand monitoring and listening platforms. "These conversations were showing up . . . if Motrin was listening, it would have been on top of it within the first hour." Corporations are still trying to figure this transparency thing out, after all. Transparency is more than apologizing and giving excuses after the fact.

Justin Goldsborough spends a lot of time surfing the Web. He has more than one thousand followers and has posted close to four thousand updates on Twitter. He's blog-savvy, social networking skilled, and Web 2.0 wise. Why? Because his role as social-media manager for telecommunications giant Sprint asks him to be so. Goldsborough's job entails not only running Sprint's internal blogging and community forum called Sprint Space but also keeping tabs on the social-media world. Goldsborough has embraced it wholeheartedly and reports active and open-minded response and permission from the big guns at Sprint. "I think that I've learned more by doing and trying things," he says. "That's one of the reasons we have had success at Sprint." Goldsborough is an active Tweeter and scans the Twitterverse for participants mentioning Sprint. When he thinks he can intervene and solve a problem, he does, often asking the person to direct-message him or e-mail him a more detailed explanation of the problem—whether about service or hardware.

Goldsborough then passes along the issue to Sprint VIP Customer Care team who follows up and updates the Twitterer's customer file.

It all starts internally for Sprint, Goldsborough says. Sprint Space, the enterprise's internal networking and blogging site, is the source of transparency for executives and employees. Company issues are blogged about on the site and employees are allowed to comment to their hearts' desire—and they will, Goldsborough says. In fact, when Sprint released its touch screen phone, the Instinct, in April 2008, the company was eager to get the product on to store shelves and into the hands of customers. So eager, in fact, that they worried about running short on inventory and for that reason, employees weren't given the Instinct upon initial release. This caused internal unease. Sprint employees, who are constantly encouraged to be "brand ambassadors," felt that they were being left in the dark about the new phone. How were they supposed to answer questions about the Instinct when they really had never seen it? The conversation about the Instinct was fleshed out in the comment section on a blog post about Sprint Space. Employees voiced concerns and disapproval about the corporate rule—as many as 450 comments on one blog post. The conversation, Goldsborough says, was so substantial that he approached senior management to take a look at what employees were saying. In response, a marketing director followed up with a blog post saying that she understands concerns, and that she is listening. She gave employees an FAQ sheet about the Instinct, but let them know that she understood. The decision, although not optimal, was with the intention to put customers first. The director encouraged Sprint to keep that in mind. "There was one guy who was really critical on the first post like I can't believe we can't get this right now. And he was the first person to comment on the FAQ post. He wrote, 'It really meant a lot to me that someone took the time to explain to me why the decision was made and I will respect it'." Sometimes all people need is to know there's someone on the other end of the line listening. Goldsborough says Sprint is trying to instill that culture—that it's okay to tell customers what they aren't going to want to hear. "It's OK to give an unpopular answer. It's *not* OK to not listen and not give an answer at all," he says. "There's fear behind 'I don't know.' People don't like to say that in a public forum. But that's the honesty that people expect to have in relationships."

Goldsborough continues with his honesty—inspiration for customer service through Twitter came from another corporation helping its customers. A company that, Goldsborough says, like Sprint hasn't historically had the best track record when it comes to customer service. That enterprise is Comcast, the high-speed Internet, cable, and digital voice provider. Frank Eliason is sort of famous on Twitter. Known to many as the "Comcast Cares" guy, Eliason has made his name and brand known on Twitter by addressing Comcast subscribers' questions and complaints. What Eliason is doing was brought into the limelight when TechCrunch blog founder Michael Arrington posted a less-than-happy post about his troubled service issues with Comcast. Arrington, also a member of Twitter, posted a Tweet about his Comcast problem. Low and behold, within minutes he was messaged by Eliason, offering to resolve the issue.

"Within 20 minutes of my first [tweet] I got a call from a Comcast executive . . . who wanted to know how he could help," Arrington wrote in his blog. "He said he monitors Twitter and blogs to get an understanding of what people are saying about Comcast, and so he saw the discussion break out around my messages."

Eliason says now that the fact the complaint was aired by a high-profile subscriber didn't matter. When he sees Comcast mentioned in any RSS or Twitter feed, he intercepts and answers as any contact center–based customer service would. "On Twitter, I'll say 'IM me your phone number so I can pull up your account.' Or if we need to do it locally, I'll send a technician out and get it scheduled. If it's going to be a longer story, I'll say, 'Hey, send us an email'."

The Comcast digital care team has been dealing with customers via social media for more than a year. Though not referring to specific social sites such as www.ComcastSucks.com, Eliason says it's important for a company to know what's being said about the business before engaging in social-media activities. In other words, think before you tweet. Eliason says Comcast hasn't yet attributed any customer satisfaction metrics to its Twitterific efforts, but its profits are on the rise.

Brands and corporations are popping up on Twitter by the handful each day. From Southwest Airlines to Home Depot to Starbucks, each brand seems to have a different strategy and motive for engaging in the microblogging site. Some, for instance, announce news and freebies, while others—more of a rarity—such as Comcast use Twitter as a mechanism for customer service. Each has a different approach. Some microblog from the brand identity, others as real people. Take Goldsborough. His name is his own and the picture is of him and his dog. When asked if he thinks it matters whether he represents himself as Justin Goldsborough or Sprint, Goldsborough says he's still trying to figure that out but, for him, he thinks a face and a name is a nice touch. All too often do people interact with automation and Web forms. Human interaction is lacking in many cases. To meet an actual person representing the company is nice, he says. It's about allowing employees to be transparent—by putting the knowledge and tools in their hands to do so. Goldsborough provides an example of when his social-media efforts came full circle. When searching Twitter posts one day, he came across a woman who was having an issue with her Instinct phone. He immediately messaged the Twitterer, but before offering to connect her with the Customer Care team, he scoured the Sprint Space blog forum. Incidentally, a coworker had recently posted about an error he was receiving with the device and steps to take to fix it. Through a quick copy and paste maneuver, Goldsborough relayed the information to his Twitter contact within minutes. Who knows how much time he saved this Sprint customer by allowing her to avoid either calling customer service or scouring the Web for an answer?

In tough economic times, transparency is especially crucial. Americans are hurt by the recession and don't want to be fed some corporate jargon about why their bank suddenly changed ownership or why their gym membership is hiked up 10 more dollars. They want the truth. Are trust and transparency synonymous? Not quite, but they are definitely blood relatives.

Corporations are cutting down workforces and reallocating resources to stay afloat. Online shoe destination Zappos.com, as an example, let go 10 percent of its workforce in November, 2008. Laying off employees is not something corporations love to speak out about, yet Tony Hsieh, the CEO of Zappos, took to his blog, offering the management's point of view on the issue. Hsieh frequently blogs on the site, and whether it's about changes to policies or internal memos he is clear on the company's motives. Hsieh wrote openly, for example, about corporate decisions involving much-loved features such as free overnight shipping and a price-protection policy: "The only difference is that we made the decisions to not advertise or promise [free overnight shipping], because . . . we found that our customers were happier when they were surprised by the fast shipping. (Of course, if you're reading this, it kind of ruins the surprise. So pretend you never read this.)"[7] In a January 25, 2009, blog post about Twitter, Hsieh wrote about the site's implications for transparency: "What I found was that people really appreciated the openness and honesty, and that led people to feel more of a personal connection with Zappos and me compared to other corporations and business people that were on Twitter," he shared. "By embracing transparency and tweeting regularly, Twitter became my equivalent of being always on camera. Because I knew that I was going to be tweeting regularly about whatever I was doing or thinking, I was more conscious of and made more of an effort to live up to our 10 core values."

Corporate blogging seems to be a recent phenomenon. But, the question remains—who is really behind that online signature? Is it a PR ploy —or the real CEO? Does a CEO stepping out and putting a face to the corporation make a company more transparent and likeable and trustable? When Sprint CEO Dan Hesse announced his e-mail address on a Sprint commercial, was that a breaking point—or an excellent marketing message? This goes back to the point about attributing a brand to a face. The corporate use of blogs and other Web 2.0 social-media tools not only increases transparency but helps customers see that the organization is more than one-dimensional or monolithic: There are actual people behind the products.

Transparency isn't just about fixing what's broken. It goes beyond explaining public-facing errors, although you'd better bet that when pornography accidentally got leaked onto live television in several Comcast cable-sanctioned areas during the Super Bowl,[8] Eliason and his Comcast colleagues used the Twitter channel to express apologies. Transparency is about being reactive, but proactive, too.

A hefty part of transparency is showing customers information in a convenient manner—even if it's induced by local legislation. Step into any chain restaurant, from a Chipotle to a Starbucks, and you can't help but notice a new set of numbers gracing chalkboards and menus—calorie content. Even if consumers know the new openness is the result of a new law, there's a deeper meaning: "We want you to be informed about what you are eating." An organization saying, "We hope you make the right choice," is a powerful part of providing a positive customer experience. After all, consumers face so many mixed messages. Is high-fructose corn syrup the root of all food evil? Or, is it truly, as the commercials proclaim, "like sugar" and "okay in small doses"? Mixed messages turn off a consumer. Rather than taking the time to research who is right and who is wrong, they might simply avoid the brands or products completely. Consumers are finicky with their attention, after all. If they are giving you time and attention, they expect something in return. Dr. Andreas S. Weigend, former Amazon.com chief scientist, calls this the "Customer Data Revolution." At a recent Predictive Analytics World conference,[9] Weigend told attendees, "The consumer data revolution is about shifting expectations. People want to get back something in return for what they are giving with data."

Want to make a consumer happy? Save them a Google search or two and empower them with information—albeit competitive—on your site. It just might work. Web sites such as farecompare.com, Amazon.com, and Zappos.com have long offered resources for comparing prices. But customers now have access to community forums and reviews for user-generated insight and feedback. Auto insurance provider Progressive has its own approach—and uses transparency as a competitive differentiator. Within the confines of its proprietary Web site, Progressive lets visitors compare rates not just among its own offerings, but against the going rates offered by the competition—an idea that likely provoked some "are you crazy?" stares. But the policy works for Progressive—and even provides a branding message.

With social networking, online communities, and blogs, customers are going to find the information they're looking for—your company might as well step up and be part of the process. Creating your own community for customer conversation is a smart Web 2.0 initiative, but it's not the only option. If you can't facilitate, you can still participate.

Size matters, too. Clate Mask, CEO and president of marketing-automation software firm Infusionsoft, says the need for transparency often goes up as the size of the company goes down. The "transparent" mind-set, he says, involves relinquishing control. "There are some limitations. A vendor just can't do everything," he says. "Part of [transparency] is opening things up and letting other people provide value." The focus, he adds, should be on information that the customer wants, "regardless of how you get it to them." It's not as if a competitor is going to snatch up every method and technique you use and make them its own. It just doesn't work that way.

Overstock.com CEO Patrick Byrne isn't afraid to let people know what makes his business tick. He's not afraid to share what didn't work and almost made his business fail, too. He admitted that turning to Teradata saved his business, saying in an interview that company's entire information architecture came close to failing. "The turkey was on fire and spewing and we caught everything in the Teradata can and actually ran the company—for six months—we were out of the Teradata box rather than the actual production systems because they were all melting down." Byrne essentially said part of transparency for him is admitting who is and should be calling the shots within the enterprise—which he says has changed drastically internally at Overstock. "The customer care environment is essentially in charge of the company. They have gone from being the corporate backwater several years ago to being the company and the one that dictates. About two years ago, because we were in some trouble, the customer care group knew where the bodies were and how to fix the company. I elevated them and put them in charge. And they fixed [our problems]." Byrne goes as far as participating in the Overstock.com community forum. Although not overly active, Byrne has, from time to time, commissioned community members for help and thoughts on issues. He shares what the company is going through quite candidly. Take a November 2008 post regarding Overstock's competition with eBay, for example. He thanked the community for ideas about getting the word out about Overstock.com's Auction wing. He writes, "I know corporate guys are always saying cheesy things about being on your side, but as those who have been here for some time know, I think, that in our case it really is true. We really are trying to do the right thing. It does not mean we can always do exactly what the community wants, but by and large, the community has set the direction for our development here. So I thank you for setting us in a direction that has ended up, in time, saving this business."

Transparency doesn't automatically guarantee your customers' trust, but it's a major building block in the equation. "One of the keys to the CRM cycle is going to be building trust over time," says Gartner analyst Scott Nelson during a one-on-one discussion of social media's impact on CRM. Most companies have yet to realize that building up a level of trust makes it, as Nelson says, "highly unlikely a customer [will] leave you and go somewhere where they're going to have start all over again."

But there's also a danger. "On the flipside, you've got to be really serious because all it takes is one breach in that trust for them to say, 'OK, you've burned me. I'm not going to trust you again.'"

Removing barriers between the buyer and seller raises many questions. How does an organization stay strategically competitive amid consumer demands for transparency? As an example of how transparency and customer data occasionally conflict, Nelson cites one mortgage company's upselling efforts: The company cross-checked the names of its home-loan customers with a list of consumers recently granted credit approvals for new-car purchases. The company then contacted those overlapping customers, informing them of a car-loan promotion.

As cunning a plan as this is, some customers might be nonplussed—or even offended—to discover their mortgage companies are keeping tabs on their other financial activities. Other customers may merely chalk it up to coincidence. Where's the line? A few years down the road, consumers may expect so much transparency that marketers will no longer be able to strategically promote and upsell.

As the issues around transparency and the use of customer data proliferate, Nelson says companies will have to be more careful about divulging such privileged information about any single individual. But the reality is that you may not be dealing with customers on an individual basis anymore—thanks to the advent of communities, forums, and social networks, consumers are as transparent to each other as you are to them.

Packs of consumers can come to your rescue if you set the scenario correctly. Remember the lead paint chaos in 2007? Moms throughout the country were panicking about toys being toxic and harming their children. Reports of inflicted toys sprouted in every news outlet—it was hard to keep it all straight. Toy manufacturer Mattel, who had dozens of toys at stake of lead paint toxicities, decided to harness the community of for support. Mattel hired social community forum vendor Communispace to set up a site for parents to congregate and communicate on the topic. Moms were able to post which toys were safe and which were not—essentially looking to each other for answers. Meanwhile, Mattel got recognition for involvement and providing the infrastructure. Forrester Groundswell awarded Mattel and Communispace for their community contributions and innovation.[10]

Anthony Lye, senior vice president of Oracle CRM, offers a very simple view of the situation. During a presentation at the Oracle OpenWorld conference, he said, "If you have a bad product, it's pretty much 'Game Over' whether you like it or not. Web 2.0 gives control to communities—and communities are a lot more aggressive than individual consumers." In other words: They outnumber you.

Yes, participation in the Web is a scary thing as many corporations see it. What if an employee went on the Web and created, say, a Wordpress blog about the enterprise, without seeking executive approval? If that blog displayed untrue information, it could tarnish the brand and enterprise reputation. For this reason, adoption of enterprise social networking has lagged. Corporations have a lot on the line and one debacle could spiral to a bigger issue or security breach. But is there too much at stake not to get involved? Goldsborough says that his company tells employees to dip a toe in Web 2.0 whenever possible—it's encouraged, not feared. If someone is a subject matter expert, they should share the knowledge. However, he points out that not all corporations have that stance. A friend of his, an employee of a fairly large enterprise, was reprimanded when he stepped into a discussion on the Web about the company he works for. His contribution was seen as risky.

Transparency—like beauty—starts from within. An enterprise must trust its employees and say we are giving you this right—please don't mess it up. But if you do, at least be honest about it. If the internal workings of an enterprise are flawed and employee satisfaction is low, it's going to show to customers in one way or another.

Is there such a thing as being too transparent? Will we ever get to a point where customers ask to be kept in the dark? Hear out this metaphor: You have had reservations at a hard-to-get-into restaurant for months. You've anticipated this event and built up your expectations. When you finally sit to dine, your waiter is practically a mirage, stopping by briefly to take your order, nodding without even writing it down. You aren't getting the attention you know you deserve, but you shrug it off in anticipation of dinner. However, the minutes pass with no acknowledgement from the server. Where is your food? Finally you get his attention to mention your absent meals. The waiter spits out an excuse and says they will be out soon. Finally a manager stops by a table to inform you that your meals weren't prepared satisfactorily so they will be remade. He apologizes for the wait and offers it on the house. In this situation, you are probably relieved to hear from someone—finally. And the free dinner is good news. But does it bother you what excuse was given? It seems quite obvious that the waiter forget to put in the order. But would it have made a difference had that been explained? Do you really need to know what went wrong? Or does the fact that someone said anything matter the most?

"You wouldn't have a customer come in your store and just ignore them," says Goldsborough. "If you don't engage them [in social media], that's the same thing as ignoring a customer."

So what's the best way to start? Can a company just *become* transparent overnight? Goldsborough says his social-media experience has been following the leaders and engaging in trial and error. However, there's myriad research devoted to "social-media" strategy. Analysts often caution enterprises to think before leaping and to consider security risks and potential breaches of trust. But what's more important—a company trusting the Internet or its customers trusting the brand? It's a toss-up, perhaps.

"We just passed a significant milestone," says Volker Hildebrand, vice president for CRM product management at SAP. "We now have 100,000 contributions to CRM discussion forums online. It's a very interesting interaction channel where we can reach out to the users—and not just the decision-makers—and basically get their feedback." The community forum, he says, is an essential feedback channel for the company: "This will also help shape our future direction."

It's one thing to pay lip service to such feedback channels; it's another thing to take action. According to a Bain & Co. survey of 362 companies, 80 percent of companies thought they were keeping their customers more than satisfied; unfortunately, only 8 percent of those customers reported receiving a "superior experience."[11] Talk about not being on the same page.

Greg Gianforte, CEO of customer experience management vendor RightNow Technologies, is among those who harp on the subject, saying that customer feedback is a critical pillar to his company's philosophy—and critical to transparency. Closing the feedback loop—linking that information back to processes—is essential, he says, and equally important is letting customers know it's happening. This idea has heightened the trend of "crowdsourcing"—asking the crowds to dictate what's important—whether it's customer service or product development ideas.[12] Crowdsourcing, a term first coined by Jeff Howe of *Wired* magazine, is the act of taking a job traditionally performed by a designated agent (usually an employee) and outsourcing it to an undefined, generally large group of people in the form of an open call.

A company can say it's transparent until it's blue in the face, but who's to say whether it's actually true? In fact, customers are more likely to tell you which companies are not transparent rather than those that actually are. And they aren't afraid to tell their friends—or complete strangers—about it, either. Here's an easy way to check on a company's transparent quality. Visit the corporate Web site's "About Us" page. If the company doesn't have one, run. Run far away. Web sites are today's white pages. They are equivalent and perhaps more powerful than a physical store front. A missing "About Us" page is like an unlisted phone number or a store without any signage. It simply does not fly. What about a company description that's so full of industry jargon and ten-cent words that it leads customers more confused than before they entered the site? Yes, that's bad too. Customers want honesty and simplification. Don't make them go to the Wikipedia page.

"We have seen an increase of our site utilization based upon delivering relevant messaging," says Debbie Doran, manager of CRM operations for travel Web site Travelocity.com. "I think our customers appreciate that more. They know that we know who they are—and that's driven customer loyalty, and has led to people coming back." In fact, Doran reveals that showing visitors relevant and compelling data and site promotions leads to a fivefold or sixfold increase in clicks. This relays the fact that customers want personalization and they don't want anyone wasting their time—and they're generally sophisticated enough to know that personalization requires the collection of personal information. At some point, however, the customer forking over data and information by the bucketload will say, "Hey, I know you have data about me, but I want to know what you know and how you're using it."

Many analysts suggest that point may have already arrived. Security will continue to be a huge issue and transparency is strongly linked to security. "A lot of it is going to come down to allowing people . . . [to know] what you know about them and [to give them] a sense of controlling that information," Nelson says. "It's more than sending them a privacy statement. It's about letting them know, 'This is what we know and we think it's accurate, will you fix it if it's not? And here's how it's being used and if at any point you feel that it makes you uncomfortable, here's how you get rid of it'."

This is especially true on social networking sites such as Facebook. In February, 2009, concerns around data ownership surfaced. Facebook released a new "terms of services" clause which led members to ask who owns the content on Facebook. The company's chief executive spoke out to reassure users that they, not the Web site, "own and control their information." Mark Zuckerberg blogged about it on February 16, 2009, asking that users be reasonable in assessing the complicated issue. He writes, "People want full ownership and control of their information so they can turn off access to it at any time. At the same time, people also want to be able to bring the information others have shared with them—like email addresses, phone numbers, photos and so on—to other services and grant those services access to those people's information. These two positions are at odds with each other. There is no system today that enables me to share my email address with you and then simultaneously lets me control who you share it with and also lets you control what services you share it with."[13] Yet, users were so unsettled by Facebook's move toward controlling their information, the site reverted back to its early terms of service—for the time being.[14]

Will customers alter what they put on the Web based on knowing what is done with it? Before, so much had been done behind closed doors. Now that organizations are making steps to show customers their inner workings, how will customers respond? Perhaps there will be a bit of backlash at first. But, really it all comes down to trust.

Gianforte, who says he made 180 customer visits over the summer, notes that customer permission will become a bigger issue as ever-more-targeted marketing incorporates privileged customer data. As an example, he cites a company that, upon receiving a change-of-address form from a customer, immediately sends along marketing materials about home-security products. This may or may not cross the line—but the consumer, not the company, maybe ought to be the one to make the call. This issue goes back to what Nelson said earlier about the trust issue. If a customer feels burned, it only takes a second time for that customer to take his business elsewhere—and in this day and age he might take his friends with him.

Goldsborough says there's no way he can respond to every blog post bashing Sprint. That's not his intention. He's there to facilitate conversation and join in—not quell it. Although the easiest examples to provide are ones where something went wrong, transparency goes beyond that. It's present in the little touches. It's a hotel providing you with the name of the housekeeper who will be tidying your room during your stay, it's knowing whether eggs in your omelet came from a grass-fed cow or not. It's your software salesman giving you his cell phone number—just in case. It's an organization explaining where budget cuts will go and how you might be affected.

Times are changing. The campaign and election of President Barack Obama alone has proven the power of the people and of social media. As Obama ushered in a new administration, he also brought the term "transparency" to light. The day Change.gov switched to WhiteHouse.gov —on January 20, 2009—site visitors saw three main tenets of the Obama administration outlined on a blog post—Communication, Participation, and Transparency.[15] "I thought to myself, 'every corporation in America needs to see this right now'," says Goldsborough. The January 20 blog post states, "President Obama has committed to making his administration the most open and transparent in history and WhiteHouse.gov will play a major role in delivering on that promise. The President's executive orders and proclamations will be published for everyone to review, and that's just the beginning of our efforts to provide a window for all Americans into the business of the government. You can also learn about some of the senior leadership in the new administration and about the President's policy priorities."

We may be at the transparency tipping point: Customers are trying to tell the businesses they interact with that they want a new kind of relationship—one that may require a new kind of thinking. That, in turn, may unlock the real beauty of CRM.

NOTES

1. Dove, "Campaign for Real Beauty," Unilever, http://www.unilever.com/brands/personalcarebrands/dove.aspx.

2. The Dove Evolution advertisement can be viewed online at http://www.dove.us/#/features/videos/default.aspx[cp-documentid=7049579]/.

3. Andrew Harrison, *Philosophy and the Arts: Seeing and Believing* (Thoemmes Press, 1997).

4. Tim O'Reilly, "What is Web 2.0," September 30, 2005, http://oreilly.com/web2/archive/what-is-web-20.html.

5. Andrew McAfee, "Enterprise 2.0, Version 2.0," May 27, 2006, http://andrewmcafee.org/2006/05/enterprise_20_version_20/.

6. Sarah Evans, "Motrin Moms: Social Media Fail Whale," Mashable, November 16, 2008, http://mashable.com/2008/11/16/motrin-moms/.

7. Tony Hsieh, "Update," The Zappos CEO and COO Blog, November 6, 2008, http://blogs.zappos.com/blogs/ceo-and-coo-blog/2008/11/06/update.

8. Rebecca Taylor, "Super Bowl Porn Incident, Still No Arrest," KVOA.com, February 7, 2010, http://www.kvoa.com/news/super-bowl-porn-incident-still -no-arrest/.

9. "Interview with Andreas S. Weigend," Transcript, Predictive Analytics, February 19, 2009, http://predictiveanalytics.org/predictive-analytics-interview -with-andreas-s-weigend-phd.htm.

10. Josh Bernoff, "2008 Forrester Groundswell Awards Winners," Groundswell, October 29, 2008, http://blogs.forrester.com/groundswell/2008/10/2008 -forrester.html.

11. Edmund Lin and James Allen, "7 Things Firms Need to Know," *Straits Times*, July 22, 2006, http://www.bain.com/bainweb/publications/publications _detail.asp?id=25130 &menu_url=publications_results.asp.

12. Jeff Howe, "The Rise of Crowdsourcing," Wired, June 2006, http://www .wired.com/wired/archive/14.06/crowds.html?pg=4&topic=crowds.

13. Mark Zuckerberg, "On Facebook, People Own and Control Their Informa- tion," Facebook Blog, February 16, 2009, http://blog.facebook.com/blog.php? post=54434097130.

14. Mark Zuckerberg, "Update on Terms," Facebook Blog, February 17, 2009, http://blog.facebook.com/blog.php?post=54746167130.

15. Macon Phillips, "Change Has Come to Whitehouse.gov," The White House Blog, January 20, 2009, http://www.whitehouse.gov/blog/change_has_come_to _whitehouse-gov/.

8

SERVICE RECOVERY, COMPLAINT HANDLING, AND THE SOCIAL MEDIA

Deborah Cowles

There was a time when dissatisfied consumers were, more or less, at the mercy of firms who produced the tangible goods and intangible services they purchased. "Consumers have traditionally had little information, limited access to one another, and few outlets for feedback and communication."[1]

Options were limited with respect to how an unhappy customer might *recover* from a firm's *failure* to meet his or her expectations. What could dissatisfied customers do? Refuse to purchase again? Write a complaint letter? Make a phone call? Perhaps tell 9 or 10 acquaintances about their dissatisfaction? Call the Better Business Bureau? Regardless of the approach taken, it was clear in most cases that the firm had the upper hand in determining if, when, and how to respond to unhappy customers.

Beginning in the late 1980s, firms began to focus more attention on recovery as a necessary ingredient in achieving and sustaining a strategic, competitive position in the marketplace. Excellent firms established unambiguous, proactive, and customer-friendly recovery policies. Building on an ambitious program of service quality research spearheaded by A. Parasuraman, V. A. Zeithaml, and L. L. Berry (e.g., 1985[2]), R. Zemke and C. Bell published their now classic article "Service Recovery: Doing It Right the Second Time" in June 1990,[3] followed closely by the also-classic article by C. W. Hart, J. L. Heskett, and W. E. Sasser, Jr., in the *Harvard Business Review* (1990), "The Profitable Art of Service Recovery."[4]

Although these and subsequent arguments for the importance of effective recovery were a welcome addition both to best business practices and to the business literature, many of the recommended service-recovery policies and procedures were developed primarily with the firm in mind. "No business can afford to lose customers, if only because it costs much more to replace a customer than it does to retain one—five times more, most industry experts agree."[5] Effective complaint handling and service recovery were found to have a significant and positive impact on (1) customer satisfaction, (2) customer retention, and (3) long-term profitability. As such, although these strategies and tactics benefited customers, they often were developed with an implicit understanding that the firm remained in the driver's seat, and that customers were, essentially, the recipients of largesse from an informed and benevolent company, which just happened to have an inspired customer-focused recovery philosophy.

With the birth and proliferation of the Internet (as we know it today) in the mid-1990s, consumer expectations with respect to service recovery began to increase. Customers expected firms to have informative, easy-to-navigate Web sites, to return customer e-mail messages in a timely manner, to offer multiple avenues of contact, to allow customers to check inventory and track shipments electronically, and to provide an increasing array of customer service options via the World Wide Web. The new millennium ushered in Web 2.0 technologies; but it was not just consumer expectations that increased as a result of these technologies. Rather, consumers soon discovered that they had newfound prowess—and a loud voice—in the marketplace with respect to complaint handling and service recovery, rooted in *social power*.

> [The Internet and the social media have] given consumers not only a collective voice but also a platform and a forum for those voices. Armed with a new suite of tools, resources, and technologies, consumers are no longer passive observers in the marketplace of ideas and commerce; they are actually defining and shaping the business landscape and the marketplace of tomorrow.
>
> The Internet, specifically the now ubiquitous open-source participatory Internet dubbed "Web 2.0," allows consumers, united by one common activity—purchasing goods and services from companies—to come together in an extended community. And increasingly, these consumers are united by a common frustration—a growing distrust of marketing and advertising. Consumer-generated media allows them to voice this distrust and to share their ideas, opinions, and emotions about every conceivable aspect of their consumer experiences—from how well a detergent removes stains to how upset they are about an outgoing CEO's compensation package.[6]

In essence, firms can no longer be content with "doing it right the second time" after a customer complains. Either (1) the consumer may not choose to give the firm a second chance, and simply take his case to the social-media audience; or (2) a great deal of damage may already be done before the consumer even seeks recovery.

SOCIAL POWER, SOCIAL PRESENCE, AND WEB 2.0

Social power, long an interest of social psychologists, caught the attention of retailers and service marketers in the 1990s as practitioners and academics alike strove to understand more completely the intricate dynamics of service interactions. "Social power has been defined as an individual's relative ability to alter others' states (material, symbolic) by providing or withholding resources or administering punishment."[7]

Service encounters are "social episodes," even if the interactions do not occur face to face or person to person (e.g., over the telephone). In 1976— long before computer-mediated communication as we have come to know it today was even conceptualized—J. Short, E. Williams, and B. Christie[8] developed "social presence theory" (SPT), whereby a medium's *social effects* are primarily the result of the degree of "social presence" it affords its users. The theory has since had considerable influence on computer-mediated communication research. *Social presence* is defined as a communicator's sense of the presence of an interaction partner in the communication process. Various media afford communicators different levels of social presence, with face-to-face communication considered to have the most social presence and text-based, written communication the least. Clearly, the participatory, interactive, and technological characteristics of the social media have the ability to convey the "sense of the presence of an interaction partner" to a greater extent than many other media. Some have argued that the social media can be more effective in facilitating communication than even face-to-face interactions. For example:

> One observation is that Second Life by-passes many of the natural reservations and constraints that we would have in "real life." It intensifies communications and can convey a sense of "closeness" with others through the use of avatars and text. SPT notes the fact that people select media for its degree of social presence and its particular suitability for the task they wish to accomplish. That is, we decide whether to meet, speak on the phone, or send an instant message depending on what we want to say and how we want to say it. Well, now we can add virtual reality and avatars to our list of media options. Second Life does convey a strong sense of social presence that readily puts people at ease. This is a peculiar phenomenon considering we are fully aware we are communicating via the artificial facial expressions and body language of avatars.[9]

Research has shown that the concept of social power has particular relevance to service settings where "(consumers offer their money, time, and effort, and providers offer the service desired by the consumers) in the hopes of achieving a mutually satisfying service encounter."[10] And, because all retail settings, where tangible goods are purchased—either online or in-store—are technically *service* settings, the concept of social power in a Web 2.0 world has relevance for virtually every consumer marketplace transaction.

In social power research, two categories of significant antecedent variables have tended to surface—*individual factors* (i.e., What consumer characteristics result in a greater or lesser sense of power?) and *interpersonal factors* (i.e., What characteristics of the consumer-retailer relationship, the service/good itself, and/or other consumers involved in the retail experience influence consumers' perceptions of social power?). Of note, a consumer's willingness to express emotions—in particular, negative emotions (e.g., "anger, frustration, irritation, hostility, nervousness, worry, tension, anxiety, shame, embarrassment, and guilt"[11]) that can result from an unsatisfactory retail experience is thought to play a central role in the outcome of the experience. To date, while no academic study specifically has addressed the emergence of Web 2.0 technologies and their impact on social power, examples abound with regard to how consumers have seized opportunities to exert the power afforded them through the social media.

Perhaps one of the earliest and best examples of a consumer taking advantage of the new power offered by the Internet can be found at the "Untied Airlines" Web site (http://www.untied.com/), as described in the *Arizona Tribune*:

> It all started with a crushed suit, a bungled flight connection and lost seat reservations [in 1996]. Those incidents, which sound like a scene taken from the 1980 screwball comedy "Airplane!," all transpired during one round-trip flight that Montreal resident Jeremy Cooperstock took between Toronto and Japan in the summer of 1996. They were also the catalyst that led to the creation of Untied.com, a Web site that serves as a clearinghouse for complaints against Chicago-based United Airlines. Untied.com is one of 40 so-called "protest Web sites" that Arizona State University professors Jim Ward and Amy Ostrom examined while researching the rising popularity of such grass-roots portals for complaining and their effect.[12]

James C. Ward and Amy L. Ostrom found in their research that consumers not only can create complaint Web sites reaching millions of other consumers, but also "sometimes attempt to create 'communities of discontent' focused on particular companies."[13] In short, this newfound power, afforded consumers via the Internet, derives not only from their ability to communicate negative word of mouth (NWOM) to thousands or even millions of other consumers, but also from their ability to "encourage other consumers to perceive themselves as a group, united in their opposition to the firm."[14]

Not everyone, however, has the resources (e.g., time, money, ability) or the inclination to develop and maintain a Web site for a lengthy period. Indeed, the vast majority of the Web sites cited by Ward and Ostrom in their 2006 study were not in existence two years after the publication of their research. In contrast, the explosion of Web 2.0 technologies has provided consumers an array of relatively convenient, inexpensive options for achieving many of the same goals sought by unhappy consumers who developed Web sites to vent their frustrations. For example:

Facebook: Facebook users have the social networking site itself, as well as a variety of other social media, to complain about Facebook tactics, policies, and poor service.

YouTube: A YouTube video shows a Comcast cable technician sleeping on a customer's couch. Whether the video is real or staged, the viral effect is the same.[15]

Twitter: "When C. C. Chapman noticed a blemish in his high-definition television's reception during the NBA playoffs recently, he blasted a quick gripe about Comcast into the online ether using the social network Twitter. Minutes later, a Twitter user named ComcastCares responded, and within 24 hours, a technician was at Chapman's house in Milford [MA] to fix the problem."[16]

Blogs: There are almost too many "customer complaint" and "bad service" blogs to count, which is why firms must monitor blog traffic to learn what is being said about the products and customer service they offer.

The following story demonstrates this new range of social-media options now available to customers who are not satisfied with a firm's service recovery practices: A person had a problem with his new Land Rover, and he felt the BMW dealership where he purchased his Land Rover was not taking his complaints seriously. So, on his blog—totally unrelated to Land Rovers, automobile dealerships, or customer satisfaction, he wrote:

Twitter friends! Please help me to demonstrate the power of social media in my fight against Land Rover and [dealer name]. This could be a really cool social media experiment! Here is the background on my battle. My wife and I dropped our 2002 Freelander off to diagnose a "check engine" light warning. When we picked up the car, my wife noticed the following new issues.

- The locks on all the doors no longer work.
- The back window won't go down.
- The built-in security system no longer functions.

When we informed Land Rover about this situation, they had the following response:

- These types of things happen to cars.
- Nothing they did would have caused this.
- That it is possible the problem existed when we brought it in (not true).
- That it is just bad luck on our part.

Their service manager refuses to help and let us know that we'll need to pay them to get it fixed. My wife is in tears over this customer service nightmare. Some people say I should call the local news channel. I say no. I say use Social Media to spark action! Please help me in my fight by doing the following few things:

- Posting a link to my blog post somewhere.
- Retweeting my call to action.
- Talking or leaving a message for the [dealer name] service manager. Let them know that consumers have power and they should take care of their customers. Let her know that this is a campaign on the behalf of [name]. Please be polite when you call.
- Twitter me with a list of the actions you took.

Not only did his tenacity payoff—(Twitter UPDATE—"We won our battle!"[17])—below are a few of the comments responding to his blogpost:

- I'm pretty [. . .] surprised by this. A brand like that should be exceeding your service expectations (I know Audi always did for me). What's sad is that kind of attitude in the service department will impact sales. I've heard some people say as much with VW. Usually, these companies have a corporate reporting place. I'd certainly tell them your opinion.
- Who would have guessed that with "German Engineering" you get "German Customer Service."
- Hi, I love Land Rover. This customer service is abysmal though—these people need to be taught a social media lesson. Do you have an email so people over here in the UK can contact this company too?

In addition, there was a link to another local Web site, "Awful Customer Service at My Dealership." The new reality that firms must accept is that information communicated on the Internet is viral in nature, and it is virtually impossible to "take back" or "eliminate" information once it is communicated. Jeremy's story illustrates consumers' growing desire and propensity to use the social power they now have as a result of social media to "withhold resources" from or "administer punishment" to companies that fail to respond to concerns and complaints in an appropriate way.

Customer Voice in the Era of the Internet and Web 2.0

Examples such as those described above demonstrate that the social media allow customers today to have their voices heard in a manner and to an extent never possible prior to the advent of Web 2.0. Whereas in the "old days," a *satisfied* customer might tell one or two people about his or her satisfaction with a product—vis-à-vis angry customers, who told 10 or 11 about their dissatisfaction—today's reality is reflected in the title of Pete Blackshaw's 2008 best seller, *Satisfied Customers Tell Three Friends, Angry Customers Tell 3,000.*[18]

Blackshaw's thesis rests not only in the marketplace's evolution into a "consumer-driven world," but also in the social power available to consumers via "the now ubiquitous open-source participatory Internet dubbed 'Web 2.0'."[19] With ever-increasing access to the social media, angry customers can voice their concerns about any marketplace transaction not just to thousands, but to multiple millions of consumers, and they can do so using any or all of the ever-growing number of social-media options.

As early as the 1970s, academic researchers were theorizing in earnest about consumer complaining behavior. As consumer markets became more competitive, companies began to increase their focus on *keeping* customers, in addition to obtaining new ones, by paying attention to consumer feedback and complaints. "In general, studies of consumer complaining behavior have identified four main purposes for complaining":[20]

- Obtain restitution or compensation
- Vent their anger
- Help to improve the service
- For altruistic reasons

A classic framework for investigating the range of options available to consumers following a dissatisfying retail incident includes categories of "exit, loyalty, and voice." In other words, unhappy consumers can simply *exit* (boycott brand/product)—i.e., elect not to frequent a retailer or purchase a particular brand in the future; they can remain *loyal* (take no action), opting to give the retailer or brand another chance in the future; or they can exercise their *voice* by complaining (either privately or publicly). With respect to this framework, little has been said regarding consumers' ability or propensity for exercising more than one of these options (e.g., exit AND voice), because "voice"—in particular, public voice—historically was the option requiring the most effort. However, in a Web 2.0 environment, meaningful and significant voice (e.g., NWOM) requires far less effort than in times past, and it has the potential for having much greater effect.

In 2004, Mattila and Wirtz[21] modified a nearly 30-year-old classification of consumer complaining behavior to include the various channels of communications that consumers can use to seek redress directly with retail firms.

> Level 1: A customer first decides if she will take action or take no action following a dissatisfying incident.
>
> Level 2: If the customer decides to take action, will the action be public or private?
>
> Level 3: If private, will the customer boycott the brand/product or spread NWOM? If public, will the customer seek redress directly, take legal action, or complain to third parties?
>
> Level 4: If the customer seeks redress directly, will the actions be interactive or remote?
>
> Level 5: If interactive, will the communication be face to face or by phone? If remote, will the communication be by letter or e-mail?

A primary distinction between pre- and post-Internet/social-media eras is the realization that NWOM is no longer necessarily—or even primarily—a *private* action, as it had been considered in the past. Online word of mouth has become popularly referred to as "word of mouse." Moreover, public actions are no longer limited to seeking redress directly, taking legal action, or complaining to third parties such as the Better Business Bureau. Rather, public actions taken via the Internet and its Web 2.0 options encompass a wide and ever-growing range of possibilities— blogs, online communities, Twitter, YouTube, Facebook, RSS, Digg, message boards, product review sites, and more.

Seeking Recovery, Getting Revenge, or What?

What motivates a consumer to seek recovery? And, is *economic* recovery all that consumers are seeking when they pick up the mantle of Web 2.0 to take their story to virtual audiences?

Most conventional theories addressing what motivates consumers to complain are rooted to some degree in *equity theory*. "According to equity theory, individuals are motivated by a comparison of the ratio of their inputs to their outcomes relative to the same ratio of comparison others."[22] In other words, a consumer compares the sum of everything he believes he has invested in a particular transaction (e.g., money, time, effort, frustration) to what he perceives he has received from the firm. If the consumer perceives that his input-outcome ratio compares unfavorably to the "comparison other" (in this case, either the firm itself or other customers of the firm), then "the individual is motivated to restore equity by any one of a number of mechanisms."[23] Given the broad scope of Web 2.0 options for seeking redress in public, it is clear that the social media can satisfy not only the four traditional motivations for complaining, listed above, but also a range of additional motivations, including gaining *public recognition* and *seeking revenge*.

In their re-conceptualization of sources of interpersonal communication and personal influence in the context of the Internet, P. Kiecker and D. Cowles[24] suggested that the Internet and the social media provide new and powerful forums for historically credible market influencers such as opinion leaders, market mavens, purchase pals, and innovators/early adopters. To a greater or lesser extent, each of these types of influencers is motivated at least in part by a desire for *public recognition*: Opinion leaders provide product-specific advice and are held in high esteem by those who accept their opinions. Market mavens are general marketplace influencers who are assumed to be opinion leaders. Purchase pals accompany shoppers who rely on their expertise and/or support in decision-making during an actual shopping trip. Innovators/early adopters like to be at the center of attention by communicating with others about their cutting-edge experience with new products.

Blogs, social networking sites, Twitter, online communities, and other social-media forums provide effective public platforms for these "credible market influencers," and consumers are ever more frequently turning to these experts for marketplace advice. Angie's List (www.angieslist.com), ServiceMagic (www.servicemagic.com), and similar product review Web sites provide—if not a public forum for opinion leaders and experts—at least a forum for consumers with experience—good and bad—with service firms. "More than 750,000 consumers use Angie's List to find high quality contractors, service companies and doctors."[25] And, it may be the case that consumers who use these service-provider databases are more likely to report poor service, as opposed to excellent service—"there are plenty of reports of bad quality service from users of ServiceMagic."[26] In short, it is very likely that human nature does not change in a virtual setting (i.e., consumers' propensity for communicating information about negative experiences); rather, consumers simply have different, more powerful communication tools available to them today compared to just a few years ago.

Web 2.0 provides a variety of platforms for customers who do not feel they have been treated fairly by firms to take their dissatisfaction to another level—*revenge*. As Jeremy's Land Rover plight and subsequent actions illustrate, there is a big difference between a consumer who complains for the purpose of seeking economic recovery and one who uses the social media to get revenge. As a result, in a Web 2.0 world, it is even more important for a firm to have in place a well-thought-out, responsive, and effective service recovery and public relations program so as to preclude consumers' elevating their actions to a level that includes using the social media for the vengeful purposes. More than ever before, consumers have the power to live the adage, "I don't get mad. I get even."

What Is a Firm to Do?

An irony in today's changing world of customer service and service recovery is the fact that consumers not only have increased marketplace power due to their access to the social media, but they increasingly expect the firms with which they do business to be engaged with the social media.[27] Ben McConnell, who, along with Jackie Huba, runs the "Church of the Customer Blog," provided the following results of a social-media study, from an Opinion Research Corporation online survey of 1,092 adults (525 men and 567 women) conducted September 11–12, 2008.[28] Sixty percent of those surveyed reported using social media to some extent, and 59 percent of users reported interacting with companies via social-media Web sites. Of those who use social media:

- 93 percent say a company should have a presence in social media.
- 85 percent say a company should not only be present but also interact with its customers via social media.
- 56 percent say they feel a stronger connection with and better served by companies when they can interact with them in a social-media environment.
- 43 percent say companies should use social networks to solve customers' problems.
- 41 percent say companies should use social media to solicit feedback about products and services.
- 37 percent say companies should develop new ways for consumers to interact with their brand.
- 25 percent say companies should market directly to consumers.

McConnell sees the social media as "the new customer service," adding that when "social media-driven customer service is combined with the work of citizen marketers, it becomes a force for more credible problem-solving (and less expensive customer service costs). With its inherent market research opportunities, social media has crossed over to the category of obvious strategy." As such, firms can integrate the social media into their strategies to turn consumers who might otherwise become angry into brand advocates:[29]

- Make it easy for someone to contact you. Develop both expertise and a presence within the social media that your customers use.
- Bring customer service in-house—customer service is not a "cost center." Train and support a sufficient number of employees to represent your brand within the social media.
- Hidden/recurring fees are not a clever way to make additional revenue. Customers are smart, and they don't like to be tricked. Such actions adversely affect perceptions of fairness and equity. Remember, if customers don't like your policies, you may be the last to know.
- Don't treat customers like hot potatoes. Dissatisfied customers will not go away, and they will only become more unhappy if they feel you're trying to avoid them.

- Review your various messaging services. Would you want to face what your customers face when they try to contact to you for any reason?
- Create relationships. "Zappos is another great example of a company that fosters a relationship between the customer service reps and the clients. People don't establish relationships with a product or a price; they have relationships with people. Without that crucial relationship, your chance of increasing repeat business is tenuous at best."[30]
- Show who you are. "Connect with your customers by giving some insight into the inner workings of the company. Blogs are great for doing this. They can take time to set up and manage, but once you get a process down, you'll find it easier to maintain, and customers feel more connected when they can read about the goings-on of a company. Any way you can build a more personal connection with customers is a good use of time and resources.[31]
- Make your site easily shop-able. Don't assume to know how Internet-savvy your customers are, and don't assume they have the latest hardware and software.
- Respond to e-mails. Consumers have ever-increasing expectations regarding e-mail response times.
- Make sure your customers know what they are getting. "When evaluating your customer service, your prevailing thought should be, 'How would I feel if I had this customer experience?' Don't be afraid to challenge processes that have been in place for years; what worked in the past won't necessarily work now."[32]

Rapidly rising consumer expectations create a very high bar for companies to meet in today's evolving social-media environment. Firms don't get to "choose" whether they want to become involved in the social media. So long as consumers have access to YouTube, Facebook, virtual worlds, Twitter, and all the rest, the social media will have an impact on how a firm should conduct business—in particular, how a firm should respond to customer complaints. The objective, however, is for firms to be, first, *proactive*, in their use of social media and, second, *responsive*—not merely reactive.

Responding to McConnell's blog posting cited above, Kathy Doering, president of Ann Michaels & Associates, Ltd. (http://www.ishopforyou .com/), a firm that provides customer-experience management services, including mystery shopping, customer feedback, and social-media monitoring, wrote: "We are using social media monitoring as a 'red flag' process and then sending in mystery shoppers to do audits for our clients. It is changing the way we do business."[33] Doering's company is just one among many arguing that firms must be proactive in their social-media involvement. Her firm and others offer "a service that monitors web-based programs for any type of feedback regarding a specific company. As consumers have highly effective forums to share their product experiences and opinions online, whether they are positive or negative, more and more large companies are realizing these consumer voices can hold enormous influence in shaping the opinions of other consumers and influence their brand loyalties and purchase decisions. With this service, we can monitor the web for complaints, compliments, and other additional feedback provided by consumers."[34]

To complicate things even further: To at least the same extent that the social media are the "new customer service," these same media represent the "new public relations." Firms have to deal not only with the dissatisfaction or possible revenge of customers they serve, but also with noncustomers who can wield the power of the social media to tarnish a firm's image, brand, and reputation in the blink of an eye. Ironically, companies must themselves be poised to "recover" from such virtual attacks or pay a heavy price for being unprepared. Domino's Pizza learned this lesson the hard way:

> Just how much damage two hooligans can do with a video camera is still unknown. But when the dust finally settles on Domino's Boogergate, it seems likely the pizza chain will be given credit for an effective, if somewhat sluggish, response. And the resulting public relations crisis can be a valuable learning experience for marketers of every stripe.
>
> . . . here's what happened: Two employees at the pizza chain uploaded a video to YouTube of one of them in a Domino's store and in a Domino's uniform sticking cheese up his nose and then putting it on a sandwich that was purportedly going to be sold to a customer. Other stomach-turning acts were also recorded for posterity.
>
> Domino's was on top of the situation within about 48 hours—too long, according to some. The offending video received nearly 1 million views before it was taken down, which already represented significant damage to the brand.[35]

For the first 24 hours, the firm's response was ineffective, even though the brand had some experience with MySpace, Twitter, YouTube, and Facebook prior to the fiasco. In fact, before the employees' YouTube posting, Domino's had nearly 300,000 Facebook fans. However, Domino's had failed to develop a crisis-management communications plan to tackle this type of user-generated, social-media sabotage, so its recovery was unnecessarily slow and the negative impact on its reputation, unnecessarily steep. A firm must examine not only its understanding of how the social media can be used to facilitate its customers' desire for service recovery, but also its preparedness to recover from a public relations/communications crisis created by individuals employing social-media tactics.

CAN SOCIAL MEDIA FACILITATE MARKETPLACE JUSTICE?

Since at least the late 1980s, scholars have based theories and models pertaining to complaint handling and service recovery processes to a greater or lesser extent on *social exchange theory* and the influence of *perceived justice* on customer satisfaction. Initially, studies emphasized the *distributive* (equity) aspect of market exchanges—that is, a customer's perceptions of the justice or fairness of the outcome of service failure/recovery encounters and/or their complaint behaviors. By the late 1990s, however, it became clear that customers' perceptions of distributive justice did not account fully for their level of post-recovery/post-complaint satisfaction.

In their award-winning article "Recovering and Learning from Service Failure," S. Tax and S. Brown[36] addressed this shortcoming by viewing complaint handling and service recovery as a longitudinal, or sequential, process. First, in terms of procedural justice, complaining customers are influenced by "the policies and rules that any customer has to go through to seek fairness."[37] Second, customers' ultimate satisfaction with the recovery will in part be determined by their interactions with the employees who participate in and other mechanisms that comprise the service recovery and complaint handling system. Finally, consumers will judge whether the compensation they receive vis-à-vis their losses, inconvenience, and energy expenditure is just and fair.

When dissatisfied customers take the time and effort to participate in a firm's complaint/recovery process, but remain dissatisfied (in particular, with the outcome of their efforts, but also with the procedures required and the interactions in which they are involved) then they feel a sense of powerlessness. Because Web 2.0 is a source of power for these unhappy customers, subsequent actions can help them restore equity to the equation, which they perceive to be imbalanced.

M. P. Bunker and M. S. Bradley describe two components of powerlessness that drive customers to third-party Internet complaint sites: "The first component follows the general definition of powerlessness and refers to consumers' beliefs that their complaints would lead to no corrective action by the company."[38] This dimension relates most closely to outcome justice. They continue: "For the second component to be discerned, the complaints had to include an element in which consumers express a form of powerlessness during the failure episode by describing a self effacing event."[39] Clearly, self-effacement would most likely occur either while participating in a firm's recovery procedures or during interactions with the firm during the complaint/recovery process.

In their research, Bunker and Bradley found that "grudge-holding was the largest reported consequence of powerlessness."[40] Prior to Web 2.0, grudge-holding largely meant "exit"—never do business with the firm again, spread NWOM. Such is not the case when consumers have access to the social media. Moreover, the same research showed that consumers who feel powerless are prone to hyperbole. Examples of such hyperbole abound on YouTube and other social media, generated by customers who were dissatisfied with a firm's service recovery policies and procedures.

Yet another study concluded that the failure of e-commerce customer service centers to meet customer expectations is a major source of online customer complaints in each of the three justice categories:[41]

Procedural Justice:	Disappointing timing/speed of delivery Difficulties in engaging a process Inability of procedures to reflect individual circumstances Lack of responsiveness
Interactive Justice:	Unsatisfactory manner of response Salesperson did not provide sufficient explanations/information Salesperson did not respond kindly
Distributive Justice:	Customer had to pay cost of returning the product Delivered product required repair One or more aspects of delivered product was inferior Unsatisfactory delivery cost

Interestingly, the nature of e-commerce itself heightens the potential for consumers to sense a lack of power. Whereas in traditional, brick-and-mortar transactions, consumers ostensibly have a physical location where they can seek redress and real people with whom they can interact, e-commerce transactions provide fertile ground for consumers to feel impotent in the face of dissatisfaction. To begin with, there are many different approaches to customer service at various retail Web sites, as well as a wider variation in guarantees, guidelines for returning products, etc. Web sites differ greatly with respect to the quality of information provided and the extent to which security and privacy aspects of transactions are handled.[42] In short, although e-commerce customer service generally has improved over the past decade or so, consumers have far more reason to feel powerless during virtual transactions, vis-à-vis in-store purchases.

Whereas, just a decade ago, Tax and Brown spoke primarily of toll-free telephone call centers and, secondarily, Internet Web sites to facilitate service recovery, today they would most surely include the plethora of options provided by Web 2.0. The next section examines how firms today are learning to integrate the social media into their service recovery and complaint handling tactics and strategies.

How Social Media Can Enhance Traditional Service Recovery

From at least one perspective, the theoretical underpinnings of service recovery today are not so different than they were two decades ago when the term "service recovery" was first coined. However, because the tools of recovery have proliferated and the power of the consumer has increased, doing service recovery right is more important today than ever before. If a consumer remains dissatisfied and feels powerless after seeking redress initially, then he or she can move on to a second stage of recovery, exerting power in the marketplace via the social media, oftentimes seeking revenge by spewing negative hyperbole to all who will listen. Social-media tools and tactics are well suited to the traditional "justice" framework of service recovery:

Procedural Justice: A firm must have in place an effective system for seeking out, receiving, and responding to customer feedback and complaints. Social media options can be integrated into this system to enhance its effectiveness. If a firm knows that its customers are social media users, it can, for example:

- Create a complaint desk in Second Life and make sure the desk is "open for business" during advertised hours.
- Widely communicate Twitter contact information.
- Create a corporate Facebook/MySpace profile that encourages customer feedback and complaints, and tackles negative feedback head on.
- Keeping in mind that transparency is paramount, position the social media up front as part of "contact us" or the firm's "customer support" function—and, it is best for Twitter addresses and blog sign-in identifiers to include information that will link the firm's communicator to the firm he or she represents.
- Educate and support both employees and, if necessary, customers with respect to how to use the social media for service recovery.

Interactive Justice: A sufficient number of employees must be able to speak for the firm via the social media, and they must be trained in how to do so, especially in terms of Twitter and responding to blogposts. For example:

- Although some firms use a single "official" Twitter contact, more frequently firms have multiple employees who serve as Twitter ambassadors. Likewise, firms must carefully control not only how many, but also who within the firm has the authority to respond to negative customer blogposts.
- First impressions are critical. If a firm makes the initial Twitter contact with a complaining customer, it should be done in a way that the customer does not feel like he or she is being stalked.
- All interactions should be authentic, helpful, timely, and polite.

Outcome Justice: If firms are effective during the procedural- and interactive-justice stages of recovery, customers will more than likely be satisfied with the outcome of their recovery efforts. However, firms still should monitor the Internet for mentions of their brands and products—especially when customers are not satisfied with the outcome of their recovery efforts:

- Two decades ago, services-marketing guru Len Berry suggested that firms "run to the problem." That is to say, ignoring problems only intensifies their adverse impact on a firm's customers, employees, sales, and long-term profitability. Today's version of running to the problem is what Paul Gillin, author of *Secrets of Social Media Marketing*,[43] recommends: Don't fear the negative.
- Gillin further advises firms that searching via Google and the other major search engines is not sufficient. A firm should monitor specialized search engines (e.g., Green Maven, Tech Stuff, CustomSearchGuide), meta-search sites (e.g., ZUULA, excite, dogpile, copernic, SurfWax), and social bookmarking sites (e.g., delicious.com, digg, clipmarks, StumbleUpon, rddit). What is being said about the firm, its brands, and its products?
- Technorati can be used to find influential bloggers who may be spreading negative (or positive) online word of mouth.
- Google's magic link command can demonstrate the viral nature of negative information following a dissatisfactory recovery outcome.

Firms must both acknowledge and respect the newfound power of consumers, rooted in consumers' access to and willingness to use the social media, which they can employ to bring about procedural, interactive, and outcome justice.

But it doesn't stop there. As opposed to viewing the social media as a "necessary evil" in the development of a service-recovery system, firms should embrace new opportunities offered by the social media *prior to* and *after* the three stages of justice. For example, because firms can monitor the social media, they do not have to wait until a complaint is registered—indeed, dissatisfied customers may never register a complaint and may never engage in the procedural-interactive-outcome justice process. Firms can preempt complaints by developing a system to monitor both favorable—and especially unfavorable—comments about a brand, a company, or customer service interactions made via the social media.

What should a company do if someone talks about them online? According to Matt Rhodes, who blogs about social media at FreshNetworks, a firm that provides social-media software and assists companies when they want to connect with and engage customers, employees, and suppliers, an unlikely source of the answer to this question comes from the U.S. Air Force's Emerging Technology Division of the Air Force Public Affairs Agency. The Air Force Blog Assessment tool, highlighted on Rhodes's site, breaks the assessment process into three stages: (1) assessment, (2) evaluation, and (3) response. The evaluation stage explains the types of sites on which blog postings might occur. These include trolls, ragers, misguideds, and unhappy customers. Trolls include sites dedicated to bashing others. Ragers are those sites which ridicule or rant about others. Misguided sites post false information. Unhappy customers are self-explanatory. Ultimately, one must decide whether to simply continue monitoring, or to attempt to respond to the post. Responses must be appropriate in terms of tone, disclosure of affiliation (transparency), source of information, and be delivered in a timely manner.

According to Rhodes, the Air Force's blog-assessment model is valuable for a number of reasons: (1) It is not always appropriate to "join" the conversation. Monitoring what is being said may be the best approach. (2) It reinforces that online honesty and transparency are critical. (3) It differentiates between different types of negative posts—they're not all the same. (4) It is easy to remember and follow. If a firm has several or many employees/representatives authorized to converse in the social-media environment, this simple model can provide a consistent voice in a complex and dynamic communications environment.

"Listening" is the term that social-media marketers use to describe this monitoring requirement. "For any brand using social media, an important first stage is to find out what people are saying about you online and then monitor these discussions and conversations. You can build on these, engage the people talking about you and learn from what they say."[44] Rhodes suggests that firms listen to 10 different types of conversations online: complaints, compliments, problems, questions/inquiries, campaign impact, crisis, competitors, crowds, influencers, and points of need.

The variety of conversations that must be monitored to satisfy both the challenges and opportunities of the social media underscores the notion that Web 2.0 demands greater cooperation and integration among previously unconnected—or, at least, less connected—functional areas of business. In short, to achieve a successful service recovery program, firms must coordinate marketing, public relations, customer service, operations, information technology, and human relations functions—no small order in an already complex, challenging, and dynamic business environment.

NOTES

1. Pete Blackshaw, *Satisfied Customers Tell Three Friends, Angry Customers Tell 3,000: Running a Business in Today's Consumer-Driven World* (Random House, 2008), 4.

2. A. Parsuraman, V. A. Zeithaml, and L. L. Berry, "A Conceptual Model of Service Quality and Its Implications for Future Research," *Journal of Marketing* no. 40 (1985), 41–50.

3. R. Zemke and C. Bell, "Service Recovery: Doing It Right the Second Time," *Training* (1990), 42–48.

4. C. W. L. Hart, J. L. Heskett, and W. E. Sasser Jr., "The Profitable Art of Service Recovery," *Harvard Business Review* 68, no. 4 (1990), 148–156.

5. Ibid., 149.

6. See Note 1.

7. K. Menon and H. Bansal, "Exploring Consumer Experience of Social Power during Service Consumption," *International Journal of Service Industry Management* no. 18 (2007), 90.

8. J. Short, E. Williams, and B. Christie, *The Social Psychology of Telecommunications*, (Wiley & Sons, 1976).

9. "Social Presence Theory & Second Life," Cyberloom, March 10, 2008, http://cyberloom.wordpress.com/2008/03/10/social-presence-theory-second-life/.

10. See Note 7.

11. Ibid., 96.

12. David Woodfill, *Arizona Tribune*, "Untied," December 2006, http://www.untied.com/site/news.html#arizonatribune.

13. "How Angry Customers Get Revenge (and Create Civic Protest)," Physorg, August 9, 2006, http://www.physorg.com/news74343253.html.

14. James Ward and Amy Ostrom, "Complaining to the Masses: The Role of Protest Framing in Customer-Created Complaint Web Sites," *Journal of Consumer Research* (2006): 220–230.

15. "Comcast Sleeping," YouTube, December 21, 2007, http://www.youtube.com/watch?v=viw2TVBygBg.

16. Carolyn Y. Johnson, "Hurry Up, the Customer Has a Complaint," *Boston Globe*, July 7, 2008, http://www.boston.com/business/technology/articles/2008/07/07/hurry_up_the_customer_has_a_complaint/.

17. Jeremy Hilton, "My Land Rover Battle," Home Culinaire, October 2, 2008, http://homeculinaire.blogspot.com/2008/10/my-land-rover-battle.html.

18. See Note 1.

19. See Note 1.

20. C. Lovelock and J. Wirtz, *Services Marketing: People, Technology, Strategy*, 6th ed. (Pearson Prentice-Hall, 2007), 392.

21. S. Mattila and J. Wirtz, "Consumer Complaining to Firms: The Determinants of Channel Choice," *The Journal of Services Marketing* 18, no. 2/3 (2004): 147–155.

22. C. L. Carr, "The FAIRSERV Model: Consumer Reactions to Services Based on a Multidimensional Evaluation of Service Fairness," *Decision Sciences* 38, no. 1 (2007): 109.

23. Ibid.

24. P. Kiecker and D. Cowles, "Interpersonal Communication and Personal Influence on the Internet: A Framework for Examining Online Word-of-Mouth," *Journal of Euro-Marketing* 11, no. 2 (2001): 71–88.

25. "Looking for the best service?" Angie's list, 2009, http://www.angieslist.com/Angieslist/.

26. " How does Service Magic Compare to Angie's List?" 2Factoidz: bite-sized knowledge, 009, http://factoidz.com/how-does-service-magic-compare-with-angies-list/.

27. Ben McConnell, "Social Media as Customer Service," Church of the Customer Blog, September 30, 2008, http://www.churchofthecustomer.com/blog/2008/09/social-media-as.html.

28. Andrea Larrumbide, "Cone Finds that Americans Expect Companies to Have a Presence in Social Media," Cone, September 25, 2008, http://www.coneinc.com/content1182.

29. Chad Little, "10 Ways to Turn Angry Consumers into Brand Advocates" iMediaConnection, March 13, 2009, http://www.imediaconnection.com/content/22292.asp.

30. Ibid.

31. Ibid.

32. Ibid.

33. "Social Media Monitoring Services," Ann Michaels & Associates, IShopForYou, 2009, http://www.ishopforyou.com/Services.html#Social_Media_Monitoring.

34. Ibid.

35. E. B. York, "What Domino's Did Right—and Wrong—In Squelching Hubbub Over YouTube Video," *Advertising Age*, Midwest Region Edition, 80, no. 14 (2009): 1.

36. S. Tax and S. Brown, "Recovering and Learning from Service Failure," *Sloan Management Review* 40, no. 1 (1998): 75–88.

37. C. Lovelock and J. Wirtz, *Services Marketing: People, Technology, Strategy*, 6th ed. (Pearson Prentice-Hall, 2007), 394.

38. M. P. Bunker, and M. S. Bradley, "Toward Understanding Customer Powerlessness: Analysis of an Internet Complaint Site," *Journal of Consumer Satisfaction, Dissatisfaction and Complaining Behavior* no. 20 (2007): 54.

39. Ibid.

40. Ibid., 67.

41. Y. Cho, I. Im, and R. Hiltz, "The Impact of E-Services Failures and Customer Complaints on Electronic Commerce Customer Relationship Management," *Journal of Customer Satisfaction, Dissatisfaction and Complaining Behavior* no. 16 (2003): 106–118.

42. Ibid.

43. P. Gillin, *Secrets of Social Media Marketing: How to Use Online Conversations and Customer Communities to Turbo-Charge Your Business* (Quill Driver Books, 2009).

44. Matt Rhodes, "The Ten Conversations to Listen for in Social Media," Fresh Networks, May 2, 2009, http://blog.freshnetworks.com/2009/05/the-top-10-conversations-to-listen-for-in-social-media/.

9

MESSAGES STILL MATTER: PR IN A DIGITAL WORLD

Bob Witeck

I remember an informal dialogue, perhaps 25 years ago, when I was asked to address a room full of college interns who were intrigued about future careers in public relations. At the time, I was only about 10 years ahead of them on my own path, but, like them, I always questioned my professional role and my mission as a public relations practitioner.

When I posed the question to the group, for example, to find out what specific difference or distinctions—if any—they make between advertising and public relations, we all laughed when one student advised that "advertising is straightforward, while public relations is *sneaky.*"

Sneaky, or not, I think I got her point. For many of us veterans as well as novices, the discipline of public relations often seems more art than science, and in this emerging digital world, it is as vital, dynamic, and challenging as ever. However, in my experience, successful public relations expertise is still primarily defined by *the power and reach of the message.* But given the dramatic changes in all digital platforms and media channels, it is far from sneaky.

I tend to agree with many experts who define successful public relations as *what others say about you* (e.g., your company, product, brand, cause) and not so much what you say about yourself (which clearly defines more conventional marketing and advertising campaigns).

Third parties, including all forms of media, define value and decide (again and again and again) the relative significance and power of messages and messengers. Others vote constantly on whether they trust you, admire you, respect you, like (or even love) you, and most of the time, whether to buy what you're selling or to side with your point of view. They judge us on relevance, timeliness, and value.

Public relations therefore encompasses all of the existing and emerging tools and strategies available to us to persuade others to share, endorse, and communicate those messages that work—that meet our objectives, whether we propose a candidate for public office, a new book, a breakfast cereal, a social change or cause, a political movement, or a corporate brand, for instance.

WHAT'S REALLY CHANGED IN THE DIGITAL AGE?

In some basic ways, little seems to have changed. Public relations practitioners still focus on communications objectives as well as target audiences, messages, messengers, and media. We recognize that our role is to get them right in balance, to create strategies that master all of these elements and succeed in crafting public perceptions and reputation for effective campaigns and to meet our communications objectives.

Many of us understandably bemoan the near-collapse of print media as well as the accelerating ownership concentration of media properties. Both are seismic business developments, and it is not yet clear how these trends and business models will unfold or what kind of media landscape yet will emerge.

Walter Isaacson, media maven and author, writes for *Time* magazine, however, "newspapers have more readers than ever. Their content as well as that of newsmagazines and other producers of traditional journalism, is more popular than ever—even (in fact, especially) among young people."[1]

Isaacson is right, but he quickly adds that far fewer of these readers are actually paying for their news, subscribing to newspapers or generally registering and compensating content providers (whether delivered to their front door or to their laptop). In the new, cruelly shrinking newsrooms in big and smaller cities and the financial stresses on journalism "as we know it," we are shifting far more resources and investments to the digital world, and consumers now insist on reading and being entertained without going to the trouble of directly buying. (For the owners of media channels, of course, this means a new and urgent focus on their business model: How to create popular *and* profitable media channels today? If you build it, will they pay?)

In that stark contemporary light, much has changed and will continue to change. And this is where digital rubber meets the digital road, and where media in all its forms challenges the messenger and seasoned public relations professional. Based on my observations and experience, I reason that the changes are perhaps most profound in these five related ways and all of them are relevant to the communicator's message: *Authenticity, transparency, trust, ubiquity,* and *eternity* (much more on that curious last point later).

Authenticity

Especially given the rise of new online channels and all genres of blogging (including the trends in marketplace America), the growing hunger and expectation for message authenticity is real, expanding, and here to stay.

In our very dynamic global economy, consumers and decision-makers are more impatient, and insist on higher standards of openness, truth-telling, and access to all essential information. (I'm not really suggesting that *telling the truth* was ever out of fashion—just that public expectations are much higher today.) They are determined to ask many more questions and to reach their own conclusions, and therefore, many consumers in the marketplace today now count on companies, leaders, and organizations to share their strengths and weaknesses, their policies and their processes, and to speak directly and unambiguously to the questions and needs of their stakeholders.

But what do we really mean by authenticity, and why is this truer than ever in the digital market? The digital market means simply that all of us are empowered to access market knowledge, pricing, decision-making, and competitive intelligence through the Web, and to expect all players to share information, resources, leadership, and data with all of us with heightened integrity. We expect these standards because we have a digital marketplace where competitors exist side by side, even if actually three-quarters around the world.

When I characterize *authenticity* with clients, I tend to focus on these kinds of questions:

- Are your messages and the many ways you share information based on core values—from the top?
- When you make mistakes or know you're wrong, do you say so out loud and work to correct rather than obscure it?
- Do you have a culture that is opaque, segmented, and compartmentalized, or is there openness and mutual support that communicates your *common ground*?

Companies and organizations with authentic messages and cultures are those that appear to connect best with their stakeholders, and are often directly associated with the other four digital trends (transparency, trust, ubiquity, and eternity).

Transparency

All communicators today must face and master an extraordinarily more transparent digital media—which implies openness along with accountability. In media communications, this simply means that there are, first, many and often competing channels for communication, from conventional radio, television, and print outlets to Weblogs, podcasts, tweets, posts, and of course, word of mouth. In the era of user-created digital content, anyone can create a unique window into a company or brand and invite others to share knowledge, impressions, or gossip.

Second, this openness with accountability also implies that much (if not all) is known about the methods of information delivery—journalistic quality, editorial judgment, and ownership, as well as media funding. For instance, is the media advertising supported or dependent on subscribers or registrants, or some kind of combination of financial support? Does the blogger have an ax to grind as a disgruntled consumer, or, more confusing, is the blogger actually an agent of the company writing under a guise or opaque identity?

Transparency is also the premium value paid by companies and organizations that communicate daily through the media and outside the media through social networks and community networks. Consider the rise of economic blockbusters like eBay and Amazon.com, which depend in great measure on showing all consumers and trading partners how to talk to each other—plainly, squarely, fairly, and fully.

Transparent communications become more important in the digital era simply because of many more, often competing, sources of information. In the Wikipedia age with its evangelizing user-generated content, the consumers of news and media insist on the highest standards of openness and accountability, albeit imperfect. They recognize, as Thomas Jefferson understood over two centuries ago, that finding the truth is truly possible only by allowing errors to be permitted and also made public—and, ultimately, correctable with new and more facts. Just as Jefferson did, we welcome a world that allows many more voices to be heard and points of view expressed in writing our rough drafts for the world.

PR practitioners and their companies that master transparency and gain a strong reputation as transparent are able to capitalize and to compete effectively by embracing this attribute. For example, for markets to work effectively, it is a truism that transparency is fundamental for all parties. It is known as the standard by which we try to reduce (if not eliminate) known biases, and to dispel the notion that we have hidden agendas or motives. In the language of software developers, WYSIWYG ("what you see is what you get").

It means that communicators, more than before, are prepared do disclose their credentials, clarify their relationships with media owners and confess any obvious biases and bents. Readers and viewers want to know the "street cred" for the writer or spokesperson, as well as the organization or media he (or she) speaks for.

Transparency also suggests that when facts are uncovered or disclosed by third parties, including journalists or consumers, or when new information later emerges, the communicator frequently pays a penalty. In those instances, consumers and audiences therefore are more swift to question a company's motives and practices and to presume that "hiding" facts is a common and duplicitous practice. With accelerating shared digital resources (inside or outside a company), the likelihood of successfully camouflaging essential (and, of course, unfavorable) facts becomes far more remote. The question is how and when, not if, the information will surface.

Not all companies nor communicators really understand yet that transparency is an iron-clad rule with social media and networks. But more are getting it, as they recognize the value of social-media channels.

No communicator likes to cede or to lose control of the message, and each is, therefore, often anxious because social media—with its cacophony of voices and opinions—enables frequent, distorted, and uninformed criticisms of their brands online. Some competitors clearly take advantage of this vulnerability and use these channels to gang up from time to time.

Consumer criticism, however, is not the real threat in the market (unless extremely unbridled, rampant, and unquestionably malicious). No product or service is perfect—and honest criticism can only be a threat if a company is blind to it or fails to understand it. Like most things in our complex world, there always is a person or a team who will try to make something quicker, smarter, better. Competition is inevitable.

That means transparency and the open conversations we embrace can and are positive benefits in our economy. As many companies are slashing budgets and trying to get back to basics, they find that trusting and engaging consumers with knowledge is a real opportunity. For seasoned communicators and public relations professionals, an analysis of compliments and criticisms helps improve messages, aids customer relationships, and sparks new thinking.

We always have known that consumers and word of mouth play a vital role in for any cause or company—building favorable reputation and market share. But transparency in social media increasingly allows consumers to share their opinions (all of them) with many more people and allows the messengers (companies and individuals) to be part of the conversation.

Trust

Trust has always been society's "glue"—the inherent bond that enables us to interact, to benefit from commerce and trade with each other, to grow the economy, to come to each other's mutual defense, and, above all, to have confidence in one another. We do so often because of basic trust in one another. It is one attribute that makes a successful communicator stand out in a pack.

For communicators in any age, trust also is the basis for credibility and helps to explain why some messengers (and messages) are widely accepted and others are not. We judge the content of the message (or the caliber of the messenger) more or less based on our trust. Do we find the message and its source believable? Is it an institution we have deemed trustworthy and accountable?

Of course, with greater transparency, the notion of trustworthiness has changed dramatically, and with nearly universal digital knowledge, we expand and demand more. In the 1950s, as early opinion polls attest, Americans were confident to place their trust almost always in their elected officials, their churches, their scout leaders, their business leaders, and their neighbors. If they wanted their news direct and unfiltered, they believed they could read one or two daily newspapers delivered to their door or turn on the evening news and have CBS News and Walter Cronkite explain the world to them. As many then agreed, Walter seemed to be the "most trusted man in America."

We are today bombarded with digital sources and information, with many expressing frustration and overload—and while others (especially younger and more educated Americans) cannot get enough. They demand information from many sources and use it to help make informed choices and to make value judgments about whom and what to trust.

Today, a very good question to ask is *who trusts whom, and why*? In 2007, Pew Research plunged into this research globally and also here in the United States. They concluded that social trust is a belief in the honesty, integrity, and reliability of others—but when querying the who and why, here's what they concluded: Generalizing for the American population as a whole, we are closely divided on the following question: "Would you say that most people can be trusted or that you can't be too careful in dealing with people?" Their 2,000 adult sample nearly split in half, with 45 percent saying the former, but 50 percent saying people are not so trustworthy—perhaps a different impression when contrasted with America at mid-century.[2]

The Pew findings also showed skews when it comes to education (50% of college graduates have high levels of social trust, compared with 28% of those with high school educations or less), and socioeconomic class (with 50% of those with professional or business class backgrounds having higher levels of social trust, when compared with 30% of those who describe themselves as working class, or 18% who say they are "struggling"). Whether there is a direct correlation, we do know that our online population and people who have access to digital information tend to have higher incomes and more education too.

Trust also plays a looming role in the perceptions we assign to the information we and others glean from the Internet and from our personal, digital universe. How reliable do we judge the Internet today as a source for answers?

Again in 2007, Pew Research unearthed significant new conclusions when they studied how Americans solve their problems and dig for specific solutions. According to Pew, when faced with a serious concern—whether financial, health, government policy, or any of 10 other possible problems—a clear majority or nearly 6 out of 10 Americans said they had turned to the Internet as their trusted source. That is more than professional experts (such as doctors, lawyers, and so on), family members or friends, publications, government agencies, television or radio, or even the public library (which was selected by just 13% of their national sample).

For communicators, we will wrestle with this delicate contradiction again and again—and recognize that online communications have empowered individuals to find and trust the varied information sources retrieved there—while still questioning our institutions and organizations that are the ultimate source of this knowledge.

Ubiquity

Mark Twain famously declared that "a lie can travel halfway around the world before the truth has time to put on its shoes." In Twain's world and very likely until late twentieth-century America caught up digitally, the real-time delivery of news was stuck and mired in many ways.

It is hard for some to recall, but before digital connections plugged us together, America throughout the twentieth century was truly a mosaic of discreet media markets and haltingly connected channels. A comment made to a small-town newspaper in Arkansas, or uttered on radio in Bangor, Maine, was not likely to be echoed, recorded, repeated or shared with other listeners and readers beyond those local audiences.

Wire services and television/radio networks helped provide some degree of universal connectivity—and to broadcast to national audiences who read the same papers and watched and listened to the same few channels that were piped in through aerials and antennae into their home receivers. That said, it meant that most of the actual and local events of each day were lost to most Americans—though we did know the major headlines and stories about war and peace, election returns, prize fights, weather disasters, and ball game outcomes. And given the generous helpings of local news, we also knew how our high school sport teams fared, whether our sanitation workers were on strike, the latest bowling scores, and schedules for holiday celebrations, among other community events.

Yet, this meant that many Americans consumed only that news that came to their door by subscribing to the newspaper or buying a television or radio (or news shared by family, friends, coworkers, and neighbors). We assumed then if it wasn't within reach of our hands, it probably wasn't relevant.

Today is the digital age of ubiquity. News, in all its profound and commercial and entertaining and even sometimes snarky packages, comes to us from next door or next continent with instant speed—and the comment made in Arkansas, if newsworthy or appropriately shocking, will be in our ears or face within minutes. It is just as likely to be communicated by a journalist as it is by an ordinary person (or as some label themselves today, by citizen-journalists). In this last election cycle, it is how politics and superstardom intersected when Barack Obama was compared to Paris Hilton—by adversarial political ads and commentary.

For communicators, this is boon and curse and suggests that we all have reach to a global audience for both good news and bad. I remember in the mid-1970s, for instance, when serving as a press secretary in Washington, DC, for a U.S. Senator, we relied on a Rube Goldberg-style delivery system to conduct television interviews with our west coast news affiliates. Simply put, I would make arrangements to have a filmmaker and crew show up at our office during the afternoon—and then record 30 minutes to 60 minutes of the Senator's responses while a journalist 3,000 miles away asked questions by phone. The unprocessed film then was flown across country within hours to arrive at the news room—for processing—and to broadcast the next evening to local audiences. Three decades ago, that costly path was how we attempted to achieve some form of television immediacy.

Today, video images and interviews are shot on digital handheld equipment by even the most amateur user—and shared globally within minutes on CNN or on YouTube, sometimes bolstering careers as often as ending others. In politics, entertainment, or business, it is this random and unpredictable ubiquity that has given every communicator a sense of power and much heightened risk.

Consider, for instance, how two of America's fabled Presidential campaigns contrast, when we understand how much the ubiquity and connectedness of media has changed in the past 60 years too.

In 1960, and until the youthful candidacy of John Kennedy, most African Americans tended to vote for Republicans because the majority of white southerners remained Democrats, and, at that time, adamantly opposed to civil rights progress. Historian and award-winning writer Taylor Branch described how very small—and largely unreported— events that pivotal year managed to transform the electorate and perhaps aided the narrow presidential election victory of JFK.

The sequence of events unfolded that year when civil rights leader Reverend Martin Luther King was stopped by a Georgia police officer who observed a white woman sitting between him and his wife, Coretta Scott King. The Kings were simply driving their friend to the hospital for cancer treatment. However, Dr. King unknowingly was operating his vehicle with an expired driver's license. As rank intimidation, Reverend King was immediately arrested and held without bail, despite the fact that the traffic infraction was a misdemeanor (and ordinarily not an offense resulting in jail). He was sentenced to 6 months hard labor at a time while his wife, Coretta, was pregnant.

African Americans were incensed by this kangaroo justice of course, along with white allies including Sargent Shriver, JFK's brother-in-law and campaign adviser. Shriver felt Kennedy should weigh in. However, other senior advisers were anxious that even a small public gesture or publicized statement of concern would risk the anger and defection of their white southern Democratic base vote. Shriver, however, offered a personal, one-on-one solution to Kennedy by urging him to make a personal phone call to Coretta King, and to make her aware he knew about her husband's plight and to offer moral support, if nothing more. Kennedy was convinced to make the call and did so to lift her spirits—and a good deal more. She was so flabbergasted to get a call from Senator Kennedy that she called her mother-in-law as soon as she got off the phone.

Bobby Kennedy served as his brother's campaign manager and was reportedly angry when he first heard about the impromptu phone call, but once he learned the specifics about the case, he then personally called the judge who had sentenced Martin Luther King and upbraided him for not granting Martin's constitutional right to bail when charged simply for a misdemeanor.

The judge rightly feared national attention and a legal rebuke and therefore ordered the immediate release of Martin Luther King, Jr. Consequently, Reverend Martin Luther King Senior (Dr. King's father)—a well-known supporter of Richard Nixon—switched course, endorsed Kennedy and persuaded scores of friends and associates to do likewise. A simple pamphlet called "The Blue Bomber" then circulated among the south's black churches, retelling the story, and enhancing the popularity and spawning a wellspring of new votes for the young Democratic candidate.

It is safe to say that white America, especially southern white households, were not part of this unique channel—and news of the JFK phone call did not travel throughout their homes or lives. It is as though Kennedy's campaign had a private connection with some voters but not with all. Yet, nearly a half-century later, during the historic Presidential campaign of Senator Barack Obama, it is impossible to avoid amplifying any comment, image, or news in the digital age.

Consider for instance, the YouTube impressions—quickly measured in the millions—spawned by Obama's Chicago pastor, the Reverend Jeremiah Wright. Each incendiary and flamboyant sermon from this deeply opinionated religious figure created firestorms of conflict, controversy, and anxiety. Many Americans questioned whether Obama shared Wright's radical and much-exposed views when he sat in his church pew.

In turn, this episode demanded the Obama campaign urgently respond and reassure voters with equal if not greater impact. Stunningly, by delivering a powerful speech on religion and race in Philadelphia in mid-campaign—and again digitally transmitted around the world instantly—Obama turned the tide of influential and popular opinion and judgment to declare himself his own man. Voters, for the most part, accepted his word.

Few can forget also Barack Obama's 2008 self-inflicted campaign misstep in California, when speaking to a private fundraiser in San Francisco.

In his comments, he appeared to label small-town Pennsylvanians as bitter and clinging to their religion and guns when times are hard. Casual comments or cynical observations like these (and worse) of course, have very often been said by political candidates and observers. Most are rarely seen or largely overlooked and underreported. In this instance, however, a citizen journalist, armed with video and audio recording technology, not only captured the comments but was able to make them accessible worldwide within minutes.

What might have been an unfortunate but forgettable gaffe turned into disastrous remarks heard round the world. For weeks to come, the Obama campaign and the candidate again found themselves in urgent recovery mode, working to repair the damaging impressions especially in rust-belt and small-town America, where anger brewed.

The two historic incidents—a half-century apart—tell the tale of a starkly changed digital media environment, where channels all have merged, and digital imagery, voice, and news travel faster and farther than we ever dreamed. For communicators, it is indeed a blessing and curse—reminding us of our responsibility to get it right because everyone else will very likely get it fast.

Eternity

If we again turn back the media pages to mid-century America, we are reminded how major wire services, big-city newspapers, and television networks amassed power and giant audiences. They not only enjoyed the reach and respect from most of us, but they also were the true "agencies of record."

What does that mean? Simply put, if these media outlets had not covered the news, reporting and archiving it, we would rarely have an extant public record or even the means to turn back the pages to explore the people, ideas, events, and calamities that made us who we are today. We relied on institutional ways to store and organize major media, and to dip into those institutional records (and libraries, of course) when we wanted to know what actually happened through the eyes of newspapers, wires, and television networks. In most instances, we depended on the preservation quality of paper, film, and chemical preservatives to keep the record whole and alive.

Why does this matter, and how has this changed? All journalists when they sit down to write a story—whether an obituary, election coverage, an accident or natural disaster, an award or criminal conviction—understand that events or hooks lead up to the latest development. For example, if you were employed at a large newspaper or wire service, or perhaps at a television affiliate, you had limited yet available ways to dredge up the past stories in a newspaper "morgue" or a video library and use the information as *then reported* to flesh out details for the latest news story.

But in any archive or ledger or news footage storage there remain gaps and holes and omissions and, certainly, losses of information as well. Not all gaps can be filled in, and, of course, not all news stories archived were completely or competently reported and preserved. And with the demise of major news organizations, even some of these relics of news archival storage today may be lost or at least overlooked.

Archiving was certainly an inconsistent and idiosyncratic practice that challenged us all to find, retrieve, and reuse media when relevant to our needs. These means were imperfect and ephemeral, which simply meant that news—in all its forms—was preserved in isolated and fragmentary ways and was not widely available to all.

In the digital era, information now may be said to be eternal and much more often universally accessible. Once captured and shared, words and images have a permanence (and again, ubiquity) that we never imagined possible. It is probably inconceivable today for professionals—or political candidates or corporations or film stars, for that matter—to rewrite messy chapters of their past or to paper over embarrassments since those very details (and graphic documentation) will likely live much longer than they will.

Although many of us today fail to commit our thoughts to paper or to write personal letters any longer, we instead have captured most of the very intimate details of our own lives and the lives of others in digital photography, social network blogs, and shared Web sites, making it quite simple to track and report on our lives forevermore.

For communicators and for our messages, we see now that the first draft of history—which has long been labeled news—may indeed be history itself. First drafts as well as final drafts today have a way of making their permanent record in digital media.

As a public relations practitioner for more than three decades, I have witnessed firsthand many of these dramatic changes and the continued evolution of media channels. Like my colleagues everywhere, I must work harder than ever to adapt to and embrace these new realities in the digital age to reach virtual and global audiences with clear, convincing, and successful messages.

NOTES

1. Walter Isaacson, "How to Save Your Newspaper," *Time*, February 5, 2009, http://www.time.com/time/business/article/0,8599,1877191,00.html.

2. Paul Taylor, Cary Funk, and April Clark, "Americans and Social Trust: Who, Where, and Why," Pew Research Center, February 21, 2007, http://pewresearch .org/assets/social/pdf/SocialTrust.pdf.

10

DIGITAL DIRECT

Lisa Spiller

The use of direct marketing in today's business world is booming! Direct marketing grew faster than almost every other marketing activity for the latter part of the twentieth century.[1] In the United States, sales attributed to direct marketing media, methods, and channels rose from $1.81 trillion in 2005 to $2.03 trillion in 2007.[2] These statistics strongly suggest that direct marketing has become an integral element in a marketer's arsenal worldwide. The economic impact of direct marketing is simply mind-boggling as is its recent transformation given this high-tech digital world in which we now live and work.

Although the traditional foundations of direct marketing are still applicable today, continuous innovations in technology are transforming the marketing landscape for all companies, organizations, associations, and consumers. This chapter examines the impact of the digital revolution on direct and interactive marketing processes and activities.

Decades ago, direct marketers gathered customer names and addresses, created mailing lists, established relationships with customers, and sold goods and services on a one-on-one basis to customers via mail and telephone. Today, much has changed while much has remained the same. Direct marketers are still concerned with creating relationships with each customer and maximizing customer value by serving individual customer needs on a personal basis; however, computer technology and new high-tech digital media have dramatically changed the speed and effectiveness of these activities. The innovation and growth of various online methods have produced new formats for conducting direct and interactive marketing today. While e-mail marketing is similar to direct mail in that it targets messages to customers and prospective customers one-on-one with great precision and effectiveness, it does so with much greater speed of transmission and enables an immediate customer or prospect response.

Direct marketing has always been accountable and measurable. Now with the various high-tech digital media formats and computer technology, it is more interactive, precise, and effective than ever before. The *new* media of yesterday have become mainstream media today. While we cannot begin to envision what innovations and changes are ahead, one thing is certain—traditional direct and interactive marketing principles will still apply. A vast majority of direct marketers are engaged in multichannel marketing. Although online channels show consistently higher growth rates, good old direct mail still plays an important role in the overall integrated marketing communications mix. The key is utilizing the right combination of high-tech and low-tech media when implementing direct and interactive marketing strategies. Let's explore the process of direct marketing and see how it has changed over the decades.

THE PROCESS AND TRANSFORMATION OF DIRECT MARKETING

The tools and tactics implemented when conducting direct marketing strategies have evolved over time with new and improved methods available to marketers. However, the primary concept and goals have remained the same.

Direct Marketing Process

Direct marketing is *database-driven* marketing. Its goal is to *create* and *cultivate* customers, regardless of whether these customers are consumers, buyers for industrial organizations, or potential donors or voters. It is a way to market a for-profit business or a not-for-profit organization. Its principles apply to marketing activities targeting both business consumers (B2B) and final consumers (B2C). At some time or another, virtually every business and every organization—charitable, political, educational, cultural, and civic—and even every individual uses direct response advertising and, indeed, has a database for so doing.

Direct marketing guru Edward Nash once said:

> Direct marketing is somewhat like laser surgery; a powerful, precise, and very effective tool in the hands of professionals, but a potential disaster in the hands of amateurs. We must approach it as if we are surgeons, not butchers, as if we are cabinetmakers, not carpenters.[3]

While new media like the Internet change the mechanism by which direct marketing activities are performed, its cornerstone database-driven direct response communications remain in effect today. Lists and data are at the very core of direct marketing. The quality of the targeted list or database segment is critical to direct marketing success. That success is determined by measuring response rates. The formula for success remains constant—reaching the *right* people with the *right* offer using the *right* creative approach.

The goal of direct marketers is to interact with customers on a one-to-one basis, with reference to the information obtained and stored about each customer in the customer database. Direct marketers then provide the customer with information and product/service offers that are relevant to each customer's needs and wants. But how do direct marketers identify and locate the "right" prospects? The answer: They rent lists. A list is a specifically defined group of organizations or individuals who possess common characteristics. Lists are available for almost anything and everything. The challenge for most direct marketers is to locate appropriate lists that will enable them to communicate with prospects that are likely to have a need or want for their products or services. Fortunately, this task, which was once carried out by sorting through packets and booklets of list cards, has become much easier due to the advances in technology, the availability of lists, and companies like NextMark, Inc.

NextMark, Inc., headquartered in Hanover, New Hampshire, is a leading provider of list commerce technology. NextMark's innovations include being the first to apply modern search technologies to the problem of finding mailing lists, the first to syndicate access to mailing list information through Web sites such as Direct Magazine, Multichannel Merchant, and the Direct Marketing Association, and the first to build the biggest and most up-to-date index of mailing lists in the world. NextMark offers a free online list finder service to provide access to insider information on virtually every list on the market—a total of more than 50,000 lists. Visit NextMark at www.nextmark.com and explore its list finder service to see how easy prospecting can be given today's digital online sophistication.

Indeed, the process of direct marketing has been affected by our digital revolution. Let's now explore its transformation.

Transformation of Direct Marketing

Social and economic changes have given impetus to the burgeoning rise of direct marketing since the mid-twentieth century and have been coupled with equally impressive advances in the technology used in various elements of direct marketing. A few of these technological and social advances are worth mentioning.

Credit Cards: Since the advent of credit cards during the 1950s, there has been enormous growth of both mail order and, more recently, online selling methods. Credit cards greatly enhanced and expedited these sales transactions. The ready availability of worldwide credit systems, together with rapid electronic funds transfer, has contributed to the feasibility and viability of direct and interactive marketing by simultaneously offering convenience and security.

Personal Computers: Perhaps nothing has revolutionized direct marketing more than computing technology. Personal computers have made possible the record keeping, work operation, and model building that are so much a part of the art and science of direct marketing. The complex maintenance of lists and the retrieval of data associated with them are but two examples of the computer's contribution. The processing of orders and the maintenance of inventories are others. And, of course, the use of highly sophisticated analysis can mean the difference between direct marketing success and failure. The computer's contributions of great speed, lower-than-human error, and low cost have made it indispensable to users of direct marketing.

Changing Consumer Lifestyles: As travel becomes more expensive and communication becomes less expensive, there is further impetus to the use of e-mail, telephone, and the Internet. Mailed catalogs, Web sites, and toll-free telephone numbers provide the convenience of shopping at home. Further, as more women have entered the work force, families are placing a greater emphasis on time utilization. Once a leisurely pastime, shopping has become more of a chore, especially for the majority of households in which both spouses work. The advent of mail order and the World Wide Web have made anytime day-or-night shopping even more convenient for these working spouses.

Negative Aspects of Retailing: Many consumers enjoy shopping in traditional retail stores. However, a strong belief in a number of negative aspects is associated with traditional retail shopping. Some of these include inadequate parking facilities; concerns about safety; long walking distances; uninformed sales clerks; difficulties in locating retail sales personnel; long waiting lines at check-out; in-store congestion; difficulty in locating certain sizes, styles, or colors of products; and the hassle of juggling packages out of the retail stores. For consumers with this mind-set, catalog and online shopping, with all of their modern methods and conveniences, have been a welcome alternative.

The Internet: The Internet has permeated virtually all direct marketing strategies and tactics. Perhaps nothing has had a greater impact on the conduct of business today. There has been a major increase in diversity of non-store retailing, especially since the advent of online shopping. Mail-order catalogs are being used, now more than ever, to generate transactions at both store locations, called "bricks" retailers, and other non-store, online retailers, called "clicks" retailers. Catalogs have been responsible for generating a great deal of Internet traffic and telephone orders, too. It is clear that the advent of the Internet, together with its World Wide Web, has ushered in a whole new type of "store."

Many of the traditional store retailers capitalized on their recognizable brands and images and expanded their distribution with mail order and Web sites. A multimedia and multichannel synergy also has developed embracing all forms of media. Personal computers have provided electronic access to what may become the most powerful medium of all: the Internet. The Internet has driven several recent trends in direct marketing, such as the interaction of *bricks* and *clicks*. Rapid advances in technology have encouraged this, as have changing lifestyles. More and more, direct marketing has become characterized as multimedia and multichannel.

Web sites make available an endless array of information for those who want it and for those who prefer to shop at their leisure and convenience, just as they have been doing for some time with mail-order catalogs and direct-mail offers. A notable example of this is Internet pioneer Amazon.com. Amazon.com has mastered the art and science of direct marketing in a way that has demonstrated the lifetime value of a customer. Amazon.com has built great market valuation in the form of a database with millions of active customer records. Amazon.com is utilizing the Internet to obtain customer knowledge, enabling the company to profile its customers and determine prospective customers. At the same time, they are predicting future behavior and using promotional strategies that will not only drive prospects to its Web site but also engage prospects in meaningful and ongoing transactions once there. Integral to Amazon's success is a database of customers and their transactions. Amazon uses its customer database for continuity selling (which encourages customers to make a repeat purchase at a regular interval of time— monthly, quarterly, etc.) and cross-selling (where related and unrelated products/services are sold to an existing customer base). Continuity selling and cross-selling to Amazon.com visitors enhance customer relationships in a variety of ways. For example, the following customized messages can be sent to each customer:

- "Customers who bought this book also bought: . . . "
- "Our auction sellers recommend: . . . "
- "Look for similar books by these subjects: . . . "
- "This book is especially popular in these places: . . . "
- "We've included the top five titles for your browsing pleasure below. (At least these were the top five as of when we sent this message.)"

In summary, the above technological and social factors have served to not only popularize the use of direct and interactive marketing over the years, but they have also affected the way direct and interactive marketing activities are carried out today. Let's now investigate how direct marketing has been affected by the high-tech digital revolution.

HIGH-TECH DIGITAL REVOLUTION

The proliferation of telephone usage (wired and wireless) has been augmented by access via computers to the Internet and its World Wide Web. Though its inventor, Tim Berners-Lee, developed the Web in 1989 to enable information to be shared among particle physicist researchers, it subsequently grew into a huge virtual marketplace. It's become an exciting environment for targeted, measurable, response-generating direct marketing.

There have been advances as well in other electronic communication involving cable, satellite, and interactive television. Certainly a major media breakthrough has been the technology of the Internet and World Wide Web. Especially in tandem with print and broadcast media, direct response advertising entices buyers to visit well-structured Web sites.

The Internet has surely changed the way most consumers make purchases and most companies conduct business today. Research shows that $19.2 billion was forecast for Internet marketing (non-e-mail) expenditures in 2007. This figure, combined with an expected annual growth rate of 15.6 percent, is expected to rise to $39.7 billion in 2012.[4]

The Internet also has the fastest growth and acceptance rates of technological media. Consider the time it has taken these technologies to reach 50 million users: telephone—40 years; radio—38 years; cable television—10 years; the Internet—5 years.[5] As of November 2007, there were more than 237 million Internet users in North America, nearly a 71 percent population penetration rate.[6] To obtain an update of these statistics, visit Internet World Statistics at www.internetworldstatistics.com. These statistics underscore the importance of the Internet to marketers. Marketers must clearly understand all aspects of the Internet if they are going to be successful in taking full advantage of this new enabling technology and integrating it into their promotional mix. Let's examine some of the applications of Internet marketing.

Direct Marketing Applications of Internet Technology

Direct marketers have been performing marketing activities for decades without the Internet, but now due to technological advances, they are able to transfer their knowledge and experience to this relatively new interactive marketing medium. It is also clear to many companies that merely having a "Web presence" is not enough. What it takes to succeed in this electronic marketplace is a clear plan for the organization to follow and execute, along with a strong commitment of both human resources and capital for the technological infrastructure to support the various online direct marketing activities.

Most companies and organizations not only have a Web site, but are actively employing direct and interactive online marketing strategies.

There are many applications of high-tech digital media—e-mail marketing, online market research, behavioral market segmentation, micro-targeting, Web advertising, Web site promotion, and e-branding are some of the chief applications. Let's briefly discuss each.

E-mail Marketing: E-mail is a part of the Internet that is separate from the Web. It is electronic communication that travels all over the world via the Internet, but is not a part of the World Wide Web. Because sending e-mail messages is easy, cheap, and fast, some companies have misused this medium. Spam, or unsolicited e-mail messages, is considered the "junk mail" of the Internet. Direct marketers can avoid sending spam by handling customer information carefully and adhering to ethical e-mail marketing practices. Providing a way for consumers to "opt-in" to a mailing list is a starting point for practicing ethical e-mail marketing. Direct marketers must keep abreast and follow the ever-changing rules for using e-mail as a marketing medium. When done right, an e-mail campaign can build profitable customer relationships at a fraction of the cost of other direct marketing methods. However, e-mail marketing programs are most effective when combined with other digital media.

Online Market Research: Technology has made marketing information readily available, easy to access, current, and affordable. It has transformed secondary data collection into a highly effective and relevant marketing activity. Much of the information available online, such as government reports, is free of charge, which enables marketers of any size to access and obtain this valuable market data. The main cost involved in conducting online market research is the human resource costs, because it requires manpower to surf the Net and identify and download relevant information.

Primary data collection has also been enhanced by technological progress. Consumers seem to be more receptive to participating in surveys conducted via the Internet as opposed to mail and telephone surveys. Thus, the Internet offers an alternative medium for executing marketing research studies on a one-to-one basis with customers. Some of the more common primary data collection techniques being implemented online include online surveys and online panels.

Behavioral Market Segmentation: Once upon a time a customer database was the primary method for obtaining behavioral data about customers to be used for market segmentation. However, advances in Internet technology have offered direct marketers additional methods by which behavioral data can be obtained. The actions taken by consumers are certainly a viable base for market segmentation. The specific types of products and services consumers have purchased, the time the transactions took place, the method or location of their purchases, and the method of payment they choose can all reveal similarities among consumers. Each behavioral factor can indicate a consumer preference that may be shared by other consumers, consequently identifying a market segment.

Direct marketers have been using behavioral data for segmenting markets for centuries. However, due to the Internet, the amount of behavioral data and the speed with which it can be obtained has increased a great deal. Today direct marketers often rely on "cookies" to segment consumers based on their online activity. A cookie is an electronic tag or identifier that is placed on a personal computer. Cookies are a tool for recognizing Web users again after they have interacted with a marketer's Web site in some capacity. The process is quite simple: whenever a Web site visitor makes a request to a Web server, that server has the opportunity to set a cookie on the personal computer that made the request. The Web site host can then use the cookie for tracking beyond the initial click to determine how often that visitor returns to the Web site, the length of time of each visit, and the particular Web pages visited, which can often detail the specific products or services in which the visitor is interested. Cookies provide valuable insight into consumer behavior, which can be used effectively to segment the consumer market.

Micro-Targeting: Targeting consumers and prospects with specific messages that resonate with each narrowly defined group or individual is micro-targeting. Micro-targeting is creating and delivering directly to customers customized messages, proof points, and offers, and accurately predicting their impact. The Internet permits marketers to send customized messages to specific groups and individuals and to use online discussions and instant messaging to support their promotional efforts.

Let's look at a specific example of how micro-targeting is being used. In today's sophisticated world, political organizations are using unique analytical tools, such as micro-targeting, to create specific offers designed to woo voters. Political micro-targeting, also referred to as "narrowcasting," is aggregating groups of voters based on data about them available in databases and on the Internet—to target them with tailor-made messages.[7] Political parties gather personal information about voters to deliver narrowly targeted messages calculated to influence their votes. Micro-targeting goes beyond traditional segmentation bases to gather data at the individual level. This information can include magazine subscriptions, real estate records, consumer transaction data, demographics, lifestyle data, geography, psychographics, voter history, and survey response data. Micro-targeting can add great value to political marketing activities.

Political micro-targeting is being used by both the Democratic and Republican political parties to determine which voters care about specific campaign issues. For example, research has shown that all people who regularly attend church are not alike. Political micro-targeting can be used to identify those churchgoers who would be more interested in hearing a Democratic message of social justice.[8] Given that direct and interactive marketing messages can be personalized and delivered to individuals on a one-to-one basis, micro-targeting is seen as a powerful tool for directing appropriate messages to voters. In conclusion, political micro-targeting helps campaigns to deliver more effective messages to specific individuals and households by tracking and analyzing information on a person-by-person basis. The Internet makes this process much more timely and effective.

Banner Advertising is the digital analog to print ads, targeting a broad audience with the goal of creating awareness about the product or service being promoted. Banner ads are similar to space ads used in print media; however, they have video and audio capabilities because they are designed for interactive media. There are a variety of sizes standardized per the Interactive Advertising Bureau. Those primary sizes include rectangles, pop ups, banners, buttons, and skyscrapers. There are also standards for digital video ad formats. Visit www.iab.net to learn more about the latest standards in banner advertising.

Because banner ads request an immediate action from the viewer, they are a direct-response ad, thus a form of direct marketing. The goal of banner ads is twofold: first, to increase brand awareness by exposing consumers to the banner ad, and second, to maximize the "click-through" rates. Click-through rates, also called "ad clicks," are defined as the number of times a user "clicks" on an online ad, often measured as a function of time ("ad clicks per day"). Typically, click-through rates are relatively low, less than 1 percent in most cases. Direct marketers must be creative to increase these rates.

Web Site Promotion: A major consideration for Internet retailers is generating traffic to their Web sites. A good many techniques have been developed to accomplish this for traditional "brick-and-mortar" retailers who have also opted to sell online. These now typically involve search engine marketing (SEM) and optimization strategies, which will be addressed in the next section.

For decades the advertising community has argued that if consumers are not aware of a company's products or services, they cannot purchase them. The same is true for a company's Web site. The theory that if you "build a better mousetrap" consumers will beat a path to your door doesn't work. Investing thousands of dollars into developing the most creative Web site means nothing—if potential customers don't know it exists. Today, many direct marketers are partnering with related product and service providers like never before. Why? Primarily due to the cross-promotion opportunities achieved by the use of Web site links made possible by the Internet.

For example, go to Apartments.com and not only can you view apartments for rent throughout the United States, but you can be linked to many services commonly related to apartment rental. The Web site provides links to moving companies, truck rental companies, banks, insurance companies, storage facilities, utility connections, furniture for rent, and much more. A good way to add links to a Web site is to explore competitor's URLs and develop a list of sites from which you should be linked. One direct marketing tip is that quality should outweigh quantity of the links offered by a Web site.

E-Branding: According to the Direct Marketing Association, the clear distinction between direct marketing and brand marketing has blurred with the digital revolution. Most companies now have a virtual storefront in the form of a Web site. Companies now have the ability to store, track, and target information on consumers like never before. Direct marketing response devices, such as URLs, toll-free numbers, and email addresses, and copy tactics like calls-to-action have found their way into television and radio spots, print ads, and almost every other type of media. Direct marketing's versatility, measurability, and undeniable return on investment have gradually garnered the respect of even the most traditional brand advertisers and agencies.[9] Direct marketers are also recognizing the importance of creating and reinforcing brand strategies at the individual level. Therefore, direct marketing and brand strategies are now viewed as complementary, and when applied correctly, they can create a synergistic marketing effect.

Today, most direct marketers incorporate high-tech digital media into their media mix to reach and interact with customers and prospects. The next section overviews these new media formats.

High-Tech Digital Media Formats

Modern direct marketing is high tech and is able to generate huge amounts of information for businesses and organizations. While information has become a key business resource, the ability to access, understand, and effectively use that information is a necessity for success in today's economy. This stresses the importance of interactivity and acknowledges that direct marketing will continue to evolve with technological advances. New high-tech digital formats and strategies are emerging daily. Some of the most recent ones include SEM, blogging, online social networking and mobile marketing. Let's now briefly explore each of these formats.

Search Engine Marketing: SEM is the entire set of techniques and strategies used to direct more visitors from search engines to marketing Web sites. Optimization is the *process* of improving Web site traffic by utilizing search engines. In general, when the link to a Web site is listed in a higher position on the search engine results page, the user is more likely to view it. Thus, search engine optimization aims at moving the Web site link to one of the top links on the search results page. The four most common purposes for SEM use include increasing or enhancing brand awareness of products or services; selling products, services or content directly online; generating leads; and driving traffic to a Web site. Research shows more than 85 percent of companies are listed on at least one search engine.[10] SEM is a new strategic marketing weapon for direct marketers in enabling consumers and prospective consumers to easily locate and visit their Web sites.

Blogging: The word "blog" is short for "Weblog." Blogs refer to Web sites that contain up-to-date, continuous information posted for all viewers to read.[11] The primary goals of blogs include creating public awareness, increasing viral marketing activity, and generating Web site traffic. Check out General Motor Company's Fastlane Blog featuring GM Vice Chairman Bob Lutz and other GM executives at http://fastlane.gmblogs .com/about.html. This blog effectively utilizes video images of new vehicles and new features. Other auto manufacturers are using blogging strategies as well. Blogging is another new high-tech media format being used by many direct marketers to generate Web site traffic and to interact with customers and prospects.

Online Social Networking: The Internet is greatly facilitating a rapidly developing new avenue for online advertising: online social networking. This marketing strategy occurs when a person or company publishes its information on an online social community such as: Facebook, YouTube, MySpace, or Friendster. Posting information on these sites allows the user to update current news, features, or interesting statistics. Viewers of the site can post comments on the page that the user created. The end result of online social networking is to increase traffic to the social community site, create inbound links, and increase traffic to the users own Web site by creating a Web page in the social community.[12] To view some examples of online social networking on MySpace, visit http://www.wolf-howl .com/seo/marketing-examples-on-myspace/. Social networking spending is expected to continue to increase. Social networking spending on advertisements may even reach $4 billion in 2011.[13] The growth of social networks has prompted popular social networking sites Facebook and MySpace to team up with agencies to use and deploy these social network communities for advertising purposes.

Online social networking, combined with the proliferation of entertainment and information, might be the drivers of high-tech digital marketing. Online social networking not only generates large quantities of Web traffic, but the information and entertainment value motivates consumers to stay online longer and to return more often. Therefore, online social networking is certainly a valuable high-tech digital format for direct marketers.

Mobile Marketing: Mobile marketing refers to marketing on mobile or cellular phones, ranging from anything including advertising to text-messaging voting campaigns. How do most people view mobile marketing? A Harris Interactive research study found that 90 percent of people interviewed said they were not interested in receiving ads on their mobile phones.[14] However, keep in mind that when the Internet first started in the 1990s, there was much debate as to whether or not companies should be able to advertise online. Now, almost everyone partakes in online advertising activities. With this in mind, mobile marketing is a form of advertising that may be the norm tomorrow. It is estimated that mobile advertising spending will reach \$4.76 billion by 2011.[15] AirG, a company that develops mobile communities for Sprint and other services, generated more than 20 billion mobile advertising impressions (basically slots for advertisers) in 2006, but sold less than 2 percent of that inventory.[16] In order to encourage consumer adoption of mobile marketing, Virgin Mobile USA announced a product to consumers promoting the opportunity to earn extra airtime minutes in exchange for allowing third parties to advertise to their mobile phones.[17] Research shows that over a third of adult mobile phone users say they are willing to accept incentive-based advertisements, with 78 percent indicating a preference for cash incentives.[18]

Even though a large number of people currently do not prefer mobile marketing, others are interested in receiving advertisements and promotions via their mobile phones. These consumers vary in their preferred contact methods for receiving mobile marketing promotions. Research shows 56 percent of consumers prefer receiving text messages, 40 percent prefer picture messages, 24 percent opt for videos, 23 percent prefer ads transferred automatically to e-mail, 22 percent prefer voicemail messages, while the remaining 7 percent prefer "other" methods.[19] Research also shows that approximately 35 percent of children age 8—12 years own a mobile phone, with 20 percent having used text messaging and 21 percent having used ringtones.[20] This demonstrates the potential impact mobile marketing can have targeting the consumers of tomorrow. Direct marketers will be quick to add this new high-tech digital format to their media mix as soon as consumers become interested in receiving direct response communication via their mobile phones.

In summary, many companies and organizations are now including new high-tech digital formats in their media mix because these formats are effective and often cost much less than more traditional media options. Let's take a look at how an entrepreneur was able to effectively use high-tech media and savvy direct and interactive marketing strategies to launch her new business venture. This is the Internet success story of Meredith Hines and TreadMoves.

TreadMoves: An Internet Success Story

TreadMoves has provided a much-needed rejuvenation for the most popular piece of home exercise equipment today—the treadmill. The TreadMoves video series, as shown in Figures 10.1, a–d, consists of many different workouts to meet the needs of different target market segments. TreadMoves provides so many new moves and combinations from which to choose that treadmill exercisers never have to do the same workout twice.

Figure 10.1a

Used with Permission of Meredith Hines, TreadMoves™

Figure 10.1b

Used with Permission of Meredith Hines, TreadMoves™

Figure 10.1c

Used with Permission of Meredith Hines, TreadMoves™

Figure 10.1d

Used with Permission of Meredith Hines, TreadMoves™

In 2001, Meredith Hines, a 24-year-old graduate student with an intense passion for health and fitness, founded TreadMoves. Hines lacked the financial backing needed to mass market her exercise videos through traditional retail channels or to advertise via traditional mass media—fitness magazines, newspapers, and television. Her challenge was to create the look of a professional and credible business on a very limited budget. Given this considerable financial constraint, certain decisions were critical to the viability of the business. Some of these key decisions included determining how to conduct marketing research, how to promote the videos to target consumer segments, how to select marketing channels for product distribution, and how to measure the effectiveness of the marketing techniques she utilized. Direct marketing techniques via the Internet provided the solution to each of her needs.

The Internet provides a wealth of general market data such as industry trends. However, gathering very specific information about customer segments and demographics is very expensive to purchase and was not an option for TreadMoves. So, the TreadMoves team used chat rooms to gather this specific type of information. In order to find the right types of chat rooms, the TreadMoves team searched the Internet for sites that hosted chat rooms related to fitness, weight loss, and exercise videos. One of the Web sites that the TreadMoves team discovered was VideoFitness.com—a Web site that is dedicated to people who work out at home with exercise videos.

This site has a very robust chat room with thousands of members who participate in discussions on a wide range of topics. The TreadMoves team read through many discussion threads (which are groups of posted comments that are responding to one original question or posted comment) to gather information about demographics and consumer behavior. This information heavily influenced the exercise content of the initial set of videos.

Once the first two TreadMoves videos were available for sale, the TreadMoves team visited the VideoFitness.com Web site and was actually able to read discussion threads about their own videos. The information gathered from these threads allowed the TreadMoves team to tailor new videos and products to the needs of their targeted customer segments and ultimately create even better products. Once the videos were on the market, it was time to actively employ promotional strategies. Promotion objectives for TreadMoves were twofold—first, to generate awareness of the videos and, second, to stimulate product purchase. Figure 10.2 demonstrates other promotional activities included the development of a Web site to be used for both promotion and selling. The TreadMoves team mailed complimentary copies of the new videos to the Webmasters of the chat rooms for them to review. Once the Webmasters posted their reviews of the workouts, the Webmasters' reviews intrigued the members of the chat rooms enough for them to visit the TreadMoves Web site and buy their own copies. Once the members of the chat rooms tried and loved

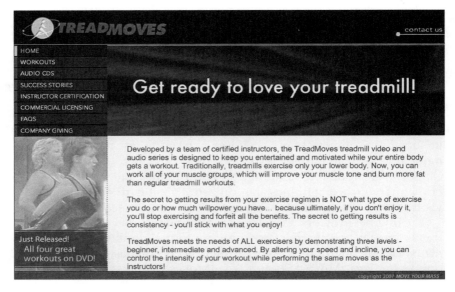

Figure 10.2
Used with Permission of Meredith Hines, TreadMoves™

the workouts, they posted their own discussion threads about Tread-Moves and generated additional traffic to the TreadMoves Web site, which further sold the videos to other chat room members.

Once the initial market introduction was made via the Internet, the team researched several other promotional methods, such as acquiring lists of e-mail addresses, placing banners on related Web pages, and buying magazine advertising space; however, the costs of each of these methods was prohibitive. Therefore, the TreadMoves team decided to focus its promotional efforts on database marketing activities. Information about each customer who purchased products from the Web site or inquired about information was captured in the database. When the second set of videos was ready for market introduction, all current customers and inquirers were sent an introductory e-mail offer to be the first to try out the new TreadMoves workouts. The response to this offer was very good—it garnered a 20 percent return within two days.

In addition, the company developed customer profiles and used them to enable the identification of prospective buyers who possessed characteristics similar to those of the TreadMoves customers. The TreadMoves team then surfed the Internet in an attempt to compile lists of prospective buyers. Each customer and prospect also received information or news related to TreadMoves. For example, when TreadMoves was ranked in the top 10 videos in 2002 by *Fitness* magazine, an e-mail message was sent to each customer and prospect in the TreadMoves database.

The TreadMoves team constantly used their database to interact with their customers and prospects. In addition to promoting new products or sharing newsworthy information, the TreadMoves Web site encouraged feedback from its customers and provided answers to customer questions about fitness. Such interaction strengthened customer relationships and enhanced the value of the TreadMoves brand. As a result of being able to demonstrate significant Web site traffic as well as a 30 percent repeat purchase rate, the TreadMoves team investigated other channels of distribution. Within two years, TreadMoves began selling via multichannel direct marketing. In addition to the TreadMoves Web site, customers could purchase the videos from multiple catalogs (such as *Collage Video*), through online retailers (such as Amazon.com), and via bricks-and-mortar retailers (such as Barnes & Noble retail stores). As of May 2008, TreadMoves has sold more than 20,000 videos worldwide and continues to get recognition from top fitness publications, such as *Fitness* magazine. Thus, direct and interactive marketing via the Internet has proven to be a very profitable marketing strategy for TreadMoves.

Conclusion

Just as the Internet has surely changed the way most consumers make purchases today, the high-tech digital revolution has certainly had a remarkable influence on the conduct of direct and interactive marketing activities. Although there are many applications of digital direct marketing today, many more have not yet been discovered or envisioned. However, as with any direct marketing medium, accountability and measurability will remain the key characteristics of all direct marketing strategies. New high-tech digital formats and strategies are emerging daily. Who knows what new digital formats and strategies future technological changes will bring?

NOTES

1. Herbert Katzenstein and William S. Sachs, *Direct Marketing*, 2nd ed. (New York: Macmillan Publishing, 1992).

2. *The Power of Direct Marketing*, 2007–2008 ed. (New York: The Direct Marketing Association, 2008), 22.

3. Edward L. Nash, *Database Marketing: The Ultimate Marketing Tool* (New York: McGraw-Hill Books, 1993).

4. See Note 2, 58.

5. Eloise Coupey, *Marketing and the Internet* (Upper Saddle River, NJ: Prentice Hall, 2001), 5.

6. *Internet Usage and Population in North America* Internet World Stats, http://www.internetworldstats.com/stats14.htm (March 7, 2008).

7. ''Political Microtargeting,'' SourceWatch, 2008, http://www.sourcewatch.org/index.php?title=Political_microtargeting (May 19, 2008).

8. "The 2008 Tools Campaign: Microtargeting," New Politics Institute, http://www.newpolitics.net/content_areas/new_tools_campaign/microtargeting (April 29, 2008).

9. *The Integration of DM & Brand*, 2007 ed. (New York: The Direct Marketing Association, 2007), xxiii.

10. *The Statistical Fact Book 2006* (New York: The Direct Marketing Association, Inc., 2006), 113.

11. What is a "Blog"?, Word Press, http://codex.wordpress.org/Introduction _to_Blogging (March 3, 2008).

12. *Online Social Marketing Guide*, Web Duck Designs, http://www.Webduck designs.com (March 10, 2008).

13. *eMarketer: Social Networking Ad Spend to Hit $4 Billion by 2011*, Mashable, http://mashable.com/2007/12/14/social-networking-ad-spending (March 23, 2008).

14. *Incentives Key to Mobile Marketing*, EMarketer, March 2007 http://www .emarketer.com (March 10, 2008).

15. Ibid.

16. Stephanie Mehta, "How Marketers Plan to Invade Your Phone," *CNN Money*, February, 2007, http://money.cnn.com/2007/02/14/magazines/fortune/mehta _pluggedin_mobilemarketing.fortune/index.htm (March 10, 2008).

17. See Note 14.

18. Ibid.

19. Ibid.

20. *One-Third of US Tweens Own a Mobile Phone*, Nielsen Mobile, December, 2007 http://www.marketingcharts.com (March 10, 2008).

11

MASS-SERVICING OF MICROMARKETS

Robert Rose

Marketing is in crisis—2009 was the year to reset. All our businesses got a little smaller in 2009—if not physically smaller, then at least a reduced appetite in our marketing or strategic plans for expansion. It was the year of change, and not just because of the U.S. presidential election but because of vast changes the year brought to entire industries. The first definition of "crisis" is "a stage in a sequence of events at which the trend of all future events, esp. for better or for worse, is determined; turning point."[1]

A Chinese proverb says "crisis is an opportunity riding the dangerous wind." So, while 2009 was a year of stressful crisis, it was also a year that teed up unprecedented opportunity for our market strategy. It established an opportunity for us to fundamentally change the way we service our markets and manage our businesses. In fact, Thomas Friedman, author of *Hot, Flat and Crowded*, came to the conclusion that "the market and Mother Nature both hit the wall in 2008/2009. We need growth; we need ways to raise people's standards of living."[2] He goes on to suggest that what we need is a "Great Disruption," something that will give us the ability to—in my words—completely reboot.

Now, the sea change is evident in traditional business, and the influences of Web 2.0 and beyond are affecting it, becoming significantly more pronounced. Entire sectors, such as periodicals, newspapers, book stores, and consumer electronic retail outlets are threatened with extinction. Others, such as record companies, broadcast television, software companies, and advertising agencies are undergoing fundamental changes. Entire job categories such as journalist, professional photographer, videographer, publisher, editor, and Web designer, are going the way of the linotypist, stenographer, and elevator operator.

The pace of change is quickening. In fact, in 2004, former U.S. Education Secretary Richard Riley was quoted as saying that "none of the top 10 jobs that will exist in 2010 exist today."[3] 2010 possibly marks the first time in history when graduates are taking jobs in categories that didn't even exist when they first entered college. Today, we are currently preparing kids for jobs that don't exist and that will use technology that hasn't yet been invented.

These changes are fundamentally affecting the way we run our businesses and are transforming our marketing strategy. One of the largest changes will be in how we approach defining and servicing our markets. The Web is completely changing the speed, efficiency, and ease with which consumers can engage with each other; as well as the products and services they consume. This new engagement of the consumer, their relationship to one another, and the networks that consume our products and services are directly correlated to every single aspect of our business. It will define how accountants will account, marketers will market, service people will service, and even how CEOs engage with their boards and shareholders.

As Jeremiah Owyang, a Forrester senior analyst, said in an interview with *CRM* Magazine in 2009 talking about the growth of Social Networking and its effect, "the community will take charge. Social networking will only continue to facilitate the power shift toward the consumer."[4] It's worth repeating: marketing is in crisis, but that crisis is an extraordinary opportunity for us.

THE NEW OPPORTUNITY

As social networks begin to form using the Web as the method to communicate, the old lines of hierarchical relationships between business and consumer begin to blur substantially. Every one of these groups becomes a powerful ally or enemy depending on our actions. All of them will be constantly in flux—developing levels of trust and transparency to filter information and determine buying decisions. They will expand and collapse with great frequency, and it will all happen with or without our participation. Seth Godin discusses this at length in his book *Tribes* when he says: "[E]veryone is not just a marketer—everyone is now also a leader. The explosion in tribes, groups, covens and circles of interest means that anyone who wants to make a difference can."[5]

It is up to us as business managers to create and build these groups so that they work optimally for us. This is not manipulation, and it's not a "Lord of the Flies" capricious takeover of power just to ensure our survival. Whether it's called a "flattened earth" by Thomas Friedman, "acquiring 1,000 fans" as Kevin Kelly has blogged,[6] "building a Tribe," as Godin has written,[7] or developing your "fanatics" as Guy Kawasaki has written[8], technology has empowered people to access markets much more efficiently. And new tools, including the Web, have made the relationship between buyer and seller much more fluid. Therefore the environment is much more competitive, much more transparent, and it provides for much greater opportunity. It is, as the Chinese proverb would say—an opportunity riding the dangerous wind.

As we look to the future, how do we approach a new market service strategy? How does this affect the market strategy function within our organization? Before we address these questions, let's frame the conversation by looking at the evolution of the Web and how it has affected our market strategy thus far.

THE THREE EVOLUTIONS OF THE WEB MARKET STRATEGY

Despite the 2.0 moniker that has been placed on it recently, in the Web's relatively short history, business strategy—and especially market strategy—has evolved at least three times and may even be currently evolving into a fourth.

Evolution 1: Microservicing Mass Markets—Catching the Wave and Surfing

The first evolution of Web strategy, circa 1995–1999, was the fascination with the new bright shiny Internet, and the natural extension of direct marketing and leveraging the Internet as a more cost-efficient method to reach a massive number of consumers. During this period, businesses were just starting to experiment with putting their businesses online—and the focus was to make Web sites functional. The main driver for Web strategy was how to extend the organization's function in this new, vast online world. Leveraging the Web site for marketing was still nascent. The strategy was almost single-minded about extending the function of the business, whether that was servicing clients with e-commerce, creating new types of markets with auctions, or removing the friction from traditional transactions such as banking, buying insurance, or registering for licenses.

It was the time likened to the "wild west." Companies became software developers overnight; hiring consulting firms or building internal technology teams to develop new Web technology to drive their businesses. The Web was owned by the IT department—and led by e-consultants. The traditional, large consulting firms all began building large e-business practices and new companies squarely focused on building Web infrastructures began to become large consultancies themselves.

During this time, marketers were barely thinking of how an online marketing strategy would advance their traditional business, and instead were trying to reinvent the business online for a mass market. This was the time of building a huge bubble, and it was the time of Super Bowl ads extolling the virtues of a dot-com strategy.

Barnes & Noble was the quintessential example of this attempt at reinvention during the first evolution. In 1999, the term "bricks and clicks" was all the rage. Traditional stores were reinventing themselves as separate, hipper, online versions. Barnes & Noble spun out BN.com as a separate online store to sell books and took the separate company public. In May 1999, BN.com went public and raised more than $430 million with its IPO, selling 24 million shares at $18 per share. By the end of the first day of trading, BN.com had a market capitalization of $2.52 billion dollars.[9]

To put that event into perspective, in 2003, after the dot-com bubble burst, BN.com found itself in danger of delisting from the NASDAQ stock exchange, and the traditional store offered to buy out the remaining shareholders of BN.com for about 14 percent of the original IPO price.[10]

That reinvention also changed the paradigm for how business could be conducted online. Certainly there were the BN.com and Pets.com sock puppet—driven debacles. But there were also the massive successes of eBay, Amazon.com, and Google that began to redefine what businesses could be online. It was during this time that some marketers began to experiment with e-mail and banner ads as a way to drive brand awareness. The focus was on how the Internet extended your reach like never before. Is it any wonder that small dot-coms thought they could take over the world but were left sorely disappointed?

It was, in short, a microservicing of mass markets. Businesses took traditional business ideas and applied them to the Web as best they could, thinking they could leverage Web technology to provide a small service to every person on the planet. Customer service at even the early successful businesses was horrible. The models were built around trying to service the new mass market in as small a way as they possibly could to take advantage of the leverage of this new "frictionless" method of selling and operating.

Then, as the 1990s ended and Web sites began to proliferate at an ever-increasing rate, search engines like Yahoo and Google began to become the main portals for users to dive into the Internet. Consumers needed to start their journey for any given Web experience with a search because there was just too much to "surf." The dot-com implosion forced companies largely to abandon their world domination dreams and look for ways simply to leverage the Internet as yet another way to do business. From the marketing perspective, marketers turned inward and began to examine how the Web could make their marketing efforts more efficient. They began to look at search engine optimization (SEO) and manipulating Web site content to rank higher in searches. The idea of paying for performance started to become more popular. Search engine marketing or "pay per click" advertising rose. In 1998, GoTo Networks—which later became Overture Services and ultimately Yahoo Search Marketing—was the first company to provide "pay per click" advertising. Google quickly followed in 2000 with its AdWords product, and sponsored search listings contained in the search results pages became an overwhelmingly successful new advertising model. [11]

Then, as the century turned in 2000, Rick Legine, Christopher Locke, Doc Searles, and David Weinberger published "The Cluetrain Manifesto" and proclaimed "These markets are conversations. Their members communicate in language that is natural, open, honest, direct, funny and often shocking. Whether explaining or complaining, joking or serious, the human voice is unmistakably genuine. It can't be faked."[12]

This declaration of the Internet as a "two-way" street coincided with the collapse of the dot-com boom and the rise of new pay for performance advertising offerings from Google and Yahoo, and it ushered us into the second evolution.

Evolution 2: The Wave Crashes and the "Search" Begins—Microservicing of Micromarkets

This second evolution, circa 2000–2006, was the extension of businesses trying to be more and more efficient and the drive for return on investment (ROI) from online initiatives. The explosive growth of Web sites caused the continued fragmentation of traffic, and the number of Web sites able to successfully sell branded banner advertising began to fall. Marketers were frustrated with the ineffectiveness of pop-ups, pop-unders, and all forms of online display advertising. New ways of blocking advertising became popular browser plug-ins. Shortsighted publishers that had considered advertising models on their Web properties now started "giving away" advertising space as value-added advertising for the print publication. Mass marketing seemed to be failing in a big way, and the idea of "one-to-one" marketing became popular.

On the other side of the business, online chat and forums became popular ways to service customers. Companies launched "community" features to try to address the "conversational nature" of markets, developing that one-to-one relationship with consumers. These forums, or threaded discussion groups, became a way where consumers could also communicate with each other on a one-to-one basis and help not only each other but also the business by providing content that was searchable.

On the marketing side, businesses soon discovered that online search marketing was starting to pay dividends. Buying on a "pay-per-performance" basis and only paying for "leads" was a novel way to save the organization money, to take advantage of "self-selecting" consumers, and to monetize every person that came to the site. The focus was on how to convert each individual visitor and how to engage this paid traffic in a way that maximized return. It was the rise of one-to-one marketing. E-mail became a primary driver. Marketers and businesses turned to the Internet as a way to leverage a budget further, and businesses began to cut traditional media in favor of new media—especially e-mail and pay-per-click campaigns.

This search for efficiency and return on investment also ignited the mass fascination with search engine optimization. As the costs for search engine marketing began to rise based on demand, the effort to drive down those costs using a concerted search engine optimization strategy took hold. If marketers could appear on the front page of Google, they wouldn't have to bother buying the key word.

This fanaticism with ROI was only increased in the early 2000s with a mild recession that was felt across most Western countries. The United States was more particularly affected in 2002 and 2003.[13]

Although most economists theorized it was more broadly based, the general feeling was that this downturn was the dot-com hangover from the bursting of the bubble. It was during this time that there was a real focus on interactivity on the Web. Self-publishing (or blogging) became immensely popular. The kinds of communities that had sprung up to service businesses now began to spring up around topics or ideas. In 2004, O'Reilly Media and MediaLive hosted the first "Web 2.0 conference." In the opening remarks, Tim O'Reilly and John Batelle outlined their definition of Web 2.0.[14]

Theirs was both a new angle and, some argued, a new paradigm of looking at the Web as a platform—as a way for consumers to commune online and for everyone to become "publishers" of content. Then, in 2006, *Time* Magazine selected "You" as their Person of The Year; consumers who were now blogging, participating in social networks, and posting videos to YouTube were redefining the Web and markets. In that *Time* magazine story, Lev Grossman wrote:

> It's a story about community and collaboration on a scale never seen before. It's about the cosmic compendium of knowledge Wikipedia and the million-channel people's network YouTube and the online metropolis MySpace. It's about the many wresting power from the few and helping one another for nothing and how that will not only change the world, but also change the way the world changes.[15]

This opening of the Web ushered in the third and current evolution of driving Market Strategy.

Evolution 3: The Growth of "Subscribe"—Mass-Servicing of Micromarkets

This third evolution, starting circa 2006 and continuing to this day, introduced market strategists to the idea of the long tail, of the power of content as conversation—the idea of engagement and of using content as media which builds a community. This idea is to use mass servicing techniques—such as product development, traditional media, branding, and even customer service—to smaller, niche markets.

In 2004, marketers were introduced to the "long tail" in a few forms. First was *Wired* magazine's Chris Anderson's seminal article and subsequent book on the subject.[16] Anderson noted how the combination of the Internet, search, and the power of content allows a long tail of consumer interaction. Anderson's writing was followed in 2008 by Kevin Kelly's article "1,000 True Fans."[17] In his groundbreaking blog post, Kelly discussed how the long tail is a "decidedly mixed blessing for creators." He pointed out that while it provides enormous access, it also adds extraordinarily high levels of competition and thus a downward pressure on price. Kelly's solution is that an artist (or company) can find 1,000 true fans and monetize those individuals.

The long tail concept is coupled with the idea of content as conversation. The explosive growth of social media publishing platforms such as Digg and Slashdot invited consumers to "rate" the news and rank importance. Social networking platforms such as Facebook, Twitter, and blogs in general taught consumers that communication, openness, and transparency through the Web within a tight social network was much more effective than e-mail for communication or searches for information gathering. Finally, these two types of platforms were mashed together and platforms such as TripAdvisor, Yelp, and Angie's List invited consumers to converse, rate, and generally socialize around ranking restaurants, hotels, and general contractors.

The participatory Web has become a publishing platform for everyone. Everyone is now capable of publishing as much content as they want, on any given topic, and without any given rules. This is the explosive growth of what Clay Shirky has called "Publish Then Filter." In *Here Comes Everybody*, Shirky writes, "The media landscape has transformed, because personal communication and publishing, previously separate functions, now shade into one another. One result is to break the older pattern of professional filtering of the good from the mediocre before publication: now such filtering is increasingly social and happens after the fact."[18]

In short, there is simply so much content on the Web that search is ineffective as a filter. Consumers are now building trusted online networks as a filter and "subscribing" to one or more information feeds—and even searching within those feeds to find what they want to learn. User-generated content platforms such as Twitter and Facebook are all built around conversation and filtering. In other words, instead of going to the New York Public Library to find what we're looking for, we're first going and looking through all our Friend's book collections. Social networks provide us a way to link together that content in a meaningful and searchable way. But what does the "subscribe" culture mean for addressing markets?

THE MASS-SERVICING OF MICROMARKETS

The shift to mass servicing of micromarkets is having a huge effect on all aspects of business. Three basic pillars help businesses to succeed in this evolution of mass-service micromarkets.

1. Everybody's a Global Brand Strategist—But There Are a Lot of Worlds to Conquer

In this new evolution, businesses need to look at their products and services as a global brand strategist while realizing they are branding across a hundred tiny worlds rather than one large one. Marketing strategy has taught us to look at our brand strategy as something to standardize and make singular, something we should slavishly guard—that our brand should be one thing to all people. The new model prescribes that a difference between "centralized" and "standardized." Our brand should be centralized, but perhaps not completely standard across all the micromarkets we may be targeting.

In a 1983 *Harvard Business Review* article called "The Globalization of Markets," Theodore Levitt made an extraordinarily strong case for the standardization of brands across the globe.[19] He reminded us of the scenes from Iran four years earlier, where young Iranians in "fashionable French-cut trousers and silky body shirts" screamed for uprising in the name of Islamic fundamentalism. They were a small group, and the coverage that this uprising received was only available through the mainstream media coverage—and only days after any event occurred. While Levitt held out the possibility that technology would actually provide the means for companies to customize products and services on a market-by-market basis, he said "possibilities do not make probabilities."

Things have changed markedly in 25 years, but Professor Levitt's strategy remains a true one. In 2009, young Iranians again took to the streets, this time to protest "democratic" election results. But this time, they took to the streets wearing American Levi's jeans. They listen to Western Rap music and eat hamburgers at "Super Star" restaurants[20]—which look strikingly like American fast food chain Carl's Jr. Iranian youth are well versed in Western culture and brands—especially those available online. They have satellite television because they've learned to hack into it. Police regularly do sweeps on "illegal" satellite dishes that pick up Western programs— one woman was quoted, "I'm going to miss 'American Idol'."[21]

Maybe most important, these events were not broadcast from mainstream television. In fact, Western media were all but banned from the country. Instead, social networks on the Web were the primary communication method for these young people. A social community sprang up almost literally overnight on Twitter and Facebook and YouTube as millions rallied behind the community of Iranians protesting for their rights. The world, as Thomas Friedman has said, is hot, flat, and crowded.

This is but one example, and it is not necessarily a community that, as business managers, we could manage or monetize. It is, however, indicative of how fast passionate communities can arise using Web technology—and how big they can become. Consider the following: Cindy Gordon, vice president of new media and marketing partnerships for Universal Studios Orlando needed to launch the new theme park, "The Wizarding World of Harry Potter." Traditional marketing methods would have prescribed a broad, approachable, brand-centric use of television, radio, print, and online. Instead, she chose to focus the brand and the marketing on seven people. These seven people were fanatical Harry Potter fans, and they got a special glimpse of the brand. Those seven people told their community of ten thousand. Those ten thousand then wrote about it and got the attention of mainstream media. By the end of the campaign, Gordon estimates that 350 million people had been exposed to the brand; all by telling seven people.[22]

Of course, how we present our brand will differ slightly depending on whom we are approaching. Certainly, the messaging and branding was different to the fanatical Harry Potter blogger than it is to the general consumer. How then do we maintain a singular brand strategy as our markets begin to split into micromarkets or communities? This trend is very real for marketers as the uniqueness of individual communities begin to pop up and threaten a brand's existence—or at the very least provide barriers from breaking into new markets.

In "Spanning Silos—The New CMO Imperative," author David A. Aaker offers a plan of how CMOs can approach the differentiation of brand standardization and brand centralization.[23] He says, "While standardization will maximize synergy and leverage, it is not always the best or even a feasible route. There is a need to have strong marketing and brand entries in each silo market. In particular, the brand that is driving the purchase and defining the use experience in each product market should be relevant and differentiated as well as visible. The brand facing customers in a silo market should be relevant to the customers; they should consider it an option when a need arises."

This is an important distinction for businesses moving forward through this evolution of mass-servicing of micromarkets. As managers of our products and services, we need to be acutely aware of the different personas and communities growing around our products and/or services. We need to be able to service them uniquely, while maintaining a consistent master brand. If Gordon had talked down to, or had approached the fanatical Harry Potter bloggers the same way as she would approach a consumer with no knowledge of Harry Potter, this experiment would have failed. In today's messaging, the brand has to be relevant to the target community.

As business managers we need to take advantage of the same communications tools that our consumers are using and understand those tools as well as, or better than, our consumers. We need to take the "global brand strategy" approach that Levitt espoused and have the flexibility to split it into what Aaker calls silos—what I'm calling micromarkets or communities.

For example, look at what Anheuser-Busch has accomplished. While retaining its master brand of "All-American," they have launched a long-tail micromarket strategy. First, they created a hard liquor brand called Long Tail libations to market niche products. As of 2010, they have two products already on the market. One of them, Purus, is a high-end vodka that is marketed as a "'green' product with 100% organic Italian wheat cultivated by village farmers in northwest Italy." That's right, Italian villagers bringing you vodka from an American beer brand.

Anheuser-Busch's marketers have also launched micro-brews across almost 80 different segments. The company now has more than 80 brands of beer including organic beer, beer directed solely at women, beer that is available only in Texas and even a "gluten-free" beer that is a "non-allergenic" beer.[24]

First we have to understand the micromarkets that are growing around our brands, and then we need to proactively develop new ones. Then we need to feed those communities with our brand and our products in a differentiated way so that we service those communities. As is often said with micromarkets and the growing trend of social media, the conversation will happen either with us or without us. To be sure, we can develop a strategy that makes us part of the conversation. In order to do that we need the second piece.

2. Take Me to Your Leader! Who Is/Are the Connector(s) in Your Company?

As we understand where the opportunities are in developing micromarkets, one of the key drivers of success will be to develop personalities that the communities can gather around. Godin describes the opportunity in *Tribes*: "It's simple: there are tribes everywhere now, inside and outside of organizations, in public and in private, in non-profits, in classrooms, across the planet. Every one of these tribes is yearning for leadership and connection. This is an opportunity for you—an opportunity to find or assemble a tribe and lead it. The question isn't, is it possible for me to do that? Now, the question is Will I choose to do it?"[25]

Rackspace is an enterprise-level hosting service company—it provides server space, bandwidth, and services to support Web site and computer application hosting. As the company puts it on its "About" page, they "deliver enterprise-level hosting services to businesses of all sizes and kinds around the world."

Because they provide a fairly commoditized set of services (e.g., computer hardware, bandwidth, and physical and digital space) they could easily be the public storage of Web hosting. But they're not. They've purposely focused all of the attention not on server specs and bandwidth charts, but on their people—their "Fanatical Support." Every employee is known as a "Racker." It permeates the entire facility. Every Racker is solely focused on customer service no matter what the set of products or features are.

In 2009, Rackspace rolled out a new program for cloud hosting—a brand new way of hosting both Web sites as well as applications that is highly targeted to a technical audience. At the same time, Rackspace began to embrace the Social Web and make strides to provide both sales and customer service through their efforts. But this wasn't going to drive a micromarket around their cloud offering. No one in the organization was really a recognized "leader" in that space. So, they enlisted the help of Robert Scoble, a technical evangelist and author. Until he was hired by Rackspace to be their new evangelist, Scoble was best known for his book on Blogging *Naked Conversations: How Blogs Are Changing the Way Businesses Talk with Customers* and for being an evangelist for Microsoft.[26]

Rackspace is creating a community (or a tribe) around the Social Web and the idea of cloud computing—and using Scoble as a leader and connector to facilitate that community. They recognize that he's respected by the target micromarket that will gravitate to cloud computing, and instead of a large media and/or marketing campaign they are relying on grassroots community building to drive the market. They are using Scoble to mass-service a micromarket.

As business leaders, we need to think in the same way when we build our mass-servicing of micromarketing strategy. We need to understand much more deeply the process of how our organization will participate in the ongoing conversation (whether it's already happening or we will make it happen) around our product or service. Then, we need to make someone responsible for leading that community and building that micromarket to feed it.

Sometimes, as in the case of Apple, this may be best left to a dynamic CEO. But in many cases, as micromarkets begin to silo themselves into smaller and smaller units, it may be up to other individuals in our organizations to lead this charge. Who are the people who can blog about our products and services? Who can lead a community around our service? Who can facilitate leadership in our industry so that we can become an emergent expert in our business?

Answering these questions is going to lead to the creation of new job functions within the organization. Just as Rackspace didn't have an official "position" that Scoble filled, the idea that we can create special "evangelist" positions will become a key piece of our marketing cost. Whether we fill that position with an existing employee and the cost becomes the allotment of time that this employee will put toward that effort or whether we need to bring in outside help is all a function of our business and marketing strategy. But consider the addition of new types of positions in your marketing arsenal: a writer who might take the editorial lead in your organization to create content and facilitate a community or a charismatic evangelist who might make up the bulk of your marketing cost instead of another few hundred thousand dollars in television buys.

Content community and conversation is the new media buy of this evolution. That brings us to our third piece.

3. Content: The Centerpiece of the Strategy

This evolution is a process and, as much as any new process, will go as fast or as slow or as wide or as deep as your organization needs. To that end, the one common element that will drive this strategy first is content.

The idea of content as the centerpiece of a market strategy will become as central as the media strategy was in the past. Every department in the organization will have a content strategy that services the communities that it targets, and will be driven by a leader who will facilitate the conversation.

Content as market strategy will take many forms. For example, Rackspace is using Robert Scoble and his blog/community Building43.com as the main conduit. The technology you utilize will also come in all flavors. The simplest, of course, is your current Web site or your blogs. But soon, other types of content vehicles will make sense—from videos posted on video sharing sites, mobile phone applications, a Social networking community, White papers, or eBooks to even more traditional media like books or a PR news release program. They will all have in common that they are not about selling. They are not about traditional marketing. They are focused on being helpful, valuable pieces of content that enrich the community and position the business as a leader in the field.

Successful programs will focus on the process of content first. You must understand five key points before you can successfully accomplish this process of content:

- Understand who YOU are. What is your organization poised to accomplish? What are the differentiating factors of your product or service? What is your organization best at providing?
- Understand who THEY are. Who and where are the communities you are serving? Have you been neglecting them for so long that they have grown roots in other places—or are they gathering around your brand in different ways? Who are the personas that make up the variety of communities? Who are their leaders and how can you reach them? If they don't exist yet, how can they be encouraged to form? What are they passionate about?
- Provide them content. This goes beyond just an editorial calendar to include how can you feed this community to start to generate a passionate following. Do you need to provide tools to facilitate their community, or just the content to foster it? This is where the business can

strategize the difference between content that is merely helpful or facilitates an interaction vs. content that is also helpful but ultimately leads to a sale. What are the biggest interests of the communities that facilitate a natural tendency to want to purchase from the business?

- Foster the communities as they arise. Communities are fluid. They naturally grow and shrink and merge. Paying close attention to how they are growing is key—and continually monitoring them is what leads to success.
- Measure. Developing a process for measuring success of how you service the micromarkets is key. There are varying ways to accomplish this, and most depend on what the servicing is and for what community. For example, if you have a content marketing strategy, you might measure lead lift according to registrations for the content. If you have a customer service content strategy, you could measure the decrease in customer service calls vs. the traffic in the engagement community.

The overall key to this strategy is that it is brand new. The function probably doesn't even exist in your organization yet. You need to be okay with that. The amount of budget that is allotted for new content creation is going to become a significant part of the "new media" budget. Subject matter experts in the organization are going to have new responsibilities, and new processes will have to be created. This transformation won't happen overnight. But it can and should happen.

Conclusion—There Isn't One. It's a Process

In the beginning of 2009, when I first got the assignment for this chapter in the book, MySpace was still a media darling, Facebook hadn't really hit its stride—and no one except the very geekiest of geeks were talking about Twitter. Assuredly as this book comes out, already new technologies, new social networks, and new trends in how businesses will address the prospect of mass-servicing micromarkets are available.

Earlier in this chapter I suggested that we were in the third evolution of market strategy using the Web, and that we may possibly be entering a fourth. This fourth evolution would take us beyond the "subscribe" mode and into something different. If the first evolution was "surf" and evolution two was "search" and evolution three was "subscribe," I think that evolution four may be "source" (which may be pushing the "s" thing a bit far). But what I mean is that even subscribing to information provided by "trusted sources" now is getting stale. Consumers are, more than ever, developing tighter and more fluid trusted networks (that may only exist for as long as they have the need) to develop relationships when and where they need it.

One of the clear trends through the first three evolutions was the explosive expansion of information that drove consumers into the "subscribe" model. The ease with which information and content can be published to the Web forces us into the "publish then filter" mode and to align our-selves with social networks that form micromarkets.

As these networks grow to unsustainable size, the trust and transpar-ency are almost inherently reduced. Influencers leave or are replaced by new influencers who form their own networks, and the tendency for change and further fragmentation is only exacerbated by the source pro-viding the content. Bernard Lunn from *Read Write Web* pointed this out in a post asking, *Is There a Reverse Network Effect with Scale?* In it he writes, "a reverse network effect may exist: as new people join, others are moti-vated to leave. This dramatically affects the length of the competitive advantage enjoyed by these ventures."[27]

Businesses that embrace the idea of mass-servicing to micromarkets and engage a facilitator and leader and foster that community with content run the real risk of creating micromarkets that have no loyalty to the overall brand. For example, in looking again at our case of Rackspace with Robert Scoble leading the servicing of a micomarket—the company runs a real risk that without Scoble, the community would fade quickly. Another risk is that the community becomes so large that it begins to fragment into smaller net-works that begin to splinter off and look for the next leader. This is a very real challenge for the mass-servicing of micromarkets: How to scale?

You can see this happening among existing social networks today. Facebook started as the quintessential micromarket—a network of Harvard students. It was then expanded to include other students in the Boston area, and ultimately to any university student. One could argue that even then it was a micromarket that could be mass-serviced. Today, with 250 million users, Facebook (and by nature the market of Facebook users) is no longer a micromarket. It's a mass market with the capability for extracting smaller, focused communities from it. In fact, this is what Facebook's scaling strategy is now completely focused on—giving adver-tisers the ability to focus marketing on extraordinarily segmented micro-markets within the universe of Facebook's groups. [28]

Remember, relative growth has no bearing on the value of the network to the consumer. As a member of Facebook, I actually get less value based on the fact that more than half a million strangers join Facebook every day. My network of friends is relatively complete, and the noise just continues to grow—and thereby the advertising is less targeted. There is an inherent tension for us as business managers, attempting to grow our micromarkets to a relative size, but managing it just to the tipping point at which the value plateaus and we'd be better off breaking it into smaller micromarkets.

THE NEXT EVOLUTION: "REAL-TIME SOURCING," OR THE RISE OF FLASH MARKETS

Because of the trends in the size of groups, the myriad tools enabling them, and the continued ease with which information is shared and connected within groups, the next evolution may actually be the rise of temporary sourcing communities, or "flash markets." New groups and markets may form right before our eyes within our own communities. A software company servicing a micromarket of ten thousand like-minded professionals may experience a huge surge in sales when external events propel these ten thousand members to discover a brand new application for this software product.

T-shirt and memorabilia creators have recognized the value of flash markets for a long time. Outside any relatively popular rock concert, you'll always find hundreds of independent entrepreneurs taking advantage of a focused micromarket and selling their T-shirts and memorabilia not officially licensed by the artist. In 2009, when Michael Jackson unexpectedly died, an enormous micromarket was fused almost over night and sales of everything related to the singer exploded.

Now as social networks and the propagation of information becomes even more frictionless, this trend may grow for other businesses as well. Micromarkets can grow and disappear very quickly—and it will be up to our micromarket leaders/facilitators to inform our processes so that we can adapt our businesses accordingly.

ENDING THOUGHTS

If 2009 was the year to reset, then 2010 is the year of new growth—and one in which we can take advantage of the fundamental opportunity that servicing micromarkets provides. If the Chinese proverb is correct and crisis is an opportunity riding the dangerous wind, developing our process with our strategy, our leaders, and our content will keep that wind at our back.

NOTES

1. "Crisis," Random House Dictionary, 2009, http://dictionary.reference.com/browse/crisis.

2. Thomas L. Friedman, "The Great Disruption," *New York Times*, March 8, 2009, http://www.nytimes.com/2009/03/08/opinion/08iht-edfriedman.1.2067 2274.html?_r=1&scp=1&sq=great%20disruption&st=cse).

3. Roberts Jones, Kathryn Scanland, and Steve Gunderson, *The Jobs Revolution; Changing How America Works*, paperback ed. (Copywriters, Inc., 2004).

4. Jessica Tsai, "Social Media: The Five-Year Forecast," CRM Media, April 27, 2009, http://www.destinationcrm.com/Articles/ReadArticle.aspx?ArticleID =53635.

5. Seth Godin, *Tribes: We Need You To Lead Us* (Portfolio, 2008).

6. Kevin Kelly, "1,000 True Fans," The Technium, March 4, 2008, http://www .kk.org/thetechnium/archives/2008/03/1000_true_fans.php.

7. See Note 5.

8. Guy Kawasaki, *The Art of the Start: The Time-Tested, Battle-Hardened Guide for Anyone Starting Anything* (Portfolio, 2004).

9. Initial Public Offering (IPO), "More E-Commerce Companies Go Public, 1997–1999," Free Encyclopedia of Ecommerce, 2009, http://ecommerce .hostip.info/pages/583/Initial-Public-Offering-IPO-MORE-E-COMMERCE-COMPANIES-GO-PUBLIC-1997-1999.html#ixzz0MOpzAhQu.

10. Daniel Gross, "Bookworm: Barnes & Noble knows how to buy and sell . . . stocks," Slate, November 11, 2003, http://www.slate.com/id/2091098/.

11. Daniel C. Fain and Jan O. Pedersen, "*Bulletin*, December/January 2006: Sponsored Search: A Brief History," Asis&T, December/January 2006, http://www.asis.org/Bulletin/Dec-05/pedersen.html.

12. Rick Levine, Christopher Locke, Doc Searls, and David Weinberger, "The ClueTrain Manifesto," 2000, http://www.cluetrain.com/.

13. Wikipedia, "Early 2000s Recession," August 14, 2009, http://en.wikipedia .org/wiki/Early_2000s_recession.

14. Wikipedia, "Web 2.0," August 18, 2009, http://en.wikipedia.org/wiki/ Web_2.0.

15. Lev Grossman, "Time's Person of the Year: You," *Time*, December 13, 2006, http://www.time.com/time/magazine/article/0,9171,1569514,00.html.

16. Chris Anderson, "The Long Tail," *Wired*, October, 2004, http://www.wired .com/wired/archive/12.10/tail.html.

17. See Note 6.

18. Clay Shirky, *Here Comes Everybody: The Power of Organizing without Organizations* (Penguin Press, 2008).

19. Theodore Levitt, "The Globalization of Markets," *Harvard Business Review*, May/June 1983: 39–49.

20. Azadeh Moaveni, "How the 'Great Satan' Became Just Great," *Time*, November 6, 2002, http://www.time.com/time/magazine/article/0,9171,386 942,00.html.

21. Azadeh Moaveni, "Stars (and Stripes) in Their Eyes: Most of the Middle East Hates America, but Iranians See a More Appealing Image. It's Their Own President They Can't Stand," *Washington Post*, June 1, 2008, http://www.washingtonpost .com/wp-dyn/content/article/2008/05/30/AR2008053002567_2.html.

22. David Meerman Scott, "The New Rules of Viral Marketing: How Word-of-Mouse Spreads Your Ideas for Free," 2008, http://www.davidmeermanscott.com/ documents/Viral_Marketing.pdf.

23. David Aaker, *Spanning Silos: The New CEO Imperative* (Harvard Business School Press, 2008).

24. Chris Anderson, "Anheuser-Busch and the Long Tail of Beer," The Long Tail, February 2, 2007, http://www.longtail.com/the_long_tail/2007/02/anheuserbusch_a .html.

25. See Note 5.

26. Robert Scoble, *Naked Conversations: How Blogs Are Changing the Way Businesses Talk with Customers* (Wiley, 2006).

27. Bernard Lunn, "Is There a Reverse Network Effect with Scale?," ReadWrite-Web, March 16, 2009, http://www.readwriteweb.com/archives/is_there_a _reverse_network_effect_with_scale.php.

28. "Facebook," Wikipedia, August 18, 2009, http://en.wikipedia.org/wiki/ Facebook.

12

FRUGALITY 2.0: MAKING SENSE OF THE IT PARADOX BY KEEPING YOUR HEAD IN THE CLOUDS

James Elliott Brown

"When the network becomes as fast as the processor, the computer hollows out and spreads across the network."

—*Eric Schmidt, CEO of Google*

ENTER THE WORLD OF FRUGALITY 2.0

A dark horizon has come upon us. As the economic downturn unabatedly grips the world, firms of all sizes are forced to reexamine their operations in hopes of finding corners to cut or expenses to slash. This reckless abandon in order to save bottom lines, however, has produced a unique and widely discussed paradox in the world of IT. Essentially, IT units must drastically lower costs yet continue to produce innovative solutions to the problems du jour facing businesses around the globe. How can a firm stay competitive and produce these innovative solutions if resources continue to grow ever thin?

The watchdogs of IT, such as Dion Hinchcliffe, have been adamant about the fact that, due to tighter budgets, 2.0 technologies will become a priority for most organizations.[1] Thus, the extensive developments in the 2.0 world are finally gaining mainstream attention as EnterpriseClass (E-Class) users seek safety in the inexpensive models that exist throughout the Web. Can these offerings combat the dilemma facing IT suppliers? Many believe so due to the savings that can result from the unique and cost-effective ideas created by the open collaboration of the Web. While a myriad of solutions are currently floating around cyberspace, perhaps the most promising trend among the wikis, mashups, and online communities is "cloud computing."

What Is It? It Sounds Too Science-Fiction for My Taste

"Cloud computing" has been assigned many definitions, the broadest of which states that it "is any situation in which computing is done in a remote location (out in the clouds), rather than on your desktop or hand-held device."[2] While definitions vary in content and scope, a common theme is that cloud computing is a paradigm composed of multiple layers, each with various traits that distinguish one from another. This paradigm, and subsequent layers, offer IT-related products that are "provided as a service allowing users to access technology-enabled services from the internet"[3] without prior training in infrastructure management.

Put simply, cloud computing is every trend of the last decade related to IT, converging "software-as-a-service, service-oriented architecture, virtualization, utility computing, outsourcing, open source, Web 2.0, social networking"[4] and freeform collaborative communication. These resources are made deliverable over the Web (the metaphorical cloud) instead of hosted in-house by each firm. Like the timeshare computing wave a decade ago, cloud computing develops a scalable public utility from what was once an individual expense.

An easy example of this digital outsourcing is Gmail, Google's e-mail service. Instead of forcing users to host their e-mail server privately, Google provides the infrastructure and storage to each user. This service is free for their basic offering, or comes in their professional level package of applications at a cost of $50 per user. Another example of a cloud utility, one that is perhaps less recognized than others, is the Internet itself. Businesses create Web sites, pay companies to host the pages, and third-party users assign a value when accessing the information.

This is the key to cloud computing—firms using an off-site network as part of their effort to parlay information to end users. Thus, cloud computing has also gained the title of 2.0's version of outsourcing, as firms are now selling their operations to off-site IT providers in order to save the resources that were once devoted to the development and management of infrastructures.

Why on Earth Should I Care about That?

This partnership, however, comes at a significantly lower cost than "going it alone." As the adoption of cloud computing grows at an exponential rate, an increasing number of firms are becoming aware of the savings that can result when the power of the cloud is tapped. For instance, it is estimated that 80 percent of corporate IT dollars are spent on data center management.[5] Imagine if that were cut to 10 percent. Now consider the savings that can result if you no longer had to pay for upgrades or individual licenses too. What difference would that make?

Many firms (particularly Small to Medium Businesses—SMBs) have leapt into the cloud to save resources while continuing to drive growth. The precipitous fall of global capital has continued this trend, leading many to estimate a doubling of current cloud computing usage by firms of all sizes. As cloud providers continue to improve their products, the ultimate goal is producing enterprise-level packages that can accommodate the needs of large firms. The trend needs significant growth, however, before the resources are truly functional at a higher enterprise level.

For many small/midsize firms, the savings that can result from incorporating cloud operations, even if on a small scale, is overwhelmingly beneficial. Thus, while concerns may outweigh savings for large enterprises, lower-level enterprises may find the benefits too great to ignore. While this may seem to be nothing more than a trend to some, those who have shifted operations into the cloud have realized the savings that can result and are heralding the benefits they have gained since doing so.

How Do I Know What It Is When I See It?

Several ideas are at play behind the concept of "cloud computing," which has grown to become an all-encompassing term. All definitions, however, are based on the following aspects (all of which can be used to identify cloud applications from the rest of the programming universe):

- Resource provided off-site by third party
- Infrastructure investment primarily on the provider, allowing for lower IT responsibilities in-house
- Low barrier to entry; relatively no skills needed to manage
- Access through the Internet (the cloud)
- Self-healing
- Self-governing
- Highly scalable and flexible
- Cost based either by usage or per person
- Cost distributed due to economies of scale
- Real-time development
- Most often centralized, but federalization (i.e., peer-to-peer) growing in popularity
- Multiple strata; many different types of clouds offered by different vendors

Who Sells Cloud Solutions?

The appeal of cloud-based solutions has spread throughout the major IT vendor circuit. The field is currently dominated by the following providers, many of which are very familiar (providing reliability due to recognition and scale):

Amazon

Amazon was one of the pioneers in cloud computing, bursting onto the scene in 2002 with Amazon Web Services (AWS). AWS is essentially a bundle of four services, including the Elastic Compute Cloud (EC^2), which taps Amazon's extensive network of servers to offer computing solutions; Simple Storage Service (S3), which provides storage at a relatively low cost on a usage basis ($0.15 per gig of space); Simple DB for database management; and Simple Queuing Service for micropayment organization.

Google

Rivaling Amazon is Google's suite of cloud resources. Google initially started with cloud applications, such as messaging, collaboration, or on-site e-mail security tools. These services are offered at a basic level for free, or a premium package can be purchased for $50 per user. In order to compute with AWS, Google has worked to expand their cloud operations through a rigorous storage acquisition strategy, buying over 500,000 servers a year over the last three years.

The stronger infrastructure, dedicated solely to cloud development, allowed Google to release the Google App Engine in April 2008. The App Engine allows users to build and host Web applications on Google's Web servers. Applications already in heavy rotation are traffic gauges, bandwidth monitors, and CPU usage displays.

Starting with slightly over 500,000 users, the App Engine member base has since amassed over 10 million clients.

Salesforce

Salesforce.com was another forefather in the cloud computing realm, and it is still driving the industry. The site offers a Web-based CRM for sales, service, marketing, and call-center operations. These services streamline customer management over the Web and are offered at a greatly discounted price in comparison to in-house operations. With over a million customers already using the service, Salesforce is now focusing on their Web application platform, Force.com. Additionally, Salesforce and Google recently teamed up, allowing interplay between Google's App Engine technology and the CRM offerings of Salesforce.

IBM and Microsoft

Slow to adapt, the dueling hegemonic powers have only recently realized the potential that exists in cloud computing. Over the last year, IBM has allocated $100 million into their "Blue Cloud" program. This program is dedicated to creating efficient data centers more than many of the other cloud providers and offers virtual Linux servers, parallel workload scheduling, and Tivoli management software.

Regarding Microsoft, Bill Gates has outlined a plan to tap the power of his firm's server base to provide radically innovative cloud solutions. For instance, the first major cloud release from Microsoft will be Azure, a cloud-based operating system. Simple versions of the Microsoft Office suite are currently available as well, along with a per-user storage of up to 500 MB.

This Is Confusing: Is There One Kind of "Cloud" or Different Types?

The world of cloud computing currently includes four distinct clouds. These include core cloud services, IaaS, Saas, and PaaS. They are each described below.

Core Cloud Services

This cloud of resources was the first form of cloud computing, after the Internet, to gain recognition from the IT mainstream. The services within the cloud are common functions, such as storage, billing, or system management. Most firms use the core cloud services as a first move into cloud computing, as it is the easiest to maintain and many concerns, such as outages, are lessened when storage is used for data of secondary or tertiary importance.

Vendor Examples: Amazon's S3, Simple DB, or Simple Queuing Service; Carbonite.com

IaaS

Infrastructure-as-a service clouds (Iaas), also known as compute clouds, provide the ties that bind any network: the raw power of servers. These clouds offer firms relatively cheap (when comparing the alternative cost of in-house servers), scalable, and quickly deliverable computing resources.

Vendor Examples: Amazon EC^2; IBM's Blue Cloud

SaaS

Software/Applications-as-a-service clouds (SaaS) offer software that is available via a third party over the Internet. They allow firms to access a wide array of programs without having to deal with the hassle of individual licensing or regular updates.

Vendor Examples: Google Docs; Skype; Salesforce.com; Open Office

PaaS

Platform-as-a-service clouds (PaaS) allow developers to build, test, and deploy custom-built applications in real time. These applications can range from games to network gauges—it's completely up to the designer. The clouds are cyber-sandboxes for firms to develop unique applications. Each vendor has its own code platform, so interchange of applications between vendors is limited.

Vendor Examples: Google App Engine, Force.com

So . . . How Will I Benefit from All This?

Firms can reap many rewards by allowing the cloud to handle some, or even all, of their IT-related business needs. These rewards include:

- Cutting cost while continuing innovation
- Low upfront and ongoing costs
- E-Class offerings
- No hardware or software needed to run
- Real-time development available
- Maximization of peaks and valleys
- knowledge saved
- Elasticity of headcount

Cutting Cost While Continuing Innovation

Making room for cloud computing offers companies the ability to utilize emerging technology in a cost-effective manner in order to drive innovation within the organization. This technology, however, breaks the standard equation of "new tech = high cost." Instead, cloud computing can be drastically less expensive than alternatives.

A perfect example can be found when comparing the costs of Google Docs and Microsoft Office. Google Docs is a cloud-based word processing service that allows users to create, store, and collaborate on various file types (most common being spreadsheets or standard documents). As with other Google products, a basic version of the service is free, or $50 per user for a premium version (i.e., more features and better suited for enterprise-level work). The Microsoft Office 2007 suite, on the other hand, can be in the range of $500 per user. While the savings earned may not always be tenfold, a drastic difference in cost is not uncommon.

Low Upfront and Ongoing Costs

Due to the preexisting infrastructure provided by cloud suppliers, perhaps the greatest savings for a firm occurs when the investment in a complex in-house network is no longer needed. The network is essentially gift-wrapped and given to them, free of the rigorous testing and trial-runs that is stereotypical of building a new infrastructure and ensuring its ability to run smoothly.

Additionally, with maintenance in the hands of the cloud suppliers and economies of scale spreading the cost among millions of users, firms have also found the ongoing costs of cloud resources to be significantly lower than maintaining a full in-house infrastructure. As technology develops, the cloud providers handle updates and renewal of software, removing the weight of network responsibility from the firm operating in the cloud.

E-Class Offerings

While hesitations remain (and will for quite some time), cloud resources are moving swiftly toward enterprise-level readiness. Many SMBs have already adopted cloud models into their infrastructure, and large firms are beginning to take notice as providers tailor services to their larger needs.

No Hardware or Software Required

A significant benefit of using cloud computing resources is that firms have access to everything they need to run their operations smoothly. Instead of regularly buying, installing, updating, and receiving licenses for new software, firms need only an Internet connection to access the power of the cloud and the regularly refreshed supplies therein.

Regarding the Office v. Google Docs example, a key component of the cost analysis is the cost of acquiring and licensing the product for each individual user. As newer versions of Office are released, licenses need to be renewed, presenting firms with significantly high ongoing costs. Cloud computing applications and software are automatically updated as providers steadily work to better their offerings for the enterprise user. Thus, regular updates of software ensure a firm is using the newest technology for the service, and these updates are included in the package deal of cloud computing.

An added benefit is that very little knowledge of the hardware/software is needed within the firm that has incorporated cloud-based operations into their infrastructure. While it would be foolish to remain completely ignorant concerning the hardware and software that is being used to support your business, the need to staff individuals that are highly trained in the software is lessened as the cloud is self-healing and self-governing. The best an on-hand expert could do is perhaps explain any problem that has occurred, but they could not necessarily solve anything as the software and hardware is held off-site. Thus, the in-house expert would be reduced to e-mailing the cloud provider in hopes of a quick resolution to any problems that develop with the software.

Real-Time Development Available

Leveraging the power of the infrastructure provided by dealers in the cloud allows firms to access a highly efficient network. Cloud utilities such as the Google App Engine offer the ability not only to create new cloud-based applications, but also to deploy them in real time. This is a particular benefit to firms that regularly update or modify applications, and need an easily adaptable platform.

Maximization of Peaks and Valleys

Let's say you own an online clothing store or an online electronics outlet. During the period of September—December your site receives approximately 50 percent more visitors than the other eight months of the year. Without cloud computing, you would need to build and maintain an infrastructure that can manage your average business needs (the eight months) but can also handle that increase in usage. Thus, while the majority of your infrastructure will remain dormant for most of the year until it is tapped for the four months of heavy usage, you will need to continually manage and update the hardware.

With cloud computing, firms can maximize the peaks and valleys of usage by paying only for what they use. Therefore, continuing this example, you would pay a certain amount that is relatively stable for eight months, then pay more during the four months as usage starts to climb toward the holidays. This scalability is provided by the massive infrastructure each cloud provider maintains, and gives on-demand flexibility in real time (i.e., it will shift resources automatically as computing need grows).

Knowledge Saved

Another widely discussed benefit of cloud computing is the freeform collaboration that results when easily accessible, Web-based resources are used as avenues for inner-office communication. Google Sites, part of the Google application package, allows teams to create discussion boards or wikis and modify them rapidly. Project updates or communication can be relayed in the single location, and information can be saved indefinitely.

During economic slowdowns, this benefit can be particularly appealing as firms start to cut back on human resources. Having working knowledge, which is regularly updated, saved on wikis and indexed online allows employees to tap the experience of coworkers who have faced and overcome common problems in the organization. Without that cache of thoughts, a knowledge gap would develop as employees leave the firm. This cache can also help save the culture of the firm, as the thought process can be identifiable through the message boards and serve as a blueprint for how the firm operates.

Elasticity of Headcount

On a related note, a firm using cloud resources may find an opportunity to be fairly elastic with their full-time staff. This includes in-house IT, which may shrink once the need to regularly maintain a network is lessened as firms leap into the cloud.

The Silver Lining Sounds Great, but What Are the Downsides?

The functionality of cloud computing, particularly for large enterprises, is still . . . well . . . cloudy due to significant concerns that arise when firms consider incorporating cloud resources. These concerns include:

- Security
- Outages
- Privacy
- Lock-in or nontransferable data
- Rewriting or licensing applications
- Negotiating service level agreements
- Network monitoring

Security

The first concern for any firm regarding cloud computing is the safety of any data that are stored in the vast emptiness of the cloud. As with any technology, Murphy's law reminds us to expect surprises. When company records or proprietary information are on the line, however, the risk becomes substantial.

Many cloud providers have dedicated their operations to ensuring the security of their services. Amazon, for instance, allows companies to encrypt their services on any level, from operating system to databases. Google also regularly monitors the security of its platform, and recently passed the SAS70 Type II audit, a comprehensive security analysis.

This is little consolation for firms with data security concerns, particularly when data are stored in shared servers instead of isolated memory banks. The heart of the matter is that security is taken out of a firm's control, and the company must instead place trust in the fact that their cloud provider can handle the responsibility and keep their information safe.

As offerings continue to move toward E-Class readiness, security will continue to be addressed. Until a proven answer to the concern is created, firms may want to utilize cloud resources primarily for secondary or tertiary information until they are comfortable moving higher-level data online.

Outages

What happens if the provider has an outage at their server farm? While infrequent, it has happened in the past, much to the chagrin of those relying on the servers to maintain daily operations. While this may occur just as frequently with an in-house network, firms have no control when an off-site infrastructure ceases to function. This has caused many firms, particularly those that rely on rapid online development and communication, to turn away from cloud operations.

Many cloud providers outline in the service level agreement (SLA) how much time they can guarantee will be free of outage (normally 99% or more). If the service fails to meet that guarantee in a certain month, users receive a lower bill or free usage for the next month. This means little, however, if the outage occurs at a crucial time for the business.

An electronics store, for instance, would not be pleased with a free month of service if their Web site crashed on Black Friday due to an outage in the cloud provider's servers. While they may not have been able to handle the bandwidth either, they could try to rectify the problem as it happened. The cloud computing model, however, would leave them powerless as consumers try to access their site and are denied entry.

Privacy

Who has access to data once in the cloud? Can employees working for the cloud provider access information? What happens when data are transferred from server to server? All of these questions must be asked in the SLA prior to incorporating cloud resources, particularly if private information is to be stored in the cloud.

Lock-in or Nontransferable Data

Another popular concern among those considering cloud computing is a fear of vendor lock-in. While a cloud provider may be appealing at first, some firms may evolve and develop a need to switch vendors within the cloud. Once that shift is underway, it is a gray area under most SLAs as to where the data go. Some firms fear information may linger in the servers of the former provider, as data are frequently shifted from server to server, leaving traces when moving.

On a related note, while many cloud providers have partnered recently (i.e., Salesforce.com and Google), allowing for interoperability, cloud resources are usually nontransferable. Thus, a firm must solidify their cloud operations under one or two vendors, or risk having to juggle multiple products from multiple providers, each with an array of SLA terms and conditions.

Rewriting or Licensing Applications

Unless they are just starting operations and select cloud resources, many firms will already have proprietary applications running prior to making the leap. If these are to be used in the cloud, a firm may have to rewrite the application's code so that it can be split and spread throughout multiple servers and accessed by multiple users.

This requirement also causes concerns over licensing rights. The cloud model allows for open access among users, and many firms are trying to understand how cloud computing and corporate security codes can work together to allow this collaboration.

Negotiating Service Level Agreements

As with any service agreement, reaching a consensus regarding terms and conditions can be painful, particularly when the alternative is running an in-house operation that does not require any negotiations. However, if firms wish to enter the realm of cloud computing, each will need to endure the process of SLA negotiation to ensure it receives a service that fits its needs. SLA negotiations can entail everything from encryptions to lock-in.

Network Monitoring

Many firms have trouble employing their network in the cloud, and devising a plan to monitor that network adds to the hassle. Providers, such as Google, have worked toward developing cloud-based monitoring tools as offerings start to target large enterprise firms.

It bears repeating that these concerns are particularly strong due to the fact that the alternative to cloud computing is keeping operations in-house. An on-site network keeps responsibility and governance within the organization. Once operations are moved into the cloud, control is lost and the hands-on approach a firm once enjoyed is gone. Security, data loss, outages . . . these are all concerns for any network, particularly one that is much smaller than the network offered by Google or Amazon. A company can control a problem, however, it if stems from *its* house. If a cloud provider fails, a firm can only sit idly by and pray for a quick resolution.

It is for this reason that large enterprise firms are slow to adopt cloud computing. While the trade-off is justified for SMBs, large enterprises have just cause to wait for cloud resources that are better suited and proven for high-level enterprise functionality.

Now I'm Interested, but What Do I Do?

To enter the world of cloud computing, the following steps may be useful:

- Assess needs
- Review providers and negotiate
- Develop plan
- Equip architecture
- Create backup plan
- Start the switch

Assess Needs

Small firms may go for the full package of cloud resources (i.e., all four layers), but larger firms may be more comfortable starting with tertiary data storage or light support for computing. Begin by asking these questions:

- What am I struggling with?
- What can be improved?
- How can each cloud lower costs?
- Will cloud computing help drive innovation?

Review Providers and Negotiate

Once you have determined your needs, you should examine how each provider fits into the picture. As many of the cloud computing resources are nontransferable, you should settle on no more than two vendors for your cloud computing activities. As many providers have partnered in the past, be aware of any benefit you can from interoperability.

Deciding which vendor is right for you is important and somewhat easy once your needs are understood. The tough part comes when you start negotiating, as firms need to clarify several aspects prior to entering the cloud. First, providers usually base their charges on either a usage or user basis (i.e., cost per gig of storage or cost per user of storage facility). Firms need to understand how they are being charged and if there are any limitations as to how much they can use the service. Also ask whether a discount can be found in bundling, as many providers prefer that you fully integrate their system instead of networking among several vendors.

In the SLA negotiations, be very clear on the providers terms and conditions for lock-in, security, and reliability. Concerning reliability, many vendors offer discounts if the service has an outage, but a firm should consider how much of a discount is worth the downtime. Keep in mind, however, that tailored SLAs usually boost the price of the service, as it no longer becomes "one cloud fits all." During the review of vendors and negotiation stage, ask the following questions:

- What happens if I want to change vendors?
- How am I charged?
- Is there a limit on scalability?
- Where are data stored?
- Is data encrypted at all times? Can I encrypt the data?
- Does the vendor offer a backup? What's involved?
- What reliability guarantees are there?
- Do I trust the vendor with my operations?

Develop a Plan

This may already be in the works as you assess your needs, but once you finalize your vendor you should start getting ready for the leap. If you plan on using storage, devise a schedule for shifting clumps of data from security levels you're comfortable moving into the cloud. You should also ready your troops for the shift, and answer any lingering questions about how operations will change. Perhaps you should also test the technology on small pockets of your staff before the full rollout, or hold training sessions with the new applications for those who will use them frequently and may not adapt quickly. All of these tasks must be done prior to making the shift if you wish to remain fluid in your operations. During plan development, address one key question:

- What can I do to make sure this works?

Equip Architecture

Unless you plan for a complete replacement, the added weight of cloud computing on your existing network may stress your bandwidth. Thus, you should consider other network designs or work a bandwidth expansion blueprint into your action plan while you try cloud computing. You may wish to deploy monitoring tools in the cloud as well, which means you need to either ensure the vendor has tools to offer, or create your own that work with the vendor's pocket of cloud. There are two key questions to answer during this stage:

- How will the trial impact my current network?
- What will I need to do if the shift is permanent?

Create Backup Plan

To put it simply, "Murphy" will show up. Be ready by working with the vendor to develop an off-site backup, or create your own backup in the event that an outage occurs and store it on-site or at a secondary off-site unit. The key question to address when creating a backup plan is as follows:

- What is the worst that can happen, and how can I be ready for it?

Start the Switch

Get your head in the clouds, and see how it feels. Most vendors offer a trial period to ensure satisfaction—take advantage of that! If it doesn't work, let it go and look for a new solution.

THE BIG IDEA

Cloud computing offers a low-cost alternative to in-house infrastructures for firms that need to lower IT resources yet continue to develop innovative solutions. This alternative grants users a dip in the communal pool of technology, providing computing power to the meek for little, if any, charge. For small to midsize firms, this trend is an amazing utility that inexpensively taps the power of a network far greater than the firm itself and is flexible enough to scale to their individual needs. As a result, according to recent surveys, 31 percent of medium-sized companies (100–999 employees) currently use software services (SaaS clouds), double the usage amount in 2004.[6] This figure is predicted to grow as the cacophony of our global economy continues to loom over enterprises of all sizes, forcing them to grow ever weary of their now-more-important-than-ever bottom line.

However, cloud computing is only just starting to provoke appeal from larger enterprises. While fears related to security and reliability will take time to overcome, the evolution of cloud computing is producing Web-based resources that are designed specifically for high-level enterprise usage. Thus, while some enterprises (such as the U.S. federal government) may not ever reach a point that the benefits of cloud computing outweigh the concerns, other major firms may find a significant boon in shifting some of their operations into the cloud in order to conserve resources.

As is the case with any form of technology, there is no guarantee that once you start using cloud computing it will either work perfectly or solve your needs. Outages may occur, data may float around in cyberspace, and you will be powerless to stop it. However, the question you must ask yourself is whether those concerns will disappear if you spend the resources necessary to build and maintain your own infrastructure and network.

I'll answer that for you: They won't.

It's a level playing field when it comes to misfortune; the only difference is that it will be your responsibility to pick up the pieces if the problem happens in your house. That can be a benefit for a simple correction, but what happens if it's a problem that needs significant work to rectify? Do you have the type of around-the-clock support that, say, Google or Amazon has ready and waiting in the event that glitch occurs?

How much is that control worth?

Enough to outweigh what you'll save by losing it?

At least consider the possibility of shifting minor operations, such as low-level data storage or team collaboration applications, into the cloud. Of course there's risk to doing so! There's no hiding it, and touting cloud computing as the perfect solution to the IT crunch is foolish, but cloud computing might be the best solution for your firm's needs at the moment. It will be a risky jump, but the trick to risk is that you have to figure out how to make it work for you. The benefits range from saving money to saving knowledge, and if you can handle the risk, the rewards may be astounding.

Perhaps one day cloud computing will be as common in the office as jammed photocopiers and lackluster birthday parties, but until that day it will remain a secret cost-cutting weapon held by a steadily growing number of companies around the world. More and more firms make the jump each day . . . will the next one be yours? I hope so. See you in the clouds . . .

NOTES

1. Dion Hinchcliffe, "8 Predictions for Enterprise Web 2.0 in 2009," January 13, 2009, http://blogs.zdnet.com/Hinchcliffe/?p=221 (January 25, 2009).

2. Steve Hamm, "Cloud Computing: Eyes on the Skies," April 24, 2008, http://www.businessweek.com/magazine/content/08_18/b4082059989191.htm.

3. Michael Castelluccio, "A Blue and White January," *Strategic Finance* 90, no. 7 (January 1, 2009): 59–60.

4. James Kobielus, "Cloud Computing in a Bubble Economy," *Network World*, December 15, 2008, 22, http://www.networkworld.com/columnists/2008/120908 kobelius.html.

5. Jeffrey F. Rayport, "Cloud Computing Is No Pipe Dream," *Business Week* (Online), December 9, 2008, http://www.businessweek.com/technology/content/dec2008/tc2008128_745779.htm?chan=top+news_top+news+index +-+temp_technology.

6. Rachael King, "Cloud Computing: Small Companies Take Flight," *Business Week* (Online), August 4, 2008, http://www.businessweek.com/technology/content/aug2008/tc2008083_619516.htm.

SUGGESTED READING

Arnold, Stephen. "Cloud Computing and the Issue of Privacy." *KM World*, July 11, 2008. 14–15, 22. http://www.proquest.com.proxy.library.vcu.edu/ (accessed March 31, 2009).

Brandel, Mary. "Stormy Weather." *Computerworld*, November 3, 2008. 22–23, 26–28.

Brynko, Barbara. "Cloud Computing: Knowing the Ground Rules." *Information Today*, November 1, 2008. 23.

Ely, Adam . "Serious About Security." *InformationWeek*, December 8, 2008. 24, 26.

"E-WORLD: 'Cloud Computing Is Silver Lining'." *Businessline*, January 19, 2009.

Foley, John . "The Cloud, Under Control." *InformationWeek*, December 8, 2008. 21–22.

Gittlen, Sandra. "Tech Tonic for '09." *Network World*, December 29, 2008. 35–36.

Guptill, Bruce, and William S. McNee. "SaaS Sets the Stage for 'Cloud Computing'." *Financial Executive*, June 1, 2008. 37–44.

Hinchcliffe, Dion. http://blogs.zdnet.com/Hinchcliffe/?p=221 (accessed February 5, 2009).

Hoffman, Thomas. " 'The Big Switch' to Cloud Computing." *Computerworld*, December 15, 2008. 36, 38.

Hoover, J. Nicholas. "Clouds Need Connections." *InformationWeek*, December 15, 2008. 16.

Hoover, J. Nicholas, Richard Martin, and Fredric Paul. "Demystifying the Cloud." *InformationWeek*, June 23, 2008. 30–37.

MacVittie, Lori. "A Primer on Cloud Computing." *Network World*, December 22, 2008. 21.

Orr, Bill. "Will IT of the Future Have Its Feet Firmly Planted in the 'Cloud'?" American Bankers Association. *ABA Banking Journal* 100, no. 9 (September 1, 2008): 50, 52–53.

Ranger, Steve. "Behind the Cloud." *Director*, August 1, 2008. 50–52.

"Soonr Unveils Mobile Cloud Computing for iPhone." *Wireless News*, January 8, 2009.

Weinberg, Neal. "Cloudy Picture for Cloud Computing." *Network World*, May 5, 2008. 19–20.

Weinberg, Neal. "Nine Hot Technologies for '09." *Network World*, December 29, 2008. 13–14,16–17.

13

ACCOUNTING IN THE CLOUDS: HOW WEB 2.0, CLOUD COMPUTING, AND SAAS ARE IMPACTING THE ACCOUNTING PROFESSION

Jason M. Santucci, Davide P. Cervone,
Bonnie W. Morris, Presha E. Neidermeyer,
and Arron Scott Fleming

INTRODUCTION TO WEB 2.0

Network-based distributed computing is impacting how all professionals conduct business, and the profession of accounting is no exception to this rule. Gone are the days of manual, stand-alone accounting systems. Today's accounting professionals are working with cutting-edge technologies that are transforming the manner in which business is transacted. Many such technologies are involved with what is referred to as "Web 2.0," "cloud computing," or "SaaS" (software-as-a-service). In this chapter we will describe some of the ideas underlying the concept of Web 2.0 and explore associated technologies and their impact on the accounting profession. We believe that Web 2.0 will have major implications to accountants, particularly in the way they share information both internally and with the world, the types of involvement that accountants will have with their clients, and the ways auditors will need to ensure data integrity for stakeholders of the organization.

How Did We Get Here? A Look Back at the Development Leading to Web 2.0 within Accounting

The transition from paper to electronic media in accounting has not always been a smooth or simple process. Initially, the switch to electronic data and record keeping occurred internally within firms, with all external reporting and transactions remaining on paper. As technology improved, electronic data interchange (EDI) was introduced as one of the first applications to be used between businesses. EDI was used to transmit data from one company's computer to those at another company through an electronic communication network. Sales and payment data were among the first transactions to be processed in this manner.

At first, many users of EDI were faced with difficulties implementing cost-effective use of the new technology because every company used its own custom data format internally, and commercial software was not available to translate between the formats used by different companies. As a result, each company was forced to build its own proprietary software to convert its local electronic data formats to and from the formats used by its trading partners. Such programs are notoriously difficult to maintain; if either company changes its internal format, for example to accommodate changing needs within the company, or even just due to a software update that uses a different storage layout, the translation program would need to be updated or possibly scrapped and completely rewritten. Such changes can be expensive and can easily introduce errors into a previously reliable process. Even the issue of what characters could be included in a document was a source of difficulty, as different computers used different encodings for the alphabet and other symbols. The two main competitors were EBCDIC (Extended Binary Coded Decimal Interchange Code, used primarily by IBM) and ASCII (American Standard Code for Information Interchange, used by nearly everyone else). These two languages did not even encompass the same set of characters, so translation between the two was not always possible, and information integrity was a challenge.

As a result of these difficulties, there was considerable incentive within a company not to update processes that were already in place and working, and innovative new ideas often were seen as prohibitively expensive. While long-term EDI might have reduced costs to the corporation if customer and sales relationships were maintained, the initial implementation process required enormous up-front costs for custom software development in order to work at all. Furthermore, any new interaction between the trading partners would require additional custom software to be written. These costs, plus the continual need to update the software as data formats changed, initially limited the use of EDI to large corporations. The development of commercially available translation and/or accounting software has allowed EDI to move from a custom solution between two parties to a process that is widely available to companies at all levels.

Over the last four-plus decades, EDI has steadily evolved from being based on proprietary formats handled by proprietary programs on proprietary networks, to standardized formats (like XML) processed by standard programs (like Internet browsers) over public networks (like the Internet), often involving value added networks (VANs) that provide companies with additional functions such as format interchange services, data synchronization, error detection and correction, and other similar support. Modern EDI applications use the Internet to process whole transactions through a series of interchanges based on XML (eXtensible Markup Language) schemas that operate smoothly and efficiently behind the scenes. Today EDI is a cost-effective and essential part of virtually all forms of business transactions.

Within accounting, EDI has impacts in a variety of fields. When transactions are being made electronically, EDI provides the mechanism for entering these individual transactions into a company's accounting system, whether that is done virtually or on-site. This represents the basis from which the internal accountants will produce the financial reports that are required of publicly traded companies and also is the starting point for auditors who must examine and pronounce an opinion on the accuracy of the financial statements produced from these data. Auditors, therefore, must have a thorough understanding of how EDI works— without this knowledge, the risk of not detecting fraud or errors increases. The current economic environment suggests the need for ever increasing understanding on the part of accountants and auditors of the manner in which EDI is operating and the ways in which the systems can, on the one hand, be subverted by the unscrupulous, and on the other, be used to improve security and accuracy.

DEVELOPMENT OF THE TERM "WEB 2.0"

The term "Web 2.0" was first coined by Dale Dougherty of O'Reilly Media, Inc., in a planning session for what was to become the 2005 Web 2.0 conference,[1] but the term does not have a precise definition; rather, it represents an approach to application design more than anything else, and it combines two ideas, one technical and one ideological.

The technical idea has to do with how users interact with the Web pages they are viewing, and how the pages react to them. Traditionally, a Web page consisted of a relatively static collection of text and imagery, together with links to other pages. A user would click on a link and a new page would appear in its place. Web site developers quickly learned that they could connect databases running on Web servers to entry forms on Web pages and generate dynamic content that responded to the data supplied by a user, giving a more interactive and user-controlled experience. Once transmitted, however, the pages themselves remained static, and the repeated cycle of click-wait-and-view made for an experience characterized by periodic changes at discrete time intervals.

In terms of user-interface design, this was a great leap backward from the richly interactive graphical interfaces used in desktop applications of the time; but access to hyper-linked data available on the Web made it well worth the loss. One of the Web 2.0 design principles is to try to bring rich interfaces like those of desktop programs to the Web, and key to that is breaking the click-wait-view paradigm by providing the smoother, seamless interaction we are used to from traditional applications.

As an example, in early versions of MapQuest you would be presented with a map of the area of interest, and if you wanted to view farther to the east, you would click on a button at the right of the map, the server would generate a new page containing the new map, and it would replace the page you were currently viewing. This was extremely useful and certainly got you the information you wanted, but it suffered from the click-wait-view processing model, which gave it a disconnected and choppy feel. Compare this to Google Maps, one of the quintessential Web 2.0 applications: to scroll to the east, you simply drag the map to the left and additional portions of the map are revealed on the right. This occurs within the original page, without the user having to wait for a whole new page to be generated and shipped over the network, which is both faster and more convenient.

This new model is made possible by JavaScript, a programming language contained in all modern Web browsers. Web pages can include programs written in that language that are run within the browser itself, making it possible for the Web pages to be dynamic, as the JavaScript programs can change the contents of the page in real time in response to the actions of the user. Traditional Web pages could react to clicks on links or on images by fetching new Web pages, but Web 2.0 pages can respond to a full range of user interactions in much more subtle and expressive ways.

A second key technical component is the ability of JavaScript programs to request data from a server without affecting the page being viewed by the user. This makes it possible for Web 2.0 applications to obtain data from remote locations "behind the scenes," as it were, and present those data to the user without the need for the click-wait-view cycle. For example, Google Maps uses this approach to obtain the information needed to extend its map when you drag it to one side, and to update the mileage information when you alter a travel route by dragging it with the mouse. Similarly, the Google home page uses it to determine a list of recommended keywords that match your current search text, which it displays as a pull-down menu below the search text box, and this information is obtained on the fly and updated as you type. By requesting small units of data that can be obtained from the server very quickly, a Web 2.0 application can remain responsive to user interactions, even though the data must be fetched over the network (which is considerably slower than accessing data from the user's local disk, for example, as would be the case if the application were not using the network). In this way, the look and feel of a desktop application is maintained, while simultaneously having the advantage of access to remote data not available on the user's own computer.

In the past, nearly all the processing involved in displaying a Web page was performed on the remote server, but with the widespread deployment of JavaScript (and its cousin, the Flash applet plugin), more and more of the processing is being off-loaded to the viewer's computer, and interactions with the server are in small chunks of data that contain only the information required by the actions of the user. This makes her experience more immediate and responsive, and it changes the way she receives and interacts with the data.

This leads to the second philosophical aspect of what it means to be a Web 2.0 application, which rejects the traditional client-server model based on a centralized server and monolithic software applications controlled by individual companies and replaces it with a decentralized system where the network *is* the application, data make up the primary resource, and the community plays a key role in generating and evaluating those data and creating that network. This paradigm switch may be more difficult to grasp than the technical features that underly it, but it is perhaps the more powerful of the two, and it requires a completely new business model from those who wish to take advantage of it.

The idea that the network is the application, in its most extreme sense, means that the application could not exist without the network; that its essential features come from the interconnections among its users and available data sources. Examples of this idea put into practice include Wikipedia, Napster, Skype, and similar applications. It is the fact that multiple people all over the world can, and do, contribute to Wikipedia that has made it the enormously successful site that it is, and this fact differentiates it from such collections as Britannica OnLine, whose data could have been delivered on a DVD as a desktop application with no network connection. Similarly, Napster combined the individual playlists of its users into a large database of music that did not reside in a single, centralized location, but as a distributed, interlinked aggregate that could not have existed without the presence of the network.

Not all Web 2.0 applications have the same level of dependence on the network. Tim O'Reilly, founder of O'Reilly Media, Inc., and a major player in defining Web 2.0, identifies four different levels of interaction[2]:

Level 3: the application can only exist in the presence of the network (e.g., Wikipedia, Skype),
Level 2: the application could exist without the network, but is greatly enhanced by it (e.g., Flickr, a shared database of photos whose true value

stems from community created information such as its database of image tags that can be used for searching and sorting of images),
Level 1: the application can and does exist offline, but gains features by being online (e.g., Writely, which could be used offline as a word processor, but gains its real power as an online collaborative editing tool), and
Level 0: online applications that would have worked just as well offline if the data were available locally (e.g., MapQuest and Yahoo! Local).

The initial incarnation of Google Maps would be at level 0, but now that users can contribute photographs and reviews that are tied to the maps, this brings it to level 2. Sites that take information from several data sources (called *mashups*) belong to level 3. O'Reilly uses HousingMaps.com, which combines online housing and condo sales information with Google Maps to enrich both, and gives its users a new way to search for and evaluate housing choices, as an example of an application at this level.

One of the ideas that is implicit in the phrase "the network is the application" is a decreased importance being put on the application itself, and the increased importance of the data it leverages. Traditional software models centered on large (read "bloated") programs that were feature-rich in an attempt to do everything; the Web 2.0 approach is more light-weight, with single-purpose components that interoperate. The application itself is no longer the central component. Indeed, since the program that is being used probably is a Web browser, in most cases the user is unaware of the application at all (she does not have to think about the JavaScript that is running behind the scenes to make it all work); her main concern is access to the data, how those data are presented, and what role she has in creating or adding to those data.

The user's perception that the application has essentially disappeared, leaving only the user and the data, leads to a final characterization of Web 2.0 applications: they are community based, harnessing the "collective intelligence" of the user community. The enormous popularity of social-networking sites, such as Facebook, LinkedIn, and Twitter, and the rise of blogs and wikis to their current status as important sources of information exemplifies the important sense in which community participation plays a role in the new paradigm of the Web. There has been a shift from centralized creation and maintenance of information, to a decentralized, cooperative means of generating and analyzing data. The new approach is based on participation rather than centralized publishing. For example, Yahoo! originated as a directory of categorized links created and maintained centrally; it was used by others, but they did not contribute to it directly. (It's true that they could suggest links to be added, but the final decisions were made by Yahoo! staff.) Contrast this to a site like Flickr, where users contribute directly to information associated with photos through the creation of tags for the images, or to Amazon, where users contribute reviews of the products for sale that are available to those thinking of making a purchase.

The traditional approach to Web site management often involved the use of a Content Management System (CMS) that provided a centralized mechanism for authorized users to create and maintain the content of the Web site, enforcing layout standards, and giving a company's site a consistent look and feel. A more community-based approach to content production is that of a Wiki, in which the users themselves create the information in a collaborative way. Wikipedia is the canonical example of this, but wikis are now in widespread use for many other, more limited, purposes. They can be used as a means of documentation (users can explain to each other how to use a piece of software or share recipes with each other, for example), or as a resource for a class (students can build a database of resources or the professor can make technical definitions or worked solutions available to the class), or as a source of local information (users could post reviews of local dining or pointers to good places to shop, or other items of local interest).

The community can do more than simply use the available data; they can add value to the data themselves. Their own input can become an important source of information itself. This can be an explicit process, as in Wikipedia, where the user actively contributes to the information available, but it can be an implicit one, where the actions that the user takes becomes part of the information. For example, when you view an item for sale at Amazon, it provides a list of items that others who viewed that page ended up purchasing. This information can give a purchaser other items to consider, and perhaps ones that are a better match for his needs, and so value is added above and beyond the description of the product itself. The data were not produced by an explicit decision of a user to provide those data, but data are generated merely by the fact that others have used the site in the past (the network is the application).

Another example of where data can be generated automatically is in article citations. If a paper appears online and another paper refers to it via a hyperlink in its bibliography, then as people follow the link, the logs on the Web server for the first paper will reveal the existence of the second paper that cites the first, and those logs can be used to create a citation index for the first paper. The needed logs are generated automatically by the fact that people are reading the citing paper and some are following the links to the cited works, and so a valuable citation database can be produced and maintained at virtually no cost in research.

The philosophy of Web 2.0 (the network is the application, it's about data not software, and users add value to the data) represents a fundamental shift from traditional software models and business models in general. Those who will thrive in the Web 2.0 marketplace are those who can adapt to this new paradigm and can find the ways in which the network, data, and community can play a cooperative role in adding value to a company's offerings.

ACCOUNTING IN THE CLOUDS

Cloud computing sounds surreal and futuristic but is very much a reality today. The word "cloud" in the term "cloud computing" is used as a metaphor for the collection of interconnected yet separate nodes linked together to provide some distributed service on the Internet (as a set of water droplets suspended separately in the air join together to form a larger configuration, a cloud); so *cloud computing* really means *Internet computing*, although cloud computing remains the predominantly used term. Four ideas comprise the cloud computing model: (1) distributed, networked servers for applications and data, (2) virtualization and grid technology for dynamic sizing (scalability), (3) application programming interfaces (APIs) and communication capability over the Internet, and (4) a usage monitoring and billing mechanism.[3] Through this model, cloud computing enables its users to cut out the need for local servers and in-house data storage that may exceed, or at times come up short of, the amount of capacity required by a particular business, by creating an enormous virtual infrastructure that is available "on demand." Cloud computing also cuts costs by removing the need for in-house, or on-site, technicians and experts that possess knowledge of how the physical databases and servers operate and how to service them, upgrade them, and back them up.

The Skype network for VOIP (voice over Internet protocol) is an example of this type of computing model. Rather than have one large, centralized directory and router for its voice transmissions, every user of Skype becomes a directory and router, helping to make connections and transfer portions of calls for other people using the network. The capacity of the network actually grows with its usage, as new users provide more routing and transfer bandwidth, and that occurs automatically, without the need for additional expenditures on servers or support personnel.

You may be more familiar with the term "on demand" when it is used in relation to cable television service or NetFlix's "watch instantly" feature. Instead of having to buy or rent a physical DVD for each movie you want to view and having to own a DVD player, these services deliver only the specific movie that you request, to your television, exactly when you want to watch it, and you only pay for the movies you request. The cloud computing model works in a similar way, where APIs and software replace DVDs and Internet servers replace DVD players. Having access to only the applications and server resources that your company needs, when you need them, is the definition of scalability and one of the major advantages of cloud computing. This can be seen in accounting via the integration of such products into the workplace. NetSuite is an example of an online business application effectively allowing customers the ability to manager their own businesses from order inception to production of financial statements through the use of NetSuite online software.

Cloud computing not only provides exactly what you need when you want it, but also provides access to software and applications from virtually anywhere with connectivity. The freedom of nearly universal accessibility provides multiple consequences and advantages for accountants and the accounting profession. First, the fact that employees can use the software and applications required to accomplish their job from anywhere can have a profound effect on the relationship between worker and office: when employees have ready access to company data over a network, it means that, no matter whether an accountant is on a business-trip, at the office, at home, or with a client, they can conduct business as normal, and so the trip, the home, the coffee shop *become* the office. Moreover, greater accessibility is not limited to individual users: companies can provide employees all over the planet with the appropriate software and applications in a much easier and cost-effective manner[4] using the cloud computing model. Other companies, such as Firefly, a UK beverage company, are experimenting with software that allows their employees around the world to share information in a manner similar to a social networking site with virtual meeting rooms, brainstorming tools, and knowledge management features, providing them more flexibility with less reliance on e-mail.[5] Accounting firms can then either establish new offices or, more likely, outsource some redundant tasks to lower costs providers.

In accounting and finance, professionals are frequently consulting with others about their financial data. The ability to remotely access such information is critical to the success of the professional advisor in the field of, for example, personal finance. Consultants frequently are obliged to access client records at off-site locations, using these data to run projections for various scenarios, such as retirement planning or investment analysis. Real-time use of a client's portfolio and changing net worth make the individual client sessions more valuable.

The cost of essentially unlimited accessibility is increased concerns about the security of the data. There are several obvious concerns: First, because the data can be accessed remotely by authorized users, unauthorized users have new avenues of attack, both directly through explicit attacks on the authentication system and indirectly through spoofing an authorized user into inadvertently providing his or her credentials. Second, because the data are transferred over public networks, there is a potential for eavesdroppers to obtain sensitive data, though encryption techniques are a well-established means of dealing with that concern. A subtler issue is that once data are made available to the public, it can no longer be controlled by the company, so decisions about what information to distribute and to whom must be made carefully. Intellectual property rights also may be an issue, especially in social-network settings where many people may be involved in collaborative authoring, or when authors write entries or reviews for larger collections of data, like online shopping sites. Finally, personal privacy rights come into play when data are collected about a user without his or her knowledge and consent. How will that data be used, and who has access to the information?

CHANGE IN ACCOUNTING PROFESSION

The movement of work from U.S. professionals to those in other countries has happened in various manufacturing, and now professional, fields. This type of labor outsourcing has occurred within a growing number of areas, from medicine, where virtual physicians read X-Rays from remote locations, to accounting, where various tasks have been sourced to locations with lower costs than in the United States. Many U.S. tax returns are now completed in India and other off-shore locations and sent back to U.S. accounting offices for delivery to clients; the only work still done in the United States amounts to taking the client information initially, and insertion of key data, such as the social security number and client name at the end of the process. While certainly in the manufacturing arena the loss of jobs has been very high, within accounting, at least at present, the type of work that has been outsourced has freed U.S. professionals to do more value-added and less-repetitive work. These new ideas are an important component of today's dynamic marketplace, much more important than retaining work that is more bookkeeping than accounting in nature. Without the constant development of new ideas it will be impossible for accountants in the United States to compete in the marketplace of the future, which is becoming more and more global every day. Knowledge and information are the most valuable assets in business today, and if used properly, technology can assist greatly in enhancing both.

To compete, while maintaining and growing the profession, the new technologies that are already being embraced outside the United States will have to be adopted by businesses, large and small alike, within the United States. Along with the advantages discussed earlier, these technologies, including application service providers (ASPs) and businesses that provide software-as-a-service (SaaS), greatly help in reducing the cost of delivering complex and specialized software to end users. The reduction in cost provided by ASPs and SaaS providers helps enable small- and medium-sized companies to access programs that they would not otherwise be able to use. As a result the Web and Web 2.0–related technologies are helping to outsource work to those in other venues and countries; that outsourcing will not necessarily hurt the accounting profession, just change it from what it is today, and if a business person in today's marketplace is not ready to handle change, they will not succeed.

CURRENT AND FUTURE OUTCOMES

A key component of Web 2.0 application is the rapid and reliable transmission of data, and that requires standardized formats that are flexible enough to express the information needs of a wide variety of users. One such standard being used in the business, financial, and accounting worlds is XBRL, or eXtensible Business Reporting Language. XBRL is a markup language that is an extension of XML and aids in transmitting business information in a standardized format, but one that is extensible and thus able to adapt to the needs of the future. This standardized format is helpful in increasing the speed that financial data can be processed and financial reporting can be completed, ultimately increasing the relevance of such data. Moreover, it provides for greater accessibility to and improved interoperability between various data sources.

XBRL, like XML, addresses one of the basic problems of the EDI approach: that computer programs could not really tell what the data meant—it was just numbers or text. Each program had to be written with a knowledge of the format and layout of the data and reports built into it, and if the layouts changed, the programs would break. With XML, the data are tagged, so that the meaning of each item is known to the program. With tagged data, programs don't need to know ahead of time what is coming because the data itself tells the program. Standardized taxonomies for reading and writing these tagged data make it easy to write software that can get the data into a form usable by the program, and standardized validators can be used to check the correctness of the formats, so that you can know with certainty that another XBRL-compliant program will be able to read it. Traditionally, 80 percent of a program would be involved in processing user input and producing output, and only 20 percent did the actual work of the program. XML is an attempt to change that ratio.

The other important feature of this approach is that when you can exchange small bits of structured data like this, and can get them from many sources, you can combine and relate data in ways that were not possible before (another key feature of Web 2.0). We can see this in accounting in several arenas both available now and, in various combinations, likely to be available from providers in the future. A current example is the Web site MyBizHomepage, which has an online platform for the financial records of small companies. Rather than being just a storage platform for these data, the site offers a free service that collects data from the small business's commercial software and makes it available via a Web browser. The implications of this ability are enormous for smaller businesses, which can use the platform for anything from creation of budgets to financial statement preparation. The speed with which the data can be transformed should help smaller businesses react in a manner equivalent to their larger competitors who have more sophisticated internal systems. The next step of such a program would be to move to a SaaS system, where the MyBiz site would act as a service provider for the firm by being the starting point for data entry, effectively bypassing the commercial software previously owned and maintained by the small business. Longer term, it's possible that the financial data contained within this site may be merged with another site, allowing for entrepreneurs to create a mashup for venture capitalists or others interested in bringing firms to be publicly traded.

The SEC (Securities and Exchange Commission) has issued Final Rule 33–9002 (issued January 30, 2009),[6] which now requires that the filings of companies publicly traded in the United States be submitted in XBRL format effective April 13, 2009. Many U.S. and foreign registrants (whose home country either mandated or voluntarily accepted XBRL financials) have been filing using this system for some time. If the global migration to one set of accounting standards (probably IFRS) is accompanied by regulations from standard-setting bodies that require reporting to be done using one reporting mechanism (probably XBRL or the next generation thereof), then the power of Web 2.0 in accounting will be dynamic. Web analysis sites complete with user-based platforms will be developed using the input from XBRL. By observing what information clients choose to view, companies will be informed of what data are integral to investor decision-making and will likely attempt to provide better insight into those particular line items. Investors could easily develop models that can be viewed and modified by others on the Web. The financial reports could be exported and tied to other economic data or investor-driven inputs in an attempt to better model financial outcomes of the company. Mashups using data from a variety of sites will likely be generated and the investing community will have better access to a wider range of interrelated data. Auditors may be required to validate the integrity of the data of these and other inputs to the decision-making process for investors.

Just as Web 2.0, cloud computing, and SaaS are having an effect on every aspect of the business world, they will impact the profession of accounting as well. These enhanced technologies will change where and how accounting professionals access data, will give their clients better and more relevant information more quickly and easily, and will offer new opportunities for job growth in the development and maintenance of these data sources and in auditing to ensure the integrity of the data they provide to the public. Integration of these technologies into the accounting profession will make its work not only less costly but also more effective and efficient in serving its clients and the public. We anticipate tremendous growth in knowledge related to the use of financial data with these developing technologies. This area will provide an important career path for those accountants who are technically innovative and interested in pushing the profession into the future.

NOTES

1. Tim O'Reilly, "What Is Web 2.0: Design Patterns and Business Models for the Next Generation of Software," *O'Reilly Network*, September 30, 2005, http://www.oreillynet.com/pub/a/oreilly/tim/news/2005/09/30/what-is-web-20.html.

2. Tim O'Reilly, "Levels of the Game: The Hierarchy of Web 2.0 Applications," *O'Reilly Radar*, July 17, 2006, http://radar.oreilly.com/archives/2006/07/levels_of_the_game.html.

3. Neal Leavitt, "Is Cloud Computing Really Ready for Prime Time?" *Computer* 42, no. 1 (2009): 15–20.

4. Firms accomplish this feat by having the software available online instead of having it locally available with installation and updating done on an individual basis for each computer with disks.

5. Miya Knights, "Using Web 2.0 for Business," *Computer Weekly.com*, December 12, 2007, http://www.computerweekly.com/Articles/2007/09/12/226726/using-web-2.0-for-business.htm.

6. The SEC will decide in 2011 whether U.S. firms will be required to use IFRS as the underlying regulation for financial disclosure in the United States, with the transition occurring between 2014–2016 for most firms.

14

WEB PANELS: REPLACEMENT TECHNOLOGY FOR MARKET RESEARCH

Anja S. Göritz

With both the steady decline in response rates in telephone interviewing and the population's increasing Internet penetration, the Internet is expected to become the most widely used mode in market and opinion research. In 2007, the market share of Internet-based market and opinion research in the United States was 41 percent,[1] whereas in Germany it was 27 percent.[2] The bulk of online interviews are now conducted in so called *Web panels* or *online panels*.[3] For conducting market research, the Internet creates an efficient venue for accessing consumer populations, asking questions in a multitude of online modes, and storing and retrieving responses.

In the classical sense, a panel is a longitudinal study in which the same information is collected from the same individuals at different points in time. In contrast to that, a Web panel has come to denote a pool of registered people who have agreed to occasionally take part in Web-based studies. As a Web panel is not necessarily a longitudinal study but a pool of readily available participants, it is more properly referred to as an "access panel." A Web panel can be employed as a sampling source for different studies. The studies can vary in design. For example, studies can be true experiments, quasi-experiments, population-descriptive, or exploratory. Moreover, studies can have different temporal makeups, for example, they can be longitudinal or cross-sectional. Of course, the studies can also vary in topic and duration.

There is a continuum between online and offline panels. With pure Web panels, the panel is operated entirely via the Internet (i.e., the recruitment of panelists, the studies, and the maintenance of the panel take place online), whereas with offline panels all processes are carried out offline. With mixed-mode panels, some processes are implemented online (e.g., running a study), some offline (e.g., recruiting panelists via Random Digit Dialing), and some processes may even be implemented in both modes (e.g., incentivizing panelists for their participation by e-mailing them a PayPal payment or by shipping a tangible gift to them). Moreover, Web panels can be distinguished according to the type of panelists they hold. For example, there are specialist panels such as panels of young parents, and there are panels that are open to people from all walks of life.

Another distinction among Web panels pertains to how the panelists were sampled.[4] On one end of the continuum there are volunteer opt-in panels, the most common form of Web panels.[5] Such panels have been built on the basis of nonprobability sampling. Typically, appeals for signing up with such a panel are posted in newsgroups, mailing lists, links, or banners, or announcements are disseminated in offline media or by word of mouth. Despite attempts to weight or stratify the participants in subsequent studies, the initial sample remains one of volunteers who have selected themselves from an unknown population.

Volunteer opt-in panels need to be distinguished from pre-recruited panels. On the one hand, there are pre-recruited panels with probability sampling of panelists. These panels have been drawn from a sampling frame of the desired population. On the other hand, there are pre-recruited list-based panels where the entire population and not only a sample is integrated into the panel (e.g., all clients of a firm or the employees of a company).

A key problem with probability-sampled panels has been the low initial response rate to the recruitment interview and the small share of interviewees who subsequently participate in the panel. After traversing the several steps necessary for recruiting panelists from probabilistic samples—where each step is a source of potential selection bias[6]—usually around 10 percent of the contacted sample can be won over as panelists.[7],[8] Not rarely though, the recruitment success has been as low as 1 or 2 percent.[9]

Although building Web panels from a probability sample is statistically sound, given the staggering refusal rate and the large expenses, probability sampled panels' actual superiority in terms of cost-benefits over opt-in panels that have been built upon a diversified recruitment strategy has yet to be shown. Thorsten Faas compared a survey in a probability sampled Web panel with a paper and pencil interview of a random sample of Internet users.[10] Despite large efforts taken to recruit the Web panel, there were considerable differences in the results. Anja Göritz followed up panelists who had been recruited from different probabilistic and convenience samples during the first two studies in a new panel.[11] These panelists' probability to load and to complete the studies was independent of the method by which panelists had been recruited. As an interim conclusion, at least for research questions that do not require representative samples, the effort for probability-sampling a panel is not warranted. Many empirical studies are suitable carried out with volunteer samples, for example, developments of scales, explorations and feasibility studies, longitudinal and cross-sectional experiments, as well as qualitative and casuistic studies.

When looking at what type of sampling and recruitment is used by actual Web panels in a survey of Dutch panels, 10 out of 12 panels use a mixture of recruitment methods.[12] In a survey of 38 German panels, Human Nasseri found that 16 panels used both opt-in as well as probabilistic methods for recruiting panelists, 12 panels recruited in a probabilistic manner exclusively, and 10 panels relied solely on opt-in procedures.[13] With regard to the recruitment being carried out offline versus online, out of the 38 German panels 26 recruited both online and offline, nine panels used online recruitment exclusively, and three panels used offline recruitment exclusively.

BENEFITS FOR MARKET RESEARCH

Studies run in Web panels are computer-assisted as well as Internet-based. Thus, they enjoy advantages of both computer assistance and Internet delivery. Compared to paper-and-pencil studies, computer-assisted studies allow multi-medial stimuli to be delivered, the data come in electronic form, skip patterns can be implemented smoothly, the order of questions and the order of answer options can be randomized, participants' input can be validated for proper syntax, and usually there is less cost for consumables. In addition to these advantages, Internet delivery allows short field times, study participation independent of the time of day and geographical location, and more cost savings because there are no expenses for interviewers and laboratories.

Adding to these benefits of both computer assistance and Internet delivery, Web panels offer specific methodological and economic advantages when compared to offline studies on the one hand and to unrestricted online studies (i.e., with ad hoc recruitment of respondents) on the other hand. For instance, market researchers can draw variable samples from a Web panel. Moreover, participants are readily available because of their pre-recruitment, thus field times can be even shorter than with unrestricted Web surveys. In Web panels the profile data of the panelists and their data from earlier studies are known. On the basis of these profile and historical data, target samples can be drawn without elaborate screening, questionnaires can be limited to novel items, and newly collected data can be checked for reliability and consistency by matching them to existing data. Furthermore, the percentage and characteristics of people who refuse to take part in a given study can be assessed because unlike in unrestricted studies the survey manager knows who was invited to the study at hand. For the same reason, preventing multiple registration and study participation by the same person is easier with Web panels than in unrestricted surveys.

Finally, Web panels have ethical advantages when compared to unrestricted surveys: Panelists can be informed as early as at their sign-up that they may be invited to studies whose purpose cannot be disclosed before the end of the research. Also, panelists who have abandoned a study prematurely can still be debriefed because they are accessible via e-mail, whereas ad hoc recruited dropouts can usually not be debriefed.

DOWNSIDES AND THREATS FOR MARKET RESEARCH

Of course, Web-based data collection has disadvantages and limits as well. Because every research environment and therefore also the Internet have peculiarities, there is the possibility of undesired interactions with the research question. For example, some respondents' computer illiteracy might impact their responses or speed in a computer-assisted task. Moreover, the Internet as a research platform is not suited for all kinds of research alike. For example, studies requiring physiological measurements or the sense of smell, taste, or touch cannot be carried out online. The downsides of the otherwise beneficial absence of an interviewer and the flexibility with regard to time and place of study participation are a reduced degree of control over both the identity of the respondents and the context of study participation.

A challenge unique to panel or longitudinal surveys is that of panel conditioning, also called panel bias. Panel conditioning occurs through panelists' ongoing survey participation. Given panelists' experience with the survey over time, their responses may increasingly differ from the responses given by people answering the same survey for the first time. Although with a Web panel, the surveys may vary in content over time, the mere act of participating in an ongoing panel may change respondents' behavior and attitudes. However, panel conditioning does not necessarily falsify responses, but can cause them to become closer to the "true values." For example, practice may reduce the unfamiliarity with the survey material or the uneasiness with the interviewing situation.

Michael Dennis reports several case studies from a Web panel where no noteworthy effects of panel conditioning could be established.[14] However, he notes that specialty and longitudinal panels, where panelists are repeatedly surveyed on the same topic and often with a long questionnaire, are at a higher risk of creating "professional respondents." Moreover, Vera Toepoel compared fresh and old panelists.[15] She found that experienced panelists take less time to fill out a questionnaire than inexperienced panelists. Furthermore, experienced panelists are more likely to engage in satisficing (i.e., doing just enough but not giving one's best). There was no difference in the number of omitted items, respondents' vulnerability to response category effects, nor in a social desirability score.

Ted Vonk, Robert von Ossenbruggen, and Pieter Willems report that the likelihood of responding to a survey request decreases with tenure in the panel.[16] The likelihood of panelists responding was 67 percent when being invited to a study within the first month of their panel membership, which dropped to 47 percent for people who had been panel members for longer than 12 months when they were invited to their first study.

To reduce panel conditioning, the frequency with which panelists are invited to studies should be kept as low as possible. At the same time, the frequency of surveys run in a panel should not be too low to keep panelists committed and aware of their panel membership. Five of 35 surveyed panels in Germany self-imposed no restrictions on the frequency of inviting panel members to complete a survey.[17] Of the remaining 30 panels, six implemented survey-free periods of two to four weeks, 15 had breaks of four to eight weeks, and nine panels had breaks of more than two months. In the Netherlands, 14 out of 19 panels adhered to a restriction policy for the frequency of inviting panelists to surveys.[18]

However, single-handed efforts by an individual panel at reducing panel conditioning may be futile because most panelists are members in several panels at the same time: 62 percent of people in 19 Dutch panels were members of more than one panel. On average each member was registered with 2.7 panels. Those who were members in multiple panels were members of 4.5 panels on average. The number of panel memberships is associated with the recruitment method: If the panel recruits potential panelists actively, the number of simultaneous memberships is significantly lower than if panelists select themselves. Moreover, the average number of panel memberships is higher among younger respondents, people who check their e-mail every day rather than less frequently, and women relative to men. The more memberships panelists hold the more likely they respond to a survey request at all and the sooner as well as faster they fill out the questionnaire.

RESPONSE RATES

Depending on the panel as well as on the length and topic of the survey at hand the response rate (i.e., of all invited persons the number of people who call up the survey) varies to a great extent. Bernad Batinić and Klaus Moser obtained an average response rate of 74 percent in 68 studies that were conducted in four different Web panels.[19] Helene Venningen yielded a response rate of 80 percent in the first study in a new market research panel.[20] Geert Loosveldt and Dirk Heerwegh, in the first two studies in their new university-based panel, yielded response rates of 70 and 56 percent.[21] In a study in an adult student panel, Adam Joinson and Ulf-Dietrich Reips observed response rates ranging from 40 to 53 percent.[22] In the same panel but another study, Adam Joinson, Alan Woodley, and Reips observed response rates ranging from 44 to 49 percent.[23] Helmut

Leopold reports a study that yielded a response rate of 45 percent.[24] The average response rate to surveys in German panels is 57 percent.[25] However, the response rate has nothing to do with data quality as panels with a low response rate usually do not remove inactive panelists from their panel database. Vonk, von Ossenbruggen, and Willems found no differences in outcomes in identical studies that were run in different panels although the response rates varied widely.[26] Some panels do not remove inactive panelists probably because the number of panel members is an important selling point in the market.

DUPLICATE PANELISTS

Multiple registrations can be detected by matching new registrations to existing profiles. According to Lorenz Gräf, 0.6 percent of the sign-ups in Web panels are duplicates.[27] In the panel at the author's university (www.wisopanel.uni-erlangen.de), 4.9 percent of people who entered the panel between 2000 and 2008 were duplicates. This figure is higher than that reported by Gräf because in the early years of this panel panelists were required to log onto the panel Web site to take part in a study. On these occasions, many panelists confounded logging on with signing up and registered anew. Since abolishing this log in to access a study, the annual percentage of duplicate registrations has decreased.

FALSE IDENTITIES

Panelists might inadvertently or deliberately fill in wrong information in the registration form. Whether a signed-up panelist of a specified name truly lives at the specified address can only be ascertained by falling back on offline validation. A simple method is to send new panelists a welcome letter or gift. Gräf has reported only two returned welcome letters out of 1000 (0.2%).[28] In Göritz, six out of 204 mouse pads (2.9%) sent to newly registered panelists were undeliverable.[29] Hence, only a small fraction of panelists seem to provide false contact data. To be on the safe side, 20 of 38 surveyed panels in Germany collected and validated panelists' postal address as part of the registration process, whereas 7 panels only collected the address but do not validate it. The remaining 11 panels in the sample did not collect the postal address.[30] In addition, one panel validated panelists' identity by means of their bank account number, whereas one other panel fell back on publicly accessible databases.

OBSOLETE E-MAIL ADDRESSES

Usually, the invitation to a study is sent by e-mail. Compared to postal mail, inviting panelists by e-mail is faster and free of charge. As a downside, e-mail invitations bounce quite often due to exceeded disk quotas and outdated addresses. In the author's panel, between 2001 and 2008, 1,622 of 11,645 e-mail addresses were invalid at registration or expired later on. This amounts to an average annual loss of 2.0 percent of the panelists due to invalid e-mail addresses. Similarly, according to Gräf, 2.7 percent of the panelists register with an invalid e-mail address.[31] These figures illustrate that it is useful to not only collect panelists' e-mail addresses at sign-up but also their postal address or their phone number or an alternative e-mail address. If the primary e-mail account becomes obsolete an otherwise lost panelist can be recovered.

INCENTIVES

To ensure panelists' long-term commitment to the panel, panelists are normally compensated for their participation. Often-used incentives, which can also be used in combination, are per-capita payments, redeemable loyalty points, lotteries, donations to charity, vouchers, gifts, and study results. Nasseri found that 17 of 38 surveyed panels in Germany incentivized their panelists with money, 15 panels relied on loyalty points, 14 used lotteries, and five panels used donations to charity, vouchers, and/or study results (multiple answers were possible).[32] Loyalty point–based incentivation is more frequent with older and internationally operating panels. This is probably due to high costs for financial transactions into foreign countries. With regard to the timing of the incentive, one distinguishes between prepaid and postpaid (i.e., promised) incentives. Prepaid incentives are given to potential respondents before their participation, whereas postpaid incentives are awarded after responses have been collected.

Both positive and negative consequences of employing incentives are conceivable. On the positive side, incentives might increase the response and the retention rate in a study. The response rate is the number of panelists who call up the first page of a study divided by the number of panelists who were invited to this study. The retention rate is the number of panelists who stay until the last page of a study divided by the number of panelists who have called up the first page of this study. Instead of retention, some people speak of dropout, which is the complement of retention. On the negative side, incentives might (1) increase the response and retention rate at the expense of other facets of data quality (e.g., more items are skipped, the consistency of responses is lower, answers to open-ended questions are shorter), (2) attract a particular clientele of respondents and thereby bias the sample's composition, (3) alienate intrinsically motivated panelists, and (4) distort the study results, for example, by altering respondents' mood. To weigh whether employing incentives can be recommended in spite of these dangers, we need to know how large the desired and undesired effects are. However, most studies that have looked into the effectiveness of incentives in Web panels gauged the impact of incentives on response and retention only. The next sections will describe

experiments run in Web panels that have examined the effectiveness of lotteries, payments effected via PayPal, donations to charity, survey results,
and prepaid incentives. To conduct a more comprehensive review on incentives a meta-analysis is planned. Readers are invited to contribute their own
study results by filling out the form at www.goeritz.net/incentives.htm.

Lotteries

Depending on respondents' expected value of winning, lotteries can be
very cheap for survey managers if only a few winners are drawn from
among thousands of respondents. But how effective are lotteries? In a
four-wave experiment, the offer to win gift certificates increased the
response rate (68%) compared with a no-incentive control group (55%)
in the first survey wave only but not in subsequent waves.[33] Retention
was not affected. Moreover, in six cross-sectional experiments,[34] response
and retention did not differ between panelists who were offered a chance
to win cash or were not offered any incentive. In corroboration, Tracy
Tuten, Mirta Galešić, and Michael Bošnjak found no significant difference
in response and retention between groups in which different sums of
money were raffled and a control group.[35] Bošnjak and Olaf Wenzel compared a lottery of loyalty points with immediate drawing and a lottery of
loyalty points where the drawing was delayed for one week with a no-
incentive control group.[36] Compared to response and retention in the control group (38% and 86%, respectively), response and retention were
markedly higher with a lottery with immediate drawing (54% and 96%,
respectively) and somewhat higher with a lottery with delayed drawing
(46% and 92%, respectively). To sum up, lotteries are sometimes effective
but primarily only when used for the first time. When employed
repeatedly, lotteries tend to be ineffective.

Payments via PayPal

Because it is cumbersome to pay Web panelists cash, incentive money
is often paid using online intermediaries such as PayPal. In a three-wave
experiment within an opt-in Web panel, Göritz, Hans-Georg Wolff, and
Daniel G. Goldstein promised one group of participants 1.50 Euros to be
paid via PayPal for their participation at each of the three waves.[37] The
control group was not offered any incentive. This was the first time that
these people were offered a payment via PayPal in this panel. The promise of the payment decreased response in the first wave (36% vs. 45%), but
increased it in the second wave (80% vs. 60%). The reversal of effect from
the first to the second wave can be explained by the fact that only those
people were invited to the second wave who took part in the first wave.
Retention was not affected. Furthermore, in a two-wave experiment,
Göritz, Wolff, and Goldstein promised one group of opt-in panelists 2
Euros to be paid via PayPal for participation in both waves.[38] The control

group was not offered any incentive. Again, these people were offered a PayPal payment for the first time. The promised payment reduced response in the first wave (39% vs. 45%), but increased retention in the second wave (98% vs. 96%). In sum, when PayPal payments are used for the first time, they can have the surprising effect of lowering response rates. It is conceivable that the more often PayPal payments are offered to the same respondents the more likely the payment eventually pays off in terms of more data sets and/or higher quality data.

Donations to Charity

A donation to charity is an incentive that causes no transaction cost. In six experiments, Göritz, Friedrich Funke, and Karsten I. Paul compared promised donations to charity against a control group.[39] Surprisingly, response was significantly lower when donations were offered than if no incentive was offered. Retention was unaffected. Thus, until more results become available it is not recommended employing donations to charity as an incentive in Web panels.

Survey Results

Under most circumstances study results are the least expensive type of incentive. In a review of several uncontrolled Web panel studies, Batinić and Moser found that studies in which results were offered elicited a lower response rate (65%) than studies without any incentive (72%).[40] Moreover, with an ad hoc sample for which the study topic was salient, Tuten et al. observed a response rate of 69.3 percent if results were offered versus 62.3 percent in the control group.[41] Moreover, retention was 59.3 percent with results versus 57.5 percent without. Finally, Marcus et al. offered either personal feedback on individual results, general survey results, or no results at all, which yielded response and retention rates of 34.6 and 80.3 percent, 33.1 and 77.8 percent, and 33.4 and 73.7 percent, respectively.[42] These inconclusive findings emphasize the need for further research on the usefulness of study results.

Prepaid Incentives

The evidence on prepaid incentives is sparser because prepaid incentives are usually more expensive. Bošnjak and Wenzel compared the (1) promise of loyalty points and (2) prepayment of some loyalty points plus promise of further points with (3) a no-incentive control group.[43] Compared to the control group (38%), response was higher with prepayment of some loyalty points plus promise of further points (53%) and somewhat higher with the mere promise of points (48%). Similarly, compared to the control group (86%) retention was higher with prepayment of some loyalty points plus promise of further points (94%) and somewhat higher with the mere promise of points (91%). Furthermore, in a five-wave experiment, Göritz sent a mouse pad to one half of newly registered panelists; the other half of newly registered panelists did not get any incentive.[44] For the five survey waves that ensued, panelists were either promised loyalty points or inclusion in a cash lottery. This was one of the few experiments where the expected value of the lottery was about the same as that of the loyalty points, and the odds of winning in the lottery were communicated to panelists. At the outset of the series of waves the prepaid gift improved participation (85% vs. 79% in the first wave), especially when the prepaid gift was combined with the lottery. This effect, however, dwindled across the waves. With regard to loyalty points versus the lottery, in the first wave there was no difference in participation. Over time, however, loyalty points became more attractive. In sum, prepaid incentives are effective, but employing them might not be cheap.

REMINDERS

If invited panelists fail to take part in a study by a certain deadline, it is possible to send them one or more reminders. In 68 Web panel studies, the more reminders were used in a survey the higher the response rate tended to be: in the 16 surveys without reminders, response was 72 percent; in the 41 surveys with one reminder it was 75 percent; in five surveys with two reminders it was 79 percent; and in six surveys that employed three reminders it was also 79 percent.[45] In a similar vein, in nine studies sending one reminder increased the response rate but did so at the price of retention.[46] The average response rate rose from 66 to 73 percent due to sending the reminder, whereas retention was significantly smaller among panelists who responded after receiving the reminder (82%) compared to initial respondents (91%). In corroboration, Leopold found the initial response rate was 40 percent and went up to 54 percent after a reminder.[47] Again, panelists who participated before a reminder dropped out of the study less often than those who participated after a reminder: 3 percent of panelists who were not reminded abandoned the survey prematurely compared to 8 percent of reminded panelists. Although these figures suggest that reminders may be worthwhile at least with regard to augmenting the response rate, one should not draw premature conclusions because there has been no systematic study of the effectiveness of reminders in Web panels if employed on a regular basis. Because reminders are intrusive—as long as no probative data urge a different approach—it is prudent to use reminders sparingly to maintain panelists' good will to participate.

FIELD TIME

Field time pertains to the time period during which a study is accessible by respondents. Web-based data collection allows the field time to be relatively short. Gräf (2001) reported five studies with field times of two or three days in which two-thirds of the invited people took part within 24 hours after receiving the invitation.[48] Three of 35 surveyed panels in Germany left a study in the field for up to four days, 19 had a typical field time of up to eight days, 11 panels of up to 14 days, and two panels of more than two weeks.[49] However, the hitherto mentioned studies do not tell us anything about the impact of the field time on data quantity and quality. To shed light on this issue, in four experiments Göritz and Stafan Stieger varied the field time across several days, and there was a control group without a deadline.[50] The longer the field time the higher the response rate. However, there was tentative evidence that the longer the field time the smaller the retention rate and clear evidence that the longer the field time the more items were omitted. Thus, there is a trade-off between obtaining more responses and obtaining lower-quality responses.

A CASE STUDY: ODC SERVICES

ODC Services, a specialist for data collection via online surveys and the owner of big European online panels, faced decreasing response rates and increasing panel attrition. As a reason ODC identified frustration on the part of panelists. The target groups for consumer surveys are often highly specified. Due to that fact, preselection is only possible to a limited degree and the number of desired test persons in the initial sample is often low. In addition to the minor prevalence of the necessary attributes, quotas are often set on various selection criteria. These restrictions lead to participants being rejected before the actual questionnaire has begun. As a result important motivators are lost. For example, panelists cannot express their opinion and they do not receive an incentive or only a fraction of the incentive they would have received for participation in the entire survey.

If panelists are not in the target group with several surveys in a row, their willingness to participate or the quality of their answers in surveys can fall. To counter this, ODC developed a simple scoring model to reflect the motivation of a panelist. To each panelist a score is assigned that takes into account the following three variables: (1) number of invitations sent out, (2) response status of panelist (negative values with non-response, quota full, screen out, or dropout; a positive value for complete response), (3) number of loyalty points received. After each survey the appropriate value is added or subtracted to a panelist's motivation score.

When inviting panelists to studies this motivation score is taken into account. To surveys with an estimated incidence level of 75 percent or above panelists with the lowest motivation scores are preferentially invited. By contrast, in surveys with a probability of belonging to the target group of 25 percent or less, participants with high motivation scores are invited. In surveys with medium incidence extreme motivation score levels are avoided.

To evaluate the effectiveness of this method, a test group of panelists (n = 1000) received motivation score–based invitations while a comparison group (n = 1000) received invitations at random during a test phase of three months. With the motivation-based invitations, there was less volatility in individual participation (SD = 1.7 vs. 2.1 on a scale ranging from 0 to 10), a higher median response rate (53.1% vs. 47.5%), and lower median attrition (0.13% vs. 0.18%) than in the comparison group.[51] Since gaining these insights, ODC Services has adopted the Panelist Motivation Score© and now sends invitations to surveys according to this model.

PRACTICAL ISSUES OF MANAGING A WEB PANEL

Studies of Web panels and practical experiences like that ODC Services bring to light several practical issues for managing Web panels. The typical process of conducting a market research study in a Web panel by order of a client is as follows:

- Clarification of request (e.g., number and kind of panelists to be invited, study starting date, field time, topic and length of study, incentives, use of reminders, any specialties)
- Inspection of client-programmed questionnaire and feedback to client; alternatively the Web panel provider programs the questionnaire as part of the order
- Drawing of the sample
- Inviting sampled panelists via e-mail; the e-mail contains the study link that has been personalized by appending a unique ID, for example, www.panelx.com/studyx.htm?a=35967
- Logging of IDs and of page-wise timestamps when respondents fill out the questionnaire
- Redirecting panelists on the final questionnaire page to the panel
- Ensuring client sends list with logged IDs plus timestamps; alternatively the panel provider compiles that list if the panel provider has programmed the questionnaire
- Sending client invited panelists' pseudononymized profile data
- Identifying of dropouts on the basis of the timestamps that were logged in the questionnaire
- Distributing incentives among eligible participants
- Documenting and performing quality control; if need be removal of flippant panelists and panelists with invalid e-mail addresses

If a company needs to conduct a small to medium amount of market research per year it usually is more cost-efficient to commission these studies from market research institutes that hold a Web panel. Some sample companies from North America and Europe that offer the services of a Web panel are Greenfield Online, Clarion Research, Research Now, Toluna, Respondi, Interrogare, Panelbiz, Harris Interactive, ODC, YouGovPsychonomics, Nielsen, and Dialego.

By contrast, if a company needs to conduct a large number of market research studies each year it may be well advised to build and manage its own Web panel. The management of the panel is rendered more convenient if the panel manager can avail of a Web based administration interface that is coupled with the panel database. Commercial panel management software is available from different companies such as Globalpark, QuestionPro, MARSC, Toluna, and Vovici. A Web search will bring up Web sites of these and other companies, and the reader can look up up-to-date information about the specification and costs. Professional panel management software seems to be widespread among large commercial Web panels. Academic and small Web panels mostly rely on homemade solutions. To decrease the adoption barrier for smaller panel operators, the author has programmed an open-source tool for Web panel management, which can be obtained for free from her personal Web page at www.goeritz.net/panelware.[52] When choosing or home-developing panel management software, one should make sure it supports the following functionalities: search panelists; view, modify, export, and delete profile data; display panel statistics; identify duplicates; draw samples; send e-mails; and create and manage e-mail templates. Professional software often provides features beyond these basics, such as parameterization as to the maximal number of surveys to send panelists, integration of online survey software to create and conduct studies seamlessly, and real-time reporting of field data and survey results.

Notes

1. Inside Research, *Newsletter*, July 2008, http://www.insideresearch.com.

2. ADM, *Arbeitskreis deutscher Markt- und Sozialforschungsinstitute e. V. Jahresbericht 2007* [Annual Report 2007], http://www.adm.com/en-US/investors/Documents/2007-ADM-Annual-Report-Eng.pdf.

3. Anja Göritz, Nicole Reinhold, and Bernad Batinić, "Online Panels," in *Online Social Sciences*, ed. Bernad Batinić, Ulf-Dietrich Reips, and Michael Bošnjak, (Seattle: Hogrefe & Huber, 2002), 27–47.

4. Mick Couper, "Web Surveys: A Review of Issues and Approaches," *Public Opinion Quarterly* 64 (2000): 464–494.

5. Human Nasseri, *Forschung mit Online-Access-Panels*. Final thesis (Diplomarbeit), University of Frankfurt/Main, Germany, 2007.

6. Sunghee Lee, "An Evaluation of Nonresponse and Coverage Errors in a Prerecruited Probability Web Panel Survey," *Social Science Computer Review* 24 (2006): 460–475.

7. Anja Göritz, "Recruitment for Online Access Panels," *International Journal of Market Research* 46 (2004): 411–425.

8. Adam Joinson and Ulf-Dietrich Reips, "Personalized Salutation, Power of Sender and Response Rates to Web-based Surveys," *Computers in Human Behavior* 23 (2007): 1372–1383.

9. Jörg Hellwig, Boris von Heesen, and René Bouwmeester, "Rekrutierungsunterschiede bei Online-Panels und ihre Folgen" [Differences in recruitment with

online panels and their consequences], in *Online-Marktforschung*, ed. Axel Theobald, Marcus Dreyer, and Thomas Starsetzki (Wiesbaden: Gabler, 2003), 241–254.

10. Thorsten Faas, "Offline rekrutierte Access Panels: Königsweg der Online-Forschung?" [Offline-recruited access panels: Silver bullet of online research?], *ZUMA-Nachrichten* 53 (2003): 58–76.

11. See Note 7.

12. Ted Vonk, Robert von Ossenbruggen, and Pieter Willems, "The Effects of Panel Recruitment and Management on Research Results," *Panel Research*, ESOMAR (2006) in Barcelona.

13. See Note 5.

14. Michael Dennis, "Are Internet Panels Creating Professional Respondents? A Study of Panel Effects," *Marketing Research* 13 (2001): 34–38.

15. Vera Toepoel, *A Closer Look at Web Questionnaire Design*. Doctoral thesis, University of Tilburg, Netherlands, 2008.

16. See Note 12.

17. See Note 5.

18. See Note 12.

19. Bernad Batinić and Klaus Moser, "Determinanten der Rücklaufquote in Online-Panels" [Determinants of response rates in online panels], *Zeitschrift für Medienpsychologie* 17 (2005): 64–74.

20. Helene Venningen, *Offline Rekrutierung für ein Web panel* [Offline recruitment for an online panel]. Final thesis (Diplomarbeit), University of Salzburg, Austria, 2002.

21. Geert Loosveldt and Dirk Heerwegh, "*Unit Non Response in Face-to-Face and Web Surveys. Some Comparisons,*" Paper presented at the Lazarsfeld Symposium in Brussels, Belgium, 2004.

22. See Note 8.

23. Adam Joinson, Alan Woodley, and Ulf-Dietrich Reips, "Personalization, Authentication and Self-Disclosure in Self-Administered Internet Surveys," *Computers in Human Behavior* 23 (2007): 275–285.

24. Helmut Leopold, *Rücklauf bei Online Befragungen im Online Access Panel* [Response in online surveys in online access panels] (Hamburg: Kovac, 2004).

25. See Note 5.

26. See Note 12.

27. Lorenz Gräf, "Internet Access Panels in der Praxis" [Internet access panels in practice], in *Online-Marktforschung*, ed. Axel Theobald, Marcus Dreyer, and Thomas Starsetzki (Wiesbaden: Gabler, 2001), 319–334.

28. Ibid.

29. Anja Göritz, "The Long-Term Effect of Material Incentives on Participation in Online Panels," *Field Methods* 20 (2008): 211–225.

30. See Note 5.

31. See Note 27.

32. See Note 5.

33. Anja Göritz and Hans-Georg Wolff, "Lotteries as Incentives in Longitudinal Web Studies," *Social Science Computer Review* 25 (2007): 99–110.

34. Anja Göritz, "Cash Lotteries as Incentives in Online Panels," *Social Science Computer Review* 24 (2006): 445–59.

35. Tracy Tuten, Mirta Galešić, and Michael Bošnjak, "*Optimizing Prize Values in Web Surveys: Further Examination of the Immediacy Effect,*" Paper presented at the General Online Research Conference in Zurich, Switzerland, 2005.

36. Michael Bošnjak and Olaf Wenzel, "*Effects of Two Innovative Techniques to Apply Incentives in Online Access Panels,*" Paper presented at the General Online Research Conference in Zurich, Switzerland, 2005.

37. Anja Göritz, Hans-Georg Wolff, and Daniel G. Goldstein, "Paying Consumers via PayPal for Their Opinions," working paper.

38. Anja Göritz, Hans-Georg Wolff, and Daniel G. Goldstein, "Individual Payments as a Longer-Term Incentive in Online Panels," *Behavior Research Methods* 40 (2008): 1144–1149.

39. Anja Göritz, Friedrich Funke, and Karsten I. Paul, "Donations to Charity as Incentives in Online Panels," working paper, University of Würzburg, Germany.

40. See Note 19.

41. Tracy Tuten, Mirta Galešić, and Michael Bošnjak, "Effects of Immediate versus Delayed Notification of Prize Draw Results on Response Behavior in Web Surveys: An Experiment," *Social Science Computer Review* 22 (2004): 377–384.

42. Bernd Marcus, Michael Bosnjak, Steffen Lindner, Stanislav Pilischenko, and Astrid Schütz, "Compensating for Low Topic Interest and Long Surveys: A Field Experiment on Nonresponse in Web Surveys," *Social Science Computer Review* 25 (2007): 372–383.

43. See Note 36.

44. See Note 29.

45. See Note 19.

46. Anja Göritz and Rik Crutzen, "Reminders in Web-based Data Collection: Increasing Response Rates at the Price of Retention," working paper.

47. See Note 24.

48. See Note 27.

49. See Note 5.

50. Anja Göritz and Stefan Stieger, "The Impact of the Field Time on Response, Retention, and Response Completeness in List-based Web Surveys," *International Journal of Human Computer Studies* 67 (2009): 342–348.

51. Christoph Bender, "A Panelists Scoring Model for an Even Allocation of Surveys with Different Incidence," Paper presented at the General Online Research Conference in Hamburg, Germany, 2008.

52. Anja Göritz, "Building and Managing an Online Panel with phpPanelAdmin." *Behavior Research Methods*, in press.

15

USING SOCIAL SOFTWARE TO IMPROVE COLLABORATION: DETERMINING FACTORS FOR SUCCESSFUL KNOWLEDGE SHARING SPACES*

Judy Payne

Leading business thinkers agree that knowing how to collaborate is the key to future business success. But collaboration is voluntary and difficult to manage for hierarchical organizations accustomed to top-down control. Could social software help organizations become better at collaborations?

This chapter describes new research conducted in partnership with 20 public, private, and third-sector organizations into how social software is being used—and how it could be used to help organizations become better at collaboration.

In the emerging era of innovation, the key organizational capability is collaboration—needed to drive the knowledge creation and transfer that are at the heart of the innovation process.[1]

At the same time, our understanding of "knowledge" is developing. Knowledge isn't something that exists somewhere, waiting for us to find it. It's more of an interpretation that groups of people give to what they see around them. Knowledge isn't a set of facts produced in a research center or university—it's produced in global teams by people with diverse skills and experiences and is subject to social accountability and

---

*This article originally appeared in *Knowledge Management Review*—November/December 2007, Volume 10 Issue 5, published by Melcrum (www.melcrum.com). It is published with permission.

acceptability. These perspectives on knowledge make it clear why collaboration is so important—it's needed to create and share knowledge. This raises serious questions about how institutions and businesses need to change and develop the ways in which they produce knowledge.

Developing the ability to collaborate effectively is difficult, because collaboration is voluntary. People won't collaborate just because they are told to, so collaboration can't be managed in a traditional hierarchical, command-and-control environment. Organizations therefore need to invest in creating conditions that will encourage collaboration: an environment of trust, self-management, behavioral protocols, shared intent, and equitable sharing of returns. This is a familiar message in knowledge management (KM), where it's widely accepted that organizations can only influence knowledge creation and sharing and that the way to do this is to provide an appropriate environment and appropriate tools.

WHAT IS SOCIAL SOFTWARE?

The language of social software is evolving and has no fixed definitions. Even the term "social software" has alternatives—including "social media," "conversational technologies," and "social computing." Wikipedia is a good source of up-to-date definitions.

There are also differences of opinion on what types of software are included under the heading "social software." Most people agree that wikis, blogs, and social networking services are "social." Some people include discussion groups, and others go further—including e-mail, instant messaging, and video conferencing within the scope of social software.

In this chapter, we are concerned with the way social software can be used in organizations and knowledge management, so we focus on software that:

- Enables content generation through conversations
- Provides a "history" or "trail"
- Supports asynchronous working (but not necessarily exclusively)

Our emphasis is therefore on wikis and blogs and social networking services such as feeds and aggregators, tagging, and folksonomies.

SOCIAL SOFTWARE AS A COLLABORATION TOOL

Although there are philosophical arguments around whether knowledge can be managed at all, in practice most organizations attempt to manage the knowledge of their employees, customers, and suppliers through a mixture of people, process, and technology tools and techniques designed to improve performance and add value.

Tools such as e-mail, instant messaging, and document management systems are usually an important part of this mix, and many organizations also use tools such as Microsoft SharePoint and Lotus Notes designed specifically to help people share knowledge and work collaboratively. These tools are not without their problems, however. The overwhelming experience of KM Forum members is that the biggest hurdle in implementing KM tools and techniques is persuading people to use them.

Social software (such as wikis and blogs) is different. Traditional tools such as Lotus Notes work from the top down, putting the group, organization, or project first. Social software is more bottom up, and works best without imposed top-down control. It can provide the conditions needed for collaboration in one hit. It might even be changing the way we socialize. If this is true, then maybe social software has the potential to help organizations develop the capability of collaboration.

Traditional software tools represent a starting point for a project and issue structure before use. Further, they have the following characteristics: (1) top down, (2) knowledge belongs to experts, (3) central control, (4) formal, (5) rigid, (6) slow, and (7) expensive. Social software tools, in contrast, are starting points for users where structure emerges with use. Further, social software tools have the following characteristics: (1) bottom up, (2) knowledge flows from everyone, (3) user control, (4) informal and easy to use, (5) flexible, (6) quick, and (7) free or inexpensive. Ultimately, we can derive these key points about social software:

- Social software allows people to collaborate peer to peer and from the bottom up, whether this fits with the organizational hierarchy or not.
- Using social software can build individuals' motivation and capability to collaborate.
- The impact and value of social software for an organization is related to the nature of the organization's hierarchy and bureaucracy and whether the software reflects or contradicts this.
- Individuals using social software (officially or otherwise) can be a catalyst for changing the bureaucracy of an organization.
- Understanding the relationships between the social software, organizational bureaucracy, and individual motivation is critical for success.

Unlike other software tools used in business, wikis, blogs, and social networking sites first became established outside the business world. Sites such as MySpace, Facebook, and the online encyclopedia Wikipedia—launched in 2001 and perhaps the best known Wiki of all—have hundreds of millions of users. The popularity of sites such as Wikipedia is not fully understood. Why do people contribute their time and knowledge freely to Wikipedia, particularly when it can be so difficult to persuade people to share knowledge at work?

Research into the motivation of Wikipedians has found that contributing content enhances individuals' sense of meaningfulness, self-determination, and relatedness. Although there's a negative effect on motivation when an author's material is edited, this reduces as people gain more experience of contributing and receiving feedback.[2] This implies that contributing to Wikipedia is building individuals' capacity to collaborate—an alluring prospect for KM.

HIERARCHY AND BUREAUCRACY

As a starting point for the study, the working group adopted principles from social-capital research. Using social-capital principles, we produced a series of interview questions to generate case studies.

The concept of social capital first appeared in community studies and is gaining currency in the business world. The concept can be roughly understood as "the goodwill that is engendered by the fabric of social relations and that can be mobilized to facilitate action."[3]

Knowledge and knowing are valuable resources, created through collaboration. Social capital affects the conditions needed for collaboration, so organizations that invest in developing social capital are more likely to be successful.

One aspect of social capital that is particularly relevant to the use of social software is the concept of hierarchy. In organizations, hierarchy and formal authority are analogous to bureaucracy, and bureaucracy can affect organizations in two ways:

- The negative view is that bureaucratic organizations stifle new ideas and demotivate their employees.
- The positive view is that bureaucracy provides clarity over responsibilities and therefore reduces role stress.

One way of resolving these opposing views is to acknowledge two types of bureaucracy: enabling (which helps employees in their work) and coercive (used by managers to command and control reluctant employees). The extent of bureaucracy in an organization does not itself lead to positive or negative effects; the important factor is the type of bureaucracy.

Wikipedia is a good example of enabling bureaucracy that has led to voluntary collaboration. Wikipedia has key policies and guidelines, developed collaboratively and enforced by participants, administrators, and (in difficult cases) an arbitration committee. The policies and guidelines are effectively the "behavioral protocols" needed to foster collaboration.

WHY DO ORGANIZATIONS USE WIKIS AND BLOGS FOR KM?

Social software increases the opportunities for people to collaborate, therefore increasing knowledge sharing and creation and generating value. It's different from traditional collaborative software because people are more likely to want to use it—but the bottom-up, enabling features of social software that make it more attractive to some individuals can make it less attractive to individuals and groups wanting to preserve their position in the existing organizational hierarchy.

Our research at Henley KM confirms what we found in the literature about the way wikis and blogs are being used. Social software is moving into the business world. Organizations are using (or planning to use) it to share documents and ideas, broadcast news and opinions, and support teams. Wikis are being used for collaborative authoring. The common underlying explanation is that organizations are using social software to improve connections between people—so they can collaborate.

Perhaps a more interesting question is, "What is stopping organizations from using wikis and blogs?" The answer to this seems to hinge on reluctance to change and nervousness about losing control, mainly from people with a stake in preserving existing structures. Our findings suggest that these people are often toward the top of existing hierarchies or in IT departments.

MOTIVATIONS TO USE SUCH TOOLS FOR KM

Using social software gives people a sense of self-determination and relatedness. Wiki users report feeling "more in touch with other people and projects" and that wikis create a "sense of team."

People also use social software because it makes their work easier. Some people don't engage at first because they are not convinced they have anything of value to contribute. Some of these people "lurk," then become active contributors. And some people don't engage at all—maybe because they feel their position in the existing social structure is threatened by social software.

WIKI SUCCESS AT A NONPROFIT

The following is a non-attributed case study from a member of the forum workgroup, followed by a further example based on the experiences at a consulting firm.

Improvement-Org works with the statutory, voluntary, and private sectors to make the best use of the full range of resources and expertise available to improve services. Its knowledge-related aims include sharing positive practice and learning about what works and what doesn't, passing on research findings to organizations to help them improve services, and encouraging organizations to work in partnership across all sectors.

Internal and External Collaboration

Improvement-Org uses social software in two ways. It uses a wiki as a real-time, collaborative authoring tool, and runs an online knowledge community where people can hold conversations, set up specialized groups, and share content and information that already exists—for example, documents, videos, and images.

Examples of collaborative authoring using the wiki range from production of a 12-chapter e-book to the creation of meeting agendas. The impetus for the book came from its authors, who wanted something more flexible than a central editor coordinating Word inputs from 12 people. Using the wiki meant that 12 authors could work on 12 chapters simultaneously. Everyone could see what everyone else was doing, so all the authors acted as reviewers and gave instant feedback. The result was rapid completion of the book, and chapters that complement each other.

A Self-Moderating Environment

Although the wiki has administrators, there is no hierarchy of editing rights for its content. At first there was a fear that the content might be low quality, but this is not the case in practice: standards for content and behavior have emerged. These standards are not written down or policed by users. An example is the way different groups of people produce collaboratively authored documents. Some groups have an initiating author who writes content, then other users comment and discuss changes before they're incorporated. In other groups users contribute and edit directly.

Improvement-Org has found that trust between users contributes to their motivation to use the wiki. Other factors that contribute to the success of the wiki are the fact that it can be accessed over the Internet and its ease of use. The custom dashboard, a Word-like interface for easy editing, and the ability to mark and watch favorite pages make the wiki attractive to users, who can personalize it and keep up to date with the specific activities that interest them.

Differences in professional status can hinder wiki use. Improvement-Org finds it difficult to get senior professionals to contribute, and has also found that some people don't contribute because they don't think they can add value. The technology itself can also be off-putting to users who are not comfortable with IT tools.

The wiki is used very heavily, but not across all user groups. About 15 percent of users contribute every day. A further 20 percent of users contribute at least once a week, and the remaining 65 percent make minimal contributions. Frequent contributors are usually the people who have been using the wiki the longest. Users new to the technology or the people network tend to lurk before they contribute. Users become more active with experience—but Improvement-org believes there is value even to users who don't actively contribute because the wiki is an effective way of transferring dynamic knowledge to passive consumers.

Although the wiki is designed for use by existing networks of people or to complete existing tasks that need collaboration, the way it is set up has created new connections because users can see what others are doing. The most active and dynamic groups seem to hold a magnetic attraction for others and pull in new users.

A Wiki Example from Consult-Co

Consult-Co is a specialist social software consulting company that works with organizations to create more effective online networks. The company has a flat structure: staff work in teams around client projects that can be consultancy, software implementation, or both.

Consult-Co has an internal wiki with blogging and comments functions, used primarily for projects. Each project has its own project space open to the client and all staff—whether they are working directly on the project or not—although this is subject to confidentiality undertakings and robust permissions management. All staff use the wiki every day.

Staff-only spaces are used for project work before it is released to clients, for keeping lists and for informal knowledge sharing and communication such as discussions about finding new office premises and sharing insights from events. The wiki is also used to develop and share best practice in Consult-Co's specialist teams. There's no separate intranet or CRM system—the wiki fulfills both these functions and enables informal peer-to-peer knowledge sharing rather than hierarchical, structured discussion.

Consult-Co describes the wiki as "central to the way we work" but stresses that the main internal communication route is face to face. The company is small and internal relationships are built face to face. The wiki just makes it easier to work together and with clients.

Client project spaces are used to share documents, develop and write specifications collaboratively with the client, and comment on project outputs. Clients contribute at each stage of a project from proposal to implementation. This creates a shared common record of the whole project, and —importantly—helps create shared expectations. Because wikis allow previous versions to be recreated, they provide an audit trail of decision-making and client sign-off. Compared with other ways of working with clients, using the wiki saves time and therefore money.

There's a strong shared understanding of how to use the Consult-Co wiki, even though nothing is written down to guide behavior. The wiki is seen very much as a work tool. Spaces "belong" to the people working on them. Others are encouraged to take an interest and contribute but they don't interfere. If someone has a question or suggestion they think might be of interest or value to others, they post it onto the wiki—otherwise they communicate one to one.

There's no need to police behavior—Consult-Co has never moderated content generated internally. It's far more likely for someone to say "let's move this discussion off email and onto the wiki" than "don't use the wiki this way." Serious discussions take place face to face, even if they continue on the wiki.

The wiki also makes it easy for new staff to find out what is going on, and provides a mechanism for leavers to share their knowledge. A recent leaver voluntarily contributed some of this knowledge and experience by creating a space on the wiki. Consult-Co sees the wiki as a potential "corporate memory" in which both formal and informal ideas and discussions are captured.

FURTHER RESEARCH INTO PARTICIPATION

A further, ongoing study by the Henley KM Forum is investigating the relationships between personality and the way people engage with social software. Why does the impact of social software vary between organizations?

Our research suggests that the impact (and value) of social software for an organization is related to the nature of the organization's hierarchy—and whether the software implementation reflects or contradicts this.

There is a big unanswered question. Is social software a set of useful tools that makes things easier for people who would collaborate anyway, or does it represent a radically different way of interacting with people that will transform organizations and make them more democratic and collaborative? Our case studies support both arguments. At Consult-Co, using a wiki internally makes collaboration more efficient—but people would have collaborated anyway. In the example at Improvement-Org, introducing a wiki created collaboration where it didn't exist before, but the hierarchy in the professions served by the Improvement-Org persists—and the most senior members of the network don't contribute. In another example among the workgroup, an executive blog seems to have made directors more responsive to staff comments.

We have also found people using social software to bypass existing organizational structures and create new ways for individuals to connect with each other. In this case individuals' desire to communicate and collaborate is greater than their loyalty to the organization and its processes. This is why social software is sometimes referred to as being "subversive."

IMPLICATIONS FOR KNOWLEDGE MANAGERS

Social software seems to have the potential to help organizations build the capability of collaboration. In some contexts at least, social software is a catalyst for making organizations flatter and more democratic in their behavior. If knowledge managers understood the relationships between social software, organizational hierarchy and bureaucracy, and individual motivation, we would be able to intervene in ways that support knowledge creation and sharing.

Table 15.1 shows what we believe would happen if a wiki was introduced to different organizations and people were free to use it as they wished. The framework can also be used to understand what KM intervention is needed to build the collaboration capability of individuals and organizations. Table 15.2 explains how a wiki can be used to build collaboration capability.

THE FUTURE?

People are using social software outside work to build their own networks, shaping their expectations of the knowledge-sharing tools available to them in a business environment and shaping their expectations of the way they, as individuals, contribute to knowledge creation and sharing. If these expectations are not met by employers, the new generation of knowledge workers has the ability to create alternative organizational structures and connections needed to switch organizations at will. Organizations that resist social software might well be missing a trick.

Table 15.1 The Likely Effects of Introducing a Wiki in Different Contexts

Individuals' Motivation and Capability	Coercive Bureaucracy	Enabling Bureaucracy
People's motivation and capability to connect and collaborate greater than motivation to preserve existing organizational structures	People would use it subversively to satisfy their own needs	Wide use of wiki for individual and work motives—for good or bad
	Some subversive use and some resistance; stalemate	People would use it to make collaboration more efficient
People's motivation and capability to connect and collaborate less than their motivation to preserve existing organizational structures	Nobody would use it (and nobody would want them to)	Nobody would use it (even though they were encouraged)

Table 15.2 Using a Wiki to Build Collaboration Capability

Individuals' Motivation and Capability	Coercive Bureaucracy	Enabling Bureaucracy
People's motivation and capability to connect and collaborate greater than motivation to preserve existing organizational structures	Give people permission to collaborate creatively within guidelines that deliver benefits to the organization as well as to individuals. Ask people to identify uses for the wiki that will deliver organizational benefits and support these uses as pilots.	Build the organization's ability for ongoing positive transformation. Use the wiki to develop radical new ideas and directions that satisfy organizational and individual needs.
People's motivation and capability to connect and collaborate equal to motivation to preserve organizational structures	Demonstrate the benefits of bottom-up collaboration to the organization. Use the wiki for tasks that require collaboration between existing teams. Encourage motivated and capable individuals to support less motivated and capable individuals.	Make existing collaboration more efficient and increase the scope of collaborative decision-making. Configure the wiki to reflect existing organizational structures and use it for everything from writing agendas to setting strategy.
People's motivation and capability to connect and collaborate less than motivation to preserve existing organizational structures	Build people's motivation and capability for collaboration. Use the wiki for small, well-defined tasks that need to be done anyway. Choose tasks that are carried out by well-defined teams. Provide training and technical support.	Build people's motivation and capability for collaboration. Use the wiki for tasks that are important to individuals even if these tasks are not high-priority for the organization. Provide training and technical support.

NOTES

1. E. Miles, C. C. Snow, and G. Miles, "The Future.org," *Long Range Planning* 33 (2000): 300–321.

2. X. M. Zhang and F. Zhu., "Intrinsic Motivation of Open Content Contributors; The Case of Wikipedia," paper presented at WISE 2006, Evanston, Illinois.

3. P. Adler and S. W. Kwon, "Social Capital: Prospects for a New Concept," *Academy of Management Review* 27, no. 1 (2002): 17–40.

About the Editor and Contributors

TRACY L. TUTEN, Ph.D., author of *Advertising 2.0: Social Media Marketing in a Web 2.0 World*, is an associate professor of marketing at East Carolina University. Frequently quoted in the press, including the *New York Times*, *Brandweek*, the *International Herald Tribune*, and the *Washington Post*, she is a leading contributor to industry views on leveraging the Internet. Her research has appeared in such journals as *Psychology & Marketing*, the *Journal of Business Research*, and the *Journal of Marketing Communication*, among others. Dr. Tuten has served consultant and guest professor roles internationally (in Korea, Germany, France, and Argentina) and in the United States with organizations that include Samsung Electronics, Royall & Company, The Martin Agency, and the NFL Coaches Association. Dr. Tuten has twice served as a Fulbright Scholar and won the 2006 Excellence in Scholarship Award during her tenure at VCU. She also won two national awards for teaching excellence (Association of Business Administration and Society for Marketing Advances), a teaching innovations award from the Society for Marketing Advances, and a university-wide teaching award at Longwood University.

JAMES ELLIOT BROWN is curious. There are so many exciting things in this world that he just can't help himself. He's always been that way, too—from the day he was born to the day he graduated Virginia Commonwealth University. Even today, as he lives in Richmond, Virginia, and serves as President of Emulsion Marketing, you can often find him staring off into the distance, pondering whatever subject is raking his brain. His current curiosities range from applying network science in order to understand viral marketing all the way to figuring out what object will fix his wobbly desk without making the whole thing lopsided. He almost has the latter in the bag. James will undoubtedly always be curious, but he's thankful that, in this case, his curiosity has led to producing work that found your eyes. He's also very happy that he wasn't born a cat—which would have meant a life of impending doom and made the publication of this research a rather odd affair. If you would like to contact James to trade curiosities or witty banter, he can be reached at JBrown@EmulsionMKTG.com.

DAVIDE P. CERVONE, Ph.D., is an Associate Professor of Mathematics at Union College in Schenectady, New York. As a postdoctoral fellow at the NSF Sponsored Geometry Center at the University of Minnesota, he wrote one of the first hypertext math research papers. Since that time, he has continued to experiment with electronic communication on the Web, and his current projects include WeBWorK (a Web-based homework delivery system for mathematics) and jsMath (a means of displaying mathematics in HTML).

ANNE GILES CLELLAND, M.A., M.S., is President and CEO of Handshake Media, Incorporated, a digital media public relations firm she founded in 2008. A writer, speaker, and consultant, she holds a Master of Arts in Education from Virginia Tech and a Master of Science in Mental Health Counseling from Nova Southeastern University. Handshake Media, Incorporated's enterprises include Handshake 2.0, a business news and public relations site, and Inside VT KnowledgeWorks, a high-tech business news site showcasing the latest in entrepreneurship, and the entrepreneurs, high-tech start-ups, and accelerated companies at business acceleration center and technology incubator VT KnowledgeWorks, located in the Virginia Tech Corporate Research Center, in Blacksburg, Virginia, USA. Handshake Media, Incorporated is a member company of VT KnowledgeWorks. Her interests include entrepreneurship, community mental health, and regional community and economic development.

IAIN J. CLELLAND, Ph.D., is Associate Professor of Management, Department of Management, in the College of Business and Economics at Radford University. His research and teaching interests include entrepreneurship, competitive strategy, environmentally sustainable business practices, business consulting, and strategic planning. He tries to keep up with his wife in triathlons, enterprise 2.0, and boundless energy.

DEBORAH COWLES, Ph.D., is an Associate Professor of Marketing at Virginia Commonwealth University in Richmond, Virginia. Dr. Cowles first became interested in the marriage of communications and computing technologies as an undergraduate journalism major at Ohio Wesleyan University. While studying in Germany, she had the opportunity to attend the 1979 World Administrative Radio Conference in Geneva, Switzerland—the every 20-year conference when the nations of the world come together to decide how to best divide up the world's radio spectrum. Through her academic and military affiliations, Dr. Cowles gained valuable experience with Internet-like communications very early on, and, as she likes to remind her students, she has been "personal computing" since the days of the 300-baud modem. After completing her master's degree in advertising at The University of Texas at Austin, she continued to focus her academic interests on the technologies that would eventually lead to the Internet in a doctoral program in marketing at Arizona State University. Dr. Cowles's research interests include services marketing, online buyer behavior, and customer relationship management. She has been teaching online courses at VCU for the better part of a decade, and she most recently developed an online version of the graduate course "Concepts & Issues in Marketing," which incorporates a module on the social media's evolving role in marketing.

ARRON SCOTT FLEMING, Ph.D., CPA, CMA, is an Assistant Professor in the Division of Accounting at the West Virginia University College ofBusiness and Economics. He is a behavioral researcher with teaching experience in accounting systems, financial, auditing, and cost accounting.

ANJA S. GÖRITZ (www.goeritz.net) is professor pro tempore of Work & Organizational Psychology at the University of Würzburg in Germany. Her research focuses on Web-based data collection, market psychology, and human-computer interaction. In 2000 she built and has since maintained Germany's first university-based online panel with more than 9,000 panelists (www.wisopanel.uni-erlangen.de). Göritz programmed several open-source tools for Web-based data collection (e.g., www.goeritz.net/brmic and www.goeritz.net/panelware). She has regularly been an instructor in the Advanced Training Institute "Performing Web-Based Research" of the American Psychological Association.

KEN MAREADY, J.D., is a start-up and technology attorney working primarily with start-ups in Virginia and North Carolina. He is Of Counsel to Hutchison Law Group, the Southeast's premier legal advisor to start-ups and other technology-based companies. He heads the firm's Blacksburg, Virginia, office, located in the Corporate Research Center of Virginia Tech. Ken advises inventors, founders, investors, and management of technology-based companies on a variety of topics including corporate structure and governance, IP protection, licensing, business and contract matters, financing, and mergers and acquisitions. He has worked in Charlotte, Raleigh, and Washington, DC, and represented clients receiving venture capital investments from funds in Silicon Valley, Boston, Atlanta, Taiwan, Germany, and elsewhere. He attended Wake Forest University School of Law, where he concentrated in business and corporate law while serving as Editor-in-Chief of the law review. He has worked in the business and technology groups of large and small law firms, also serving for two years as general counsel to a venture-backed technology company. He has served actively on Venture Capital and Private Equity committees of the American Bar Association and has lectured and coached for university and entrepreneurial interest groups.

ANDREW McAFEE, Ph.D., joined the faculty of the Technology and Operations Management Unit at Harvard Business School in 1998. His research investigates how managers can most effectively select, implement, and use Information Technology (IT) to achieve business goals. Dr. McAfee was the recipient of a U.S. Department of Energy Integrated Manufacturing Fellowship for his doctoral research, which focused on the performance impact of enterprise information technologies such as SAP's R/3. His current research is an exploration of how Web 2.0 technologies can be used within the enterprise.

LAUREN McKAY is a staff writer for monthly print publication *CRM* magazine and its Web counterpart, destinationCRM.com. Lauren has covered the customer relationship management industry for *CRM* since 2008 and specializes in Enterprise Strategy. Prior to *CRM*, Lauren contributed as an intern to *Working Mother*, a parenting and lifestyle publication. A Kansas City, Missouri, native, Lauren attended the University of Missouri–Columbia where she received her B.A. in Journalism. At the university, Lauren reported and edited for the local newspaper and city magazine. As evident from her Twitter profile, Lauren enjoys participating in and researching social media. She lives in Brooklyn, New York.

BONNIE W. MORRIS, Ph.D., CPA, is the Go-Mart Professor of Accounting Information Systems in the Division of Accounting at the West Virginia University College of Business and Economics. Recently, her research has focused on continuous auditing, interorganizational information sharing, and employee fraud. Her teaching specialties are accounting information systems, IT auditing, and fraud data analysis.

PRESHA E. NEIDERMEYER, Ph.D., CPA, is an Associate Professor in the Division of Accounting at the West Virginia University College of Business and Economics. Her research specialty is defined by current events in business and accounting. She is the coauthor of the book *Use What You Have: Resolving the HIV/AIDS Pandemic* and coeditor of the book *Work, Life, and Family Imbalance.* Her teaching specialties include financial and international accounting. She is an active participant in various organizations benefiting charities in Africa.

JUDY PAYNE is a management consultant and a director of the Henley Knowledge Management Forum at Henley Business School, United Knigdom. She specializes in collaborative working, knowledge management, and learning. Judy believes that the best way to help people is to enable them to help themselves and each other. Judy uses facilitation and process consultation skills to work with consultancy clients, the Henley Knowledge Management Forum, and MBA dissertation candidates. She is fascinated by social networking and undertakes research at Henley Business School into the way organizations use social software. Judy is also an e-facilitator with experience of encouraging and supporting virtual collaboration using social software tools.

ROBERT ROSE heads Big Blue Moose, which provides technology-driven marketing solutions for corporate clients. He served as Crown-Peak's Vice President of Marketing and Strategy from 2002–2009. While at CrownPeak, he revamped the company's brand and messaging strategies. Previous to joining CrownPeak, Robert served as Vice President of Strategic Planning for Ignited Minds, an advertising agency specializing in strategic marketing consulting to the entertainment and consumer electronics sectors. There he directed the company's business development efforts, new Internet service offerings, and contributed to the firm's creative, results-oriented Internet marketing strategies. Robert has been providing strategic marketing and technology-related consulting for Web start-ups since 1994. He served on the board of the SIIA's Software Division from 2003 to 2006 and was one of the founding members of the Executive Council on Software as a Service.

Prior to technology and the Internet invading his life, Rose was a screenwriter and musician in Hollywood. He helped create a television series for Showtime Networks Inc., wrote a number of plays that premiered in both Los Angeles and Off-Broadway in New York, and scored the music for numerous film and theatrical productions in both cities. Despite that, Robert still lives in and loves Hollywood with his wife Elizabeth and their Golden Doodle Daisy.

JASON M. SANTUCCI, MPA, is a Graduate Research Assistant in the Division of Accounting at the West Virginia University College of Business and Economics. His research interests include capital markets and fraud accounting. He plans on beginning work toward his Ph.D. in accounting in the Fall of 2010. In his spare time he enjoys spending time outdoors, cycling and running, and experimenting with electronics.

LISA SPILLER, Ph.D., is a Professor of Marketing in the Joseph W. Luter III College of Business and Leadership at Christopher Newport University in Newport News, Virginia. She has been teaching direct marketing courses to undergraduate business students for 25 years and has helped her university pioneer a major in direct and interactive marketing. Dr. Spiller's marketing students have won the coveted Collegiate Gold ECHO Award from the Direct Marketing Association in 2003, 2005, and 2007 and the Collegiate Silver ECHO Award in 2002. Her students have also received the Gold Collegiate Marketing Award for Excellence and Innovation (MAXI) from the Direct Marketing Association of Washington Educational Foundation (DMAW-EF) in 2004, 2005, 2006, and 2007; the Collegiate Silver MAXI Award in 2002 and 2003; and the Guy Yolton Creative Direct Mail Award in 2002, 2004, 2005, and 2007.

Dr. Spiller was named the Direct Marketing Educational Foundation (DMEF) Robert B. Clark Outstanding Direct Marketing Educator in 2005. She was the inaugural recipient of the DMAW-EF O'Hara Leadership Award for Direct and Interactive Marketing Education in 2008. Professor Spiller has received awards for her teaching, including the inaugural CNU Alumni Society Faculty Award for Excellence in Teaching and Mentoring in 2007; Faculty Advisor Leader Awards from the DMA in 2002, 2003, 2005, and 2007; a Distinguished Teaching Award in 1997 from the DMEF; and the Elmer P. Pierson Outstanding Teacher Award in 1987 from the University of Missouri, Kansas City.

Professor Spiller received her B.S.B.A. and M.B.A. degrees from Gannon University and her Ph.D. from the University of Missouri, Kansas City. Prior to joining academia, Spiller held positions as a marketing director with an international company and account executive with an advertising agency. Through the years, she has served as a marketing consultant to many organizations. Professor Spiller possesses a true passion for teaching and has been a strong advocate of direct and interactive marketing education throughout her entire academic career.

BOB WITECK is Chief Executive Officer and a founding partner of Witeck-Combs Communications, Inc., with over 30 years of professional communications experience both in the private sector and in public service. He is a seasoned communicator, counselor, public affairs professional, and crisis communications expert. Witeck-Combs Communications, founded in 1993 and headquartered in Washington, D.C., is a strategic communications firm helping companies design strategies to strengthen reputations and address communications challenges. The firm's clients have included SPARC (the Scholarly Publishing and Academic Resources Coalition), American Airlines, the Christopher Reeve Foundation, Marriott Corporation, the Historical Society of Washington, D.C., MTV Networks, Volvo Car Corporation, and IBM, to name a few. Before opening his independent practice with Wes Combs in 1993, Bob Witeck was Senior Vice President for Hill & Knowlton Public Affairs, the international public relations and public affairs firm. On Capitol Hill for over a decade, Witeck also served as Communications Director for the U.S. Senate Committee on Commerce, Science and Transportation and as a Senate Press Secretary and Legislative Assistant. He is a graduate with distinction of the University of Virginia, where he was named an Echols Scholar.

Index